GOVERNING THE PAST

The way we govern the past to ensure peaceful futures keeps conflict anxieties alive. In pursuit of its own survival, permanence, and legitimacy, the project of transitional justice, designed to put the 'Never Again' promise into practice, makes communities that ought to benefit from it anxious about potential repetition of conflict. This book challenges the benevolence of this human rights-led global project. It invites readers to reflect on the incompatibility between transitional justice and the grand goal of ensuring peace, and to imagine alternative and ungovernable futures. Rich in stories from the field, the author draws on personal experiences of conflict and transition in the former Yugoslavia to explore how different elements of transitional justice have changed the structure of Bosnia and Herzegovina and neighbouring societies over the years. This powerful study is essential reading for students, scholars, and practitioners interested in human rights and durable international peace.

MAJA DAVIDOVIĆ is Senior Lecturer in International Relations in the School of Law and Politics at Cardiff University. She has won the Open Society Foundations Civil Society Scholar Award and been awarded a British Academy Small Grant.

GOVERNING THE PAST

'Never Again' and the Transitional Justice Project

MAJA DAVIDOVIĆ
Cardiff University

CAMBRIDGE
UNIVERSITY PRESS

CAMBRIDGE
UNIVERSITY PRESS

Shaftesbury Road, Cambridge CB2 8EA, United Kingdom

One Liberty Plaza, 20th Floor, New York, NY 10006, USA

477 Williamstown Road, Port Melbourne, VIC 3207, Australia

314–321, 3rd Floor, Plot 3, Splendor Forum, Jasola District Centre, New Delhi – 110025, India

103 Penang Road, #05-06/07, Visioncrest Commercial, Singapore 238467

Cambridge University Press is part of Cambridge University Press & Assessment, a department of the University of Cambridge.

We share the University's mission to contribute to society through the pursuit of education, learning and research at the highest international levels of excellence.

www.cambridge.org
Information on this title: www.cambridge.org/9781009583930

DOI: 10.1017/9781009583923

When citing this work, please include a reference to the DOI 10.1017/9781009583923

First published 2025

Cover image: Huntstock/Stockbyte/Getty Images

A catalogue record for this publication is available from the British Library

Library of Congress Cataloging-in-Publication Data
Names: Davidović, Maja author
Title: Governing the past : "Never again" and the transitional justice project / Maja Davidović, Cardiff University. Other titles: Never againand the transitional justice project
Description: Cambridge, United Kingdom ; New York, NY : Cambridge University Press, 2025. | Includes bibliographical references and index.
Identifiers: LCCN 2025002844 (print) | LCCN 2025002845 (ebook) | ISBN 9781009583930 hardback | ISBN 9781009583947 paperback | ISBN 9781009583923 epub
Subjects: LCSH: Transitional justice–Bosnia and Herzegovina–Case studies | Transitional justice–Case studies | Human security–Bosnia and Herzegovina–Case studies | Bosnia and Herzegovina–History–1992
Classification: LCC JC599.B67 D38 2025 (print) | LCC JC599.B67 (ebook) | DDC 327.1/720949742–dc23/eng/20250331
LC record available at https://lccn.loc.gov/2025002844
LC ebook record available at https://lccn.loc.gov/2025002845

ISBN 978-1-009-58393-0 Hardback

CONTENTS

ACKNOWLEDGEMENTS

From a mere idea, through completing a PhD thesis, to rethinking and publication, this book comes out at the end of a (more or less) six-year-long process. While the book is my responsibility and mine alone, it could not have existed without my mentors, colleagues, friends, and family.

First, a big thank you to my mentors. To Catherine Turner for believing in me when I was at my best and at my worst, creating opportunities for me that I could only dream of, and teaching me how to think, read, and write better and with more confidence. To Stefanie Kappler for her continuous support and advice that so often helped when I felt stuck. She always made time for me even when free time was incredibly scarce, and I am forever thankful for that. To Marysia Zalewski for making Cardiff feel like home from my very first day there.

This book would not exist without all the people working in Bosnia and Herzegovina and Serbia on different transitional justice matters who accepted my invitations and offered me not only their precious time but also honest, detailed, and incredibly valuable responses, and shared contacts, food, and book recommendations with me. Hvala svima/хвала свима! I hope to see you all again in Sarajevo, Banja Luka, Brčko, Potočari, Bijeljina, Istočno Sarajevo, Belgrade, or elsewhere.

At different stages of the project, I benefited from guidance, feedback, advice, and help from a range of colleagues and friends. I am grateful to, in no particular order, Padraig McAuliffe, Roger MacGinty, Anne Flaspöhler, Emil Archambault, Marianne Doherty, Claire Thurlow, Elisa Wynne-Hughes, Branwen Gruffydd Jones, Harmonie Toros, Thomas Leahy, Luisa Calvete Portela Barbosa, and Darko Stojilović.

Importantly, I thank the Open Society Foundation for supporting the field research component of this book with their Civil Society Scholar Award. The grant made all the difference. I am also grateful to my editor Tobias Ginsberg for believing in this project.

Lastly, the biggest 'thank you' goes to my loving family. My parents, Slađana and Aleksandar Davidović, my working-class heroes, have wholeheartedly trusted me and supported every idea and initiative I took, even when nobody else they knew in their small Serbian town could relate. For always letting me be my own person, inspiring me to dream big, and making me feel like I am invincible, I thank them greatly. Big thanks also go to our lovely dog Maks who is a serious research assistant and who has given me so much joy whenever I visited Serbia in the past six years. Our younger dogs, Maša, Tedi, and Meda, did much less assisting but nevertheless deserve a mention as well.

I am grateful also to my Welsh family for everything they have done to support me in the past six years. To Jo-Anne and Pete Westlake for making the UK feel more like home and caring for me so deeply. To Amy and Fraser Davies for making me an auntie, which is my favourite role in the world. To Renee and Ronan Davies for all the love, joy, and giggles, and for keeping me grounded.

And how do I begin to thank Steve Westlake, my partner and best friend? He encouraged me to believe that I can do all the things that used to appear so unreachable, and I always had his love and support to turn to while writing this book. Steve stood by me through thick and thin and was always there to happily dance with me upon receiving the good news, no matter how big or small, and no matter where, as we moved from Budapest to Belgrade to Durham to Sarajevo to Bristol and, finally, to Cardiff. I cherish our life together more than anything and I share this success with him.

ABBREVIATIONS

ARBiH	Army of the Republic of Bosnia and Herzegovina
BiH	Bosnia and Herzegovina
BIRN	Balkan Investigative Reporting Network
CNA	Centre for Non-violent Action
CRPC	Commission for Real Property Claims of Displaced Persons and Refugees
DPA	General Framework Agreement for Peace in Bosnia and Herzegovina/ Dayton Peace Agreement
FBiH	Federation of Bosnia and Herzegovina
GNRs	Guarantees of non-recurrence
HVO	Croatian Defence Council
ICC	International Criminal Court
ICMP	International Commission on Missing Persons
ICRC	International Committee of the Red Cross
ICTY	International Criminal Tribunal for the former Yugoslavia
IHL	international humanitarian law
IHRL	international human rights law
IJC	Independent Judicial Commission
IPTF	International Police Task Force of the United Nations
IRC	International Rescue Committee
MHRR	Ministry of Human Rights and Refugees of Bosnia and Herzegovina
MPI	Missing Persons Institute
OHR	Office of the High Representative of the United Nations in Bosnia and Herzegovina
OSCE	Organization for Security and Co-operation in Europe
RDC	Research and Documentation Centre
RS	Republika Srpska
SDP	Social Democratic Party
SFRY	Socialist Federal Republic of Yugoslavia
TRC	Truth and Reconciliation Commission
UNDP	United Nations Development Programme

UNSC	United Nations Security Council
VRS	Army of Republika Srpska
WCC	War Crimes Chamber of the Court of BiH

Prologue

On 16 March 2013, the city of Thessaloniki organised its first-ever Holocaust Memorial Walk. The walk was held in commemoration of the 70th anniversary since the first deportations of the city's Jewish population to Auschwitz. It was set to begin, symbolically, at Liberty Square, where after a few official speeches, the crowd would walk to the old railway station from which the first carriages departed to Auschwitz. As a twenty-one-year-old student at one of Thessaloniki's colleges, with a developing passion for human rights, I was among the first to arrive at the square. My best friend and I watched the crowd grow larger by the minute, until we could no longer see where it ended. Some newspapers later reported that 2,500 people took part in the memorial walk.[1] I was at the front line.

It was a monumental day for the city. The walk represented the re-embracing of the crucial role that Jewish communities played in this city's history before they perished in the Holocaust. For the first time in 101 years, it was said, the sitting Prime Minister of Greece had set foot in a synagogue and vowed 'Never Again'.[2] 'We have to be very careful to remember the message of "Never Again"', Prime Minister Samaras was quoted saying on this occasion, as 'the fight against neo-Nazis is more important than ever'.[3] Samaras was referring then to the increasingly popular support the neo-Nazi party Golden Dawn was gaining among the Greek public, shifting the focus from global memories of the Holocaust to local issues.[4] The new Greece, scarred by the financial crisis and led by Samaras, was reconnecting with the old Greece, scarred by

[1] Gavin Rabinowitz, 'Greek Jews Get Sudden Boost in Neo-Nazi Fight' (*The Times of Israel*, 29 March 2013) www.timesofisrael.com/greek-jews-get-sudden-boost-in-neo-nazi-fight/ accessed 2 May 2023.

[2] ibid.

[3] ibid.

[4] ibid.

Nazi Germany, its Jewish population almost entirely destroyed, to address some of the challenges the country was going through at that time and perhaps to justify its foreign policy preferences, too. Holocaust commemorations presented Greek political elites with an opportunity to position Greece as a fervent advocate against racism and anti-Semitism and an ally of Israel. At the same time, numerous refugees who found themselves on Greek soil were facing increased attacks on their rights and freedoms.

As for myself, I came to the memorial walk to honour the victims. At this point in my studies, I began to nurture an interest in genocide studies, planning to pursue further education in that area. I took advantage of any opportunity to learn more about the Holocaust and completed coursework on the topic. The motive for dedicating my life to this field of academic inquiry was personal. By that time, I had developed a deep awareness of the Srebrenica genocide committed by the Republika Srpska Army (VRS) at the last stage of the war in Bosnia in the name of Serb independence and the 'cleansing' of Serb territories. A child of the 1990s and a Serb, I learned about the Srebrenica genocide in my late teens; not in school, nor from my family, but through informal education to which I was exposed by accident. I felt shame around this ignorance and a conviction that I, as any 'ordinary' individual, had a role to play in preventing future genocides in the region I called home.

When, right before the Holocaust memorial walk was about to start, two of my classmates and I were given a large banner to carry and lead the entire march with, I felt a deep connection with the past. The banner read, '*Ποτέ ξανά! Never Again!*' The message was explicit: Never Again will we let the Holocaust happen! My friends and I carried it, slowly and diligently, for the entirety of the two-mile walk to the old train station. The next day, pictures of us and the banner made numerous newspapers. Of all the people, I never learned why the banner was given to the three of us. Perhaps because we were 'the youth', the future. Our participation in commemorative activities was key for ensuring that the youth have a brighter and more peaceful future than our ancestors did.

These connections and disconnections between the past and the future, and the conundrum of how to prevent something that had already happened in the past, continued to puzzle me as I developed my career as a transitional justice scholar. I have heard the 'Never Again' promise repeatedly being made by politicians across contexts, in relation to both past and emerging mass violations of human rights, for genocides, crimes against humanity, and ethnic cleansings. I have seen memorials to the victims of the Holocaust, the Srebrenica genocide, and the Armenian genocide, all carry the same plea to remember and prevent the most horrendous of atrocities from being repeated. Yet, I was left wondering, as a scholar and a 'youth': what does 'Never Again' look like in practice, beyond promises and memorials? When wars end, when genocides are committed, how do societies ensure they are not repeated? How does the international community govern such prevention of further atrocities, but also how do survivors of such mass atrocities do so on an everyday basis? Eleven years after the Holocaust Memorial Walk, I wrote this book in response to these and other questions. Remembering the message of 'Never Again' day in and day out, I have taken these questions to Bosnia and Herzegovina and have sought to illustrate distinct experiences of 'Never Again' after genocide, reassessing the meaning of 'non-recurrence' in the light of the global project of transitional justice.

1

Introduction

Urgencies of the Past and the Future

1.1 Two Global Imperatives

Preventing mass atrocities from resurging has been a global imperative since the end of World War II when the international community vowed that atrocities such as the Holocaust would 'never again' be repeated. Since then, the vow of 'Never Again', like the one myself and other participants of the memorial walk in Thessaloniki made in 2013, has symbolised different political actors' commitment to non-recurrence of gross human rights violations across the world. This commitment was followed by concrete developments in law and practice, particularly as international human rights law (IHRL) burgeoned.[1] When, in the last decade of the twentieth century, some of the most horrendous war crimes since World War II were committed in places like Rwanda and former Yugoslavia, mass atrocities became a key threat to international security and new regulatory models were sought after.[2] Consequently, multiple mechanisms have been devised to aid the goals of preventing both the occurrence and the recurrence of mass atrocities as the international human rights regime further

[1] The 1948 Convention on the Prevention and Punishment of the Crime of Genocide is a symbol of such global actions, as the treaty was created as a direct response to the Holocaust meant to signal the international community's commitment not to let such atrocities happen again. See the United Nations Office on Genocide Prevention and the Responsibility to Protect, *Genocide Convention*, www.un.org/en/genocideprevention/genocide-convention.shtml accessed 9 May 2024.

[2] Jelena Subotic, 'Truth, Justice, and Reconciliation on the Ground: Normative Divergence in the Western Balkans' (2015) 18 Journal of International Relations and Development 361, p. 363; Kathryn Sikkink, 'From State Responsibility to Individual Criminal Accountability: A New Regulatory Model for Core Human Rights Violations' in Walter Mattli and Ngaire Woods (eds.), *The Politics of Global Regulation* (Princeton University Press 2009) pp. 121–50.

developed and the international criminal justice regime began to be devised. One of the more prominent policy models underpinned by these legal regimes has been transitional justice, as a set of tools, mechanisms, and practices which states transitioning from conflict and/or authoritarianism are advised or even conditioned to implement in order to 'deal' with their problematic pasts and prevent recurrence of atrocities.

This book tells a story about the efforts to prevent renewed conflict through the global project of transitional justice and uncovers what is often invisible in the evaluation of transitional justice processes – securities of the self, identities, anxieties, and uncertainties – and how they matter for any attempt to ensure a long-lasting 'Never Again'. The purpose is to rethink the scope and meaning of non-recurrence as a largely neglected yet core aspect of transitional justice by empirically investigating how post-conflict societies make sense of it in the everyday and how the very project of transitional justice shapes such everyday understandings. Ultimately, I reassess transitional justice as a force of global governance. To do this effectively, I draw on my extensive field and desk research in Bosnia and Herzegovina (BiH), a country devastated by war thirty years ago and one of the key recipients of transitional justice-related interventions in the 1990s and early 2000s; a transitional justice laboratory.

The book is interested in transitional justice as a rapidly growing *global project* consisting of legal norms, mechanisms, and policies on correct and appropriate 'dealing' with the past exported to dozens of countries transitioning from conflict and/or authoritarianism. Since the 1980s, the imperative to 'deal' with past state-sponsored violence by confronting it and not greeting it with widespread impunity, like was the case for much of human history, has been growing in both scope and reach. Over time, transitional justice began to be characterised through its constitutive elements as it travelled from Latin America in the 1980s, to Eastern Europe, the Balkans, Rwanda, and South Africa in the 1990s, until it was fully integrated into the work of the United Nations and, subsequently, numerous international organisations in the early 2000s. The mechanisms and tools of transitional justice, most notably criminal trials, truth and reconciliation commissions, reparations, and measures of institutional reform such as vetting begun to be discussed as a 'package' of measures, underpinned by specific international normative commitments, for instance, the anti-impunity norm or the right to truth. While there is an understanding that not all possible measures of transitional justice could be applied in all contexts,[3] for a couple of decades there has been an increased understanding, if not a consensus, around the idea that past violence and injustice must be dealt with and accounted for.[4] To ensure that the past is dealt with, numerous external actors rush to aid the country affected by such violence, occasionally even before peace is negotiated. In this sense, transitional justice became a matter of global governance.

The two global imperatives of 'Never Again', or ensuring a peaceful future, and 'transitional justice', or dealing with the past, come hand-in-hand. As this book will show, each of the core tools of transitional justice has been advocated for in both academic and policy circles for its potential to contribute to non-recurrence of mass atrocities or the overall conflict in the specific context to which transitional justice has travelled. Not only is dealing with the past through transitional justice tools seen as overall beneficial for 'Never Again' but also non-recurrence itself has become an overarching telos of transitional justice. Ensuring non-recurrence of violations, scholars have claimed, remains 'the most important aim of transitional justice'.[5] Consequently, at the level of international transitional justice policy and advocacy there is an understanding that transitional justice 'can contribute to prevention' of recurrence.[6] As a form of global governance, transitional justice exists, inter alia, to put 'Never Again' to practice. Yet, the compatibility between the two global imperatives is rarely questioned by scholars and policymakers.

In forthcoming chapters, I reevaluate the connections and disconnections between these two contemporary imperatives by interrogating people's experiences of the 'Never Again' promise and perceptions of what hampers its fulfilment in post-conflict times and tracing the influences of the transitional justice project on such experiences and perceptions. I do not treat transitional justice as an a priori benevolent force of

[3] United Nations Secretary-General, 'The Rule of Law and Transitional Justice in Conflict and Post-Conflict Societies' (United Nations Security Council 2004) UN Doc. S/2004/616*.

[4] Jelena Subotic, 'The Transformation of International Transitional Justice Advocacy' (2012) 6 International Journal of Transitional Justice 106.

[5] Michelle D Bonner, '"Never Again": Transitional Justice and Persistent Police Violence in Argentina' (2014) 8 International Journal of Transitional Justice 235, p. 237.

[6] In a 2021 report, the International Center for Transitional Justice outlined four potential contributions of transitional justice processes to prevention, based on five country case studies. Roger Duthie, *Transitional Justice and Prevention: Summary Findings from Five Country Case Studies* (International Center for Transitional Justice 2021) p. 1.

global governance. Instead, the book opens space for thinking through what, if anything, transitional justice does for non-recurrence. Departing from previous studies,[7] I proceed not by delving into the claims of whether individual mechanisms such as trials and truth commissions are beneficial for a meaningful 'Never Again' but by exploring whether the way we govern 'dealing with the past' is. In doing so, I provide an in-depth interrogation of the structural elements and characteristics of transitional justice as a global project embedded in neoliberal legalism.

In dissecting the project of transitional justice, I rethink what the project is for, to propose that beyond ensuring the values of justice, truth, and reconciliation, the project first and foremost serves to govern uncertainties which arise in transitional periods of rupture between the seemingly old and the seemingly new, periods in which transitional justice thrives. As an overarching telos of transitional justice, ensuring non-recurrence requires providing assurances about this uncertain future. Doing so establishes transitional justice as a mechanism of security.[8] In addition to physical (in)securities, the book also focuses on the largely neglected nexus between transitional justice and *(in)securities of the self*, that is, ontological (in)security, as transitional justice interacts with multiple collective actors trying to make sense of the transition and embarking on different and often competing quests for knowledge about the past, certainty about the future, and a secure sense of self in the world.

Examining transitional justice developments over thirty years in post-war BiH, I arrive at my core claim that in pursuit of its own survival, permanence, and legitimacy, the transitional justice project helps make the populations who are supposed to benefit from it anxious about potential '*again*' or repetition of conflict. The book shows that after years of transitional justice interventions, many of the practices people in BiH identify as threatening meaningful assurances of non-recurrence can in fact be understood as ontological security-seeking practices, triggered, or worsened by the global project. These behaviours, in turn, create an

[7] For example, Cyanne E Loyle and Benjamin J Appeal, 'Conflict Recurrence and Postconflict Justice: Addressing Motivations and Opportunities for Sustainable Peace' (2017) 61 International Studies Quarterly 690; Chris Mahoney and others, 'Conflict Prevention and Guarantees of Non-Recurrence. Background Paper for UN-World Bank Pathways for Peace Study' (1 May 2017). Available at SSRN: https://ssrn.com/abstract=3158012 accessed 13 May 2024.

[8] Michel Foucault, *Security, Territory, Population: Lectures at the Collège de France, 1977–78* (Palgrave Macmillan 2007) p. 20.

environment which signals continuous anxiety about the uncertain future of peace in the country. These, I suggest, are the results of certain applications of the kind of transitional justice project that has been globalised. I proceed by outlining the key questions, claims, and contributions of the book and providing a brief overview of the birth and development of transitional justice as a global project, a vehicle of peace, as well as security.

1.2 Key Questions

While preventing mass atrocities from being repeated remains the organising telos of the transitional justice project, the merits of the causal relationship between the two imperatives remain disputed. Many of the claims of positive influences of individual transitional justice mechanisms on the objective of non-recurrence are speculative rather than empirically grounded. That a mechanism has an effect on non-recurrence is a claim used to investigate whether transitional justice 'works' or not, and subsequently evaluate the effectiveness of the project. Yet, when evaluated according to introspective criteria accomplished through the fulfilment of the project's own promises, non-recurrence becomes detached from the people for whom the promise of 'Never Again' was made in the first place. Missing from the burgeoning transitional justice scholarship are holistic – as opposed to piecemeal – explorations of the subjective value awarded to the principle of non-recurrence by different stakeholders, and of non-linear and perhaps non-causal interactions between how these lived experiences of non-recurrence are constructed and all the different elements of the global project of transitional justice. This book sits in this gap.

The two core questions this book explores are (1) how does the global project of transitional justice shape the lived experiences of and efforts towards conflict non-recurrence in societies subject to transitional justice interventions and (2) which structural elements of the transitional justice project shape these experiences and efforts for better or for worse? In doing so, the book grapples with broader questions. What do meaningful guarantees of conflict non-recurrence entail for post-conflict societies? What are some of the factors shaping people's perceptions of the likelihood of renewed conflicts? Following these explorations are musings on some narrower questions about BiH as an instrumental case rooted in its decades-long experience of being a testing ground for distinct ideas about what transitional justice is and how it should look. What has the transitional justice project in BiH included, and what has it excluded and why? This question is explored in Chapter 3. What does non-recurrence look like as an everyday experience in BiH, and how do different tenets of the transitional justice project shape these experiences? These questions are investigated in Chapters 4, 5, and 6. And finally, in Chapter 7: what role do 'ordinary people' have in creating and sustaining meaningful assurances that renewed conflict would be unlikely, with or without transitional justice?

I wish to make a brief comment here on the distinctions between mass violations and conflict. A BiH prosecutor once told me that the best we can hope to prevent is mass violations of human rights and humanitarian law and not renewed conflict, because war is, after all, legal. As this book will show, the same logic largely applies to the concept of 'guarantees of non-recurrence' (GNRs), a claimed yet under-conceptualised pillar of the transitional justice project and a legal norm found in public international law, IHRL, and international humanitarian law (IHL). The rationale underpinning GNRs in international law is to ensure that a specific violation of the said law is not repeated in the future. What specific measures GNRs necessitate changes from one legal regime to another and from one case to another. In public international law, GNRs may be attached to a single violation by the injuring state, for example, wrongful execution of a national of another state, and may require an apology or a specific legal amendment. Yet, in the other two legal regimes, the violations for which GNRs ought to be offered are often systemic and mass-scale, for example, state-sponsored enforced disappearances of civilians, or torture of prisoners of war. The point of this tool then is to help change the conditions which seemingly enabled or brought the violation in question through a range of measures of legal and institutional reform. Thus, GNRs cannot be about ensuring that an injuring actor never goes to war again but rather that, if it does, gross violations of IHL are avoided.

My book does not separate the two on the basis of (il)legality. The violations I am discussing here can exist outside the context of war, but war, in my experience and as per evidence from across the world, cannot exist in a 'pure' form without any of violations of IHL.[9] Hence, even

[9] See, for instance, Lamp (2011) who argues that the traditional enforcement mechanisms of IHL are inherently challenged by the so-called new wars, or Owens (2003) proposing that 'small' massacres of civilian population are becoming normalised in post-9/11 wars. Nicolas Lamp, 'Conceptions of War and Paradigms of Compliance: The "New War"

where transitional justice interventions seek to prevent mass breaches of international law, as per the logic of the legal norm of GNRs, by no means a coherent practice at the level of international policy as Chapter 2 will show, they also, by extension, seek to prevent renewed conflict which would serve as a backdrop, escalation, or justification for these violations. Furthermore, the lived experiences of war and its aftermaths suggest that there is a conflation between prevention of conflict and prevention of mass violations of IHL or IHRL; that 'Never Again' invariably means no more war. When we shift the focus from international law to everyday life in post-conflict societies, as my book does with close examinations of BiH, we can see that people do not typically express anxieties around a specific form of violation, for example, torture or rape being repeated, although this of course could be pertinent to survivors of these specific violations. Instead, as multiple chapters of this book will illustrate, they express anxieties around a renewed conflict in which genocide and multiple other atrocities such as torture or rape could flourish. Inevitably, then, the scope of this book is larger than the norm of GNRs.

1.3 The Argument

In this book, the global project of transitional justice is not characterised as a benevolent form of governance, as claims of a positive relationship between it and prevention of further conflict continue to be questioned. Based on extensive field research on transitional justice in BiH, I position the project of dealing with the past as a structure which can have negative impacts on people's uncertainties about 'Never Again', leaving any meaningful assurances of non-recurrence on shaky ground. My principal argument is that the transitional justice project, with its core tenets on how to 'deal' with the past and its own survival needs, does not mitigate anxieties around renewed conflict in different political communities; on the contrary, it often worsens them. In post-conflict BiH, this book shows, the transitional justice project has made a bad situation worse, and, while the actual likelihood of renewed conflict is debated, unpredictable, and not a claim this book makes, the anxieties around the uncertain future of sustainable peace in this country persist.

Challenge to International Humanitarian Law' (2011) 16 Journal of Conflict and Security Law; Patricia Owens, 'Accidents Don't Just Happen: The Liberal Politics of High-Technology "Humanitarian" War' (2003) 32 Millennium: Journal of International Studies 595.

I arrive at this argument by examining the intersections between transitional justice and security and underpinning my thinking with structuration theory. I widen the scope of analysis by integrating not only physical but also ontological (in)security needs which the transitional justice project neglects but with which it inevitably interacts. The book paints a picture of post-conflict BiH in transition as a space with multiple and often competing security claims, both those of physical survival and of being. Out of this space emerges a proposition that there is no one security for BiH but instead multiple quests for survival, certainty, and continuity, among which the transitional justice project has its own demands in order to remain an effective form of global governance over the pasts deemed 'problematic'. At the same time, different political communities that interact with the components of transitional justice develop competing security claims in this shared but volatile post-conflict space as they are pressured to question their relationships with their past selves and identities in the international system through trials, commissions, and other transitional justice mechanisms.

Looking at the long-term trajectory of transitional justice governance in BiH, rather than solely at the immediate transitional period, this book demonstrates that, in seeking to sustain its own relevance and legitimacy, the global project provides extraneous pressures on ontological insecurities in these actors. In this book, I show that many of the practices people identify as threatening assurances of non-recurrence can in fact be understood as ontological security-seeking practices by collective political actors in BiH. These, in turn, keep the society in a state of continuous anxiety about the uncertain future of peace.

Asserting that the project originally designed to ensure that mass violations are not repeated serves as a source and aide of anxieties and grievances around potential renewed conflict represents a major contribution to scholarly understanding of transitional justice as *a structure of global governance*. Examining nearly three decades of transitional justice in BiH allows the book to make this argument in relation to three core characteristics of the global project. First, the global project relies on international institutions for its survival and legitimacy and as such engages in an exercise of linking local transitional justice processes to those institutions. In doing so, it exhibits a misunderstanding of security as lived experience and portrays a false premise that security, certainty, and identities can only effectively be governed through institutional structures. Second, as a family of norms, the transitional justice project operates based on normative hierarchies. This norm arrangement prioritises certain prescribed or proscribed behaviours expected from the transitioning state over others and places the institutionalised forms of anti-impunity over other behaviours found in the norm cluster. Institutions of criminal justice arise as authoritative sources of truth and history in a process that is violent and exclusionary towards other complementary truth recovery processes. Lastly, as a global intervening force ought to represent a rupture between the old and the new, a progress from violent and 'bad' pasts to peaceful and 'good' futures, the transitional justice project is coated in civilisationism. Upon structural failures, the agents of the project shift responsibility onto the subjects of transitional justice who cannot seem to reach the standard of civilisation and in doing so stigmatise certain actors in international society, (re) constructing them as different, less desirable, and 'deviant'.[10]

These characteristics of transitional justice shape how the mechanisms and tools of the global project are put into practice and how they operate in specific contexts such as BiH. I demonstrate links between such tools and mechanisms of transitional justice and production of anxieties about potential renewed conflict, proposing how the global project has been complicit in political communities' ongoing ontological security-seeking exercises, namely (1) revisionist production of fractured and false truths about the war; (2) securitisation of ethnic-based identities through history teaching; and (3) glorification of war crimes and denial, trivialisation, and minimisation of atrocity crimes, all of which exacerbate collective anxieties around potential new conflict. In Chapter 4, I show how the normative hierarchy upon which the project operates and the positioning of the International Criminal Tribunal for the former Yugoslavia (ICTY) as a key source of the historical status quo has not produced an 'objective truth', as originally claimed, but instead has enhanced the building of multiple, competing, and often parallel truths about the war. This normatively hierarchical relationship between different mechanisms of transitional justice has also influenced other sectors of social life in BiH. In Chapter 5, I demonstrate how the global project has aided the proliferation of ethnonationalist histories as (1) the above-mentioned parallel truths are integrated into history education and (2) public education operates based on ethnic divides due to the original design for post-war BiH. In this chapter, the other two characteristics of the project also come

[10] Rebecca Adler-Nissen, 'Stigma Management in International Relations: Transgressive Identities, Norms, and Order in International Society' (2014) 68 International Organisation 143.

into play. To fill in the gap in dissemination of common truth, the ICTY has undertaken a civilising mission to educate local populations. Yet, this has been done in rather detrimental ways that link complex social phenomena such as memory and identity back to the institution and do not resonate with the prevention needs of the BiH society. Similarly, in Chapter 6, all characteristics are at play. I discuss how quick, ineffective, and untransparent practices of legal and institutional reform by the international community left BiH with a legal structure which allows glorification of war criminals as well as their reintegration into the BiH socioeconomic and political lives. In an already familiar pattern, the detrimental consequences and by-products of such reforms were labelled as 'uncivilised' behaviours of ethnonationalist elites with the purpose of relieving the international community of any responsibility and reinstating the relevance of the very same international community who steps in to fix such 'uncivilised' behaviours.

Finally, in exploring how different agents give meaning to practices for 'Never Again' *with*, *despite*, and possibly *against* the global project of transitional justice in Chapter 7, I discuss whether the global project of transitional justice can become a space for bettering, rather than worsening, ontological security needs. I propose a reconsideration of non-recurrence in post-conflict societies as best studied through the encounters between the global and local, physical and ontological, ideational and material. Through these encounters, I uncover elements and characteristics not awarded high value within the transitional justice project such as *interpersonal*, *transethnic*, *reflective*, and *dialogical*. Ultimately, I reconceptualise non-recurrence beyond governance as coexistence, binding, and healing and as a form of *work* different sections of the post-conflict society ought to undertake beyond or possibly without the transitional justice project.

1.4 Methodology

This book arrives at its conclusions through a case study of post-war BiH. In this research design, BiH appears as an instrumental case,[11] a case by no means representative of all transitional justice experiences across contexts but emblematic of the transitional justice project. In many ways, BiH stands out when compared to other countries with developed

[11] John W Creswell, *Qualitative Inquiry and Research Design: Choosing Among Five Approaches* (3rd ed., SAGE 2013) p. 98.

transitional justice programmes and processes: the conflict is commonly characterised as 'international' as opposed to civil, it is only one of the two countries where the UN Security Council (UNSC) established an ad hoc international criminal tribunal, and it is a country whose constitution is not only tied to but an integral part of the peace agreement that put an end to the conflict. Why is, then, BiH, I claim, a vehicle for understanding the intersections between the transitional justice project and prevention of renewed conflict? Although BiH does not have a coherent transitional justice policy, it has a very developed transitional justice infrastructure consisting of processes, projects, and practices relating to all core pillars of transitional justice with long-lasting involvement of a range of international, regional, and domestic actors. In fact, BiH is one of the countries with the most resource investment in transitional justice by the international community. As Campbell succinctly puts it, BiH became a country that 'exemplifies contemporary transitional justice' with its multiple projects, many of which have already completed their mandates.[12] Moreover, BiH was one of the first states to witness transitional justice as a newly developed field of research and policy and was since used to test many policy ideas initially proposed by transitional justice research, including those making causal links between different mechanisms such as criminal trials and the objective of non-recurrence. Transitional justice projects and processes in BiH have been developing for thirty years, which allows me to comment on the longue durée of the transitional justice project.

The research design is qualitative, contemporary, and exploratory, seeking to produce context-dependent knowledge that tells the reader something about transitional justice as a whole. I draw on my extensive field research with practitioners working in the spheres of transitional justice in BiH. This includes observing and interviewing practitioners representing forty-three institutions, organisations, and mechanisms within all sectors relating to the issues and aspirations of transitional justice: courts, truth commissions, government agencies working on reparations, international organisations conducting institutional reform, civil society organisations, museums, and research centres.[13] These actors

[12] Kirsten Campbell, 'Reassembling International Justice: The Making of "the Social" in International Criminal Law and Transitional Justice' (2014) 8 International Journal of Transitional Justice 53, p. 66.

[13] A list of organisations which participated in this research, as well as those that were only studied through desk research where interviews were not available, can be found in Table

represented organisations which were established solely for a transitional justice-related reason (e.g., the 2004 Srebrenica Commission) and those who do not exclusively work towards transitional justice matters but have engaged in transitional justice-related activities through different projects or aspects of their mandate (e.g., municipal courts with a special jurisdiction to adjudicate atrocity crimes cases). The interviews and observations took place in 2019 and early 2020, in the last weeks of Europe's freedom from COVID-19 (or so we thought).

This field research has been complemented by in-depth desk research on transitional justice in BiH from its inceptions to recent developments. Part of this research was to screen all identified institutions, organisations, and mechanisms working on different aspects of transitional justice for references to non-recurrence and 'Never Again', and another part was developing a genealogy of the transitional justice project in BiH, outlined in Chapter 3. I relied on academic articles and books, international (non-)governmental organisations' reports and policy papers, legal documents such as peace agreements and UN General Assembly and Security Council resolutions, available in English and Bosnian/Croatian/Serbian, and interviews with practitioners formerly involved in the early days of transitional justice. In addition to academic, desk, and field research, the book demonstrates active monitoring of current affairs regarding transitional justice in BiH up until 2023 as evidenced through my engagement with numerous news sources from local and region media outlets such as *BIRN*, *N1*, *Radio Slobodna Evropa*, *AlJazeera Balkans*, and others.

How did a project designed to investigate non-recurrence bring me to anxiety and ontological (in)security? Without any preconceived, authoritative definitions of 'non-recurrence', I applied a flexible method of thematic data analysis which allowed for questions to evolve, and it made space for unforeseeable events and developments. This is how, over time, 'anxiety' emerged as a prominent theme in interlocutors' framing of their own experiences and understandings of non-recurrence. 'If we don't do this, or change that in our society, then repetition is likely' or 'this will go on until the next war' are kinds of statements I heard often. Methodologically speaking, what were the markers of such anxiety? In this book, I was interested in identifying anxiety as a mood – a social phenomenon generating collective disposition – rather than an

A.1 in Appendix. Depending on their preferences, participants are cited under their full names, institutional affiliation, or fully anonymously.

individually held emotion.[14] The general 'mood' of anxiety was not inferred from behaviour, that is, a practice that appears to be ontological security-seeking,[15] but rather was discursively manifested in the analysed texts as well as in the interviews through phrases, constructions, and stories which pointed to a feeling or perceptions of feelings of unease and uncertainty about the collective future of peace. The way people spoke about such uncertainties and unease pointed to an intersubjective construction of 'anxiety' as it was also about other actors' actions based on personal experiences or interacting with them or those who represented them (e.g., interaction with some young people leads to statements about 'the youth'). The next step was to investigate the context in which these moods were expressed: in relation to what situations, practices, actors, or a lack thereof do people talk about these moods? As the contexts were identified, traces of the transitional justice project were searched for among them. Not everyone talked about the same kind of mechanisms, tools, and practices; in fact, a few people spoke of none. Yet, where they did, these experiences were grouped and organised into themes, as presented in Chapters 4, 5, and 6.

1.5 Impact and Significance

This is the first book-length, holistic, and empirically grounded English language investigation of the intersection between the imperatives of 'Never Again' and transitional justice. It is significant for both scholarly knowledge and policymaking in four core ways.

First, the book contributes to the ongoing challenges of the presumed benevolence of the transitional justice project both conceptually and empirically. Although it can sometimes fail to realise some of its goals on account of a range of domestic and/or international factors, the transitional justice project is largely treated as a benevolent project that engages in positive actions. In other words, transitional justice is commonly treated as a separate entity (defined or undefined) that *achieves*,[16]

[14] Bahar Rumelili, '[Our] Age of Anxiety: Existentialism and the Current State of International Relations' (2021) 24 Journal of International Relations and Development 1020.

[15] Nina C Krickel-Choi, 'The Concept of Anxiety in Ontological Security Studies' (2022) 24 International Studies Review 1.

[16] For example, Nicola Summers, 'Colombia's Victims' Law: Transitional Justice in a Time of Violent Conflict' (2012) 25 Harvard Human Rights Journal 219.

contributes,[17] *shapes*,[18] or *promotes*[19] goals, values, and a range of social phenomena. 'Dealing' with the past in a combination of these proposed ways is therefore not only inherently 'good', although it may be challenging, but also necessary.

Scholarly concerns about whether and how transitional justice 'works' as a whole or through its parts have been long present. It would be impossible to list here all the critiques of transitional justice, nor there is a need to. Transitional justice as a whole has been repeatedly called legalistic, limited, linear, incapable of addressing systemic violations or root causes of such violations, and ultimately incomplete.[20] The issue is that many such critiques still largely confirm the belief of transitional justice as being inherently, or at least, on balance, benevolent; that some transitional justice is better than none, although some have of course proposed that its goals may be irreconcilable or even impossible to achieve.[21] Even within the growing scholarship on transformative (transitional) justice, there are debates about whether the goals of transformative justice, such as emphasising local agency and resources and challenging the existing power structures, can be sought within transitional justice as an existing project or outside it.[22] Because transformative justice writings rest on well-established critiques of transitional justice (e.g., that it is elite-oriented[23] and that it does not address structural violence[24]), it is ultimately a radically transformed transitional justice

[17] For example, Patricia Lundy and Mark McGovern, 'Whose Justice? Rethinking Transitional Justice from the Bottom Up' (2008) 35 Journal of Law and Society 265.

[18] For example, Jon Elster, *Closing the Books: Transitional Justice in Historical Perspective* (Cambridge University Press 2004).

[19] For example, Lisa J Laplante, 'Transitional Justice and Peace Building: Diagnosing and Addressing the Socioeconomic Roots of Violence through a Human Rights Framework' (2008) 2 International Journal of Transitional Justice 331.

[20] For example, Kieran McEvoy, 'Beyond Legalism: Towards a Thicker Understanding of Transitional Justice' (2007) 34 Journal of Law and Society 411; Padraig McAuliffe, 'Transitional Justice and the Rule of Law: The Perfect Couple or Awkward Bedfellows?' (2010) 2 Hague Journal on the Rule of Law 127; Matthew Evans, 'Structural Violence, Socioeconomic Rights, and Transformative Justice' (2016) 15 Journal of Human Rights 1.

[21] Bronwyn Anne Leebaw, 'The Irreconcilable Goals of Transitional Justice' (2008) 30 Human Rights Quarterly 95; Catherine Turner, *Violence, Law and the Impossibility of Transitional Justice* (Routledge 2016).

[22] Paul Gready and Simon Robins, 'From Transitional to Transformative Justice: A New Agenda for Practice' (2014) 8 International Journal of Transitional Justice 339, p. 340.

[23] Erin Daly, 'Transformative Justice: Charting a Path to Reconciliation' (2002) 12 International Legal Perspectives 73.

[24] Daire McGill, 'Different Violence, Different Justice? Taking Structural Violence Seriously in Post-Conflict and Transitional Justice Processes' (2017) 6 State Crime Journal 90.

where 'both the problem it seeks to address, and related responses and interventions' are rethought and reframed.[25] The underlying logic is the same – a conviction that transitional justice can and should *contribute* and make positive impacts on its subjects[26] – whereby the project is reaffirmed.

This book, on the contrary, does not concern itself with 'what works best' in a given repertoire of tools or norms. Instead, it seeks to contribute to scholarly discussion about how the given repertoire works, and continues to work, and to what end. Nagy opened a research path for considering transitional justice as a global project imbued with power, leaving certain rights, harms, and peoples behind.[27] Similarly to Nagy, Miller conceptualised transitional justice as an 'enterprise' on the premise that there is certainty around the objectives of transitional justice yet simultaneously a sense of 'uneasiness' about its means, results, and efficacy.[28] Practitioners understand the limits of the 'enterprise' but continue to portray it as the only or at least necessary response to violence.[29] Rowen also theorised the seemingly paradoxical characteristics of transitional justice, proposing that the project is malleable.[30] Both Rowen and Miller's work allow for a view of the transitional justice project as purposefully contradictory, both universal and context-specific, both flexible and precise all the while being treated as an inevitable response to mass human rights violations.

This book contributes to these discussions by proposing new ways to think through the limits, powers, and products of transitional justice as a global project. I build on the work of Nagy, Miller, and Rowen to suggest that the fact that there has been no consensus over how to do transitional justice or what transitional justice is good for begs the questions of not only the scope of transitional justice and whether it is inclusive of and

[25] Gready and Robins, 'From Transitional to Transformative Justice', p. 355.

[26] Maja Davidovic and Catherine Turner, 'What Counts as Transitional Justice Scholarship? Citational Recognition and Disciplinary Hierarchies in Theory and Practice' (2023) 67 International Studies Quarterly 1.

[27] Rosemary Nagy, 'Transitional Justice as Global Project: Critical Reflections' (2008) 29 Third World Quarterly 276.

[28] Zinaida Miller, 'Embedded Ambivalence: Ungoverning Global Justice' (2020) 11 Transnational Legal Theory 353.

[29] ibid, p. 355.

[30] Jamie Rebecca Rowen, *Searching for Truth in the Transitional Justice Movement* (Cambridge University Press 2017); Jamie Rebecca Rowen, '"We Don't Believe in Transitional Justice": Peace and the Politics of Legal Ideas in Colombia' (2017) 42 Law & Social Inquiry 622.

effective in addressing structural violence and gender inequality,[31] or violence against Indigenous people,[32] but also *what transitional justice is for*. It is through my examination of what the project is for that I carve a new pathway for exploring how the project, with its specific set of characteristics and practices of dealing with the past, shapes collective senses of self, self's position in the world, and future trajectories. This helps me expose the often-hidden harmful effects of the project on the sphere of ontological, and not purely physical, securities. By grounding the book in structuration theory, I also elaborate on the temporality of transitional justice to propose that, while transitional justice as a project is short-lived in a specific context, as a structure, it needs permanence over time and despite contexts. In that sense, 'dealing' with the past as a form of global governance aspires to be long-lasting, exhibiting both rigidity and flexibility to do so. In broader terms, the book is positioned as a contribution to knowledge about the productive work of such a global project, but also the constructions of its benevolence and necessity, in contexts to which it is exported.

Second, I comprehensively and empirically cover a topic that prominent scholars have highlighted as being 'a missing part' of the transitional justice puzzle.[33] The book expands on existing reviews of GNRs in transitional justice[34] by proposing that non-recurrence in transitional justice is broader in scope than GNRs; exploring the lived experiences of prevention of renewed conflict in a post-conflict context, and reconceptualising the links between the global project of transitional justice and non-recurrence. The book shows how lived experiences of conflict prevention are enabled and constrained by the structure of the transitional justice project and, at the same time, have the capacity to shape the tenets of the project itself. Preventing renewed conflict in a

31 Nagy, 'Transitional Justice as Global Project', p. 287.

32 Miller, 'Embedded Ambivalence'.

33 Clara Sandoval-Villalba, 'Reflections on the Transformative Potential of Transitional Justice and the Nature of Social Change in Times of Transition' in Roger Duthie and Paul Seils (eds.), *Justice Mosaics: How Context Shapes Transitional Justice in Fractured Societies* (International Center for Transitional Justice 2017); Pablo De Greiff, 'The Future of the Past: Reflections on the Present State and Prospects of Transitional Justice' (2020) 14 International Journal of Transitional Justice 251.

34 Naomi Roht-Arriaza, 'Measures of Non-Repetition in Transitional Justice: The Missing Link?' in Paul Gready and Simon Robins (eds.), *From Transitional to Transformative Justice* (Cambridge University Press 2019); Alexander Mayer-Rieckh, 'Guarantees of Non-Recurrence: An Approximation' (2017) 39 Human Rights Quarterly 416.

post-war context, therefore, cannot happen in isolation from social life nor from the rules and resources that bind the structure of transitional justice across space and time. It is these insights that allow me to propose a conceptualisation of non-recurrence in post-conflict societies beyond governance, a task perhaps more important than trying to salvage the transitional justice project through improvements. Non-recurrence is a goal above all goals that can continue to exist without the transitional justice project, but the transitional justice project needs non-recurrence as its overarching telos.

Third, the book also speaks to existing scholarship on ontological (in)security in International Relations and links it to transitional justice. The nexus between the two has rarely been explored. I build on the works by Mälksoo,[35] Subotic,[36] and Rumelili[37] by desegregating 'the state' and showing that there may be multiple ongoing battles for ontological security within a single state, as multiple actors compete for justice, truth, and peace in post-conflict spaces. While the former Yugoslav states eventually complied with their international transitional justice obligations, different actors within and beyond the state developed mnemonical security-oriented approaches to dealing with the past and sought to fix certain narratives of the past in social memories. The book enriches scholarly knowledge on this topic by providing an in-depth, long-term examination of a single case study; tracing how anxieties and ontological (in)securities develop over time and what factors support these developments; and exploring how multiple different mechanisms of conflict resolution and dealing with the past shape ontological (in)securities after a conflict. The book also responds to the critiques suggesting that ontological security studies are not interested in change[38] by exploring how different agents give meaning to practices for 'Never Again' and act in anxious times *with*,

[35] Maria Mälksoo, 'The Transitional Justice and Foreign Policy Nexus: The Inefficient Causation of State Ontological Security-Seeking' (2019) 21 International Studies Review 373.

[36] Jelena Subotic, *Yellow Star, Red Star* (Cornell University Press 2019).

[37] Barak Rumelili, *Conflict Resolution and Ontological Security: Peace Anxieties* (Routledge 2015).

[38] Trine Flockhart, 'The Problem of Change in Constructivist Theory: Ontological Security Seeking and Agent Motivation' (2016) 42 Review of International Studies 799; Karl Gustafsson and Nina C Krickel-Choi, 'Returning to the Roots of Ontological Security: Insights from the Existentialist Anxiety Literature' (2020) 26 European Journal of International Relations 875.

despite, and *against* the global project of transitional justice. The book is significant in its critique of the global project of transitional justice as an aide of ontological insecurities, and for its imagining of what a less anxious future of BiH could look like.

Finally, although not written with an intent to change policy outcomes, the book makes for an important read for policymakers in BiH as well as those working on 'dealing with the past' more broadly. On the outside, BiH might be considered an 'over-researched' context that, with nearly thirty years of peace, is no longer of interest to donor communities. At the same time, BiH is continuously perceived as 'a failed state' or 'frozen conflict' that continues to test the security assurances on the margins of the European Union. The book provides a fresh outlook on this well-studied case. For those worried about the future of BiH, this book offers a more elaborate response to the question of whether and why peace in contemporary Bosnia may be in danger by looking beyond domestic ethnonationalist practices. It does so by examining the extraneous factors that have aided different forms of such ethnonationalism and elaborating on global ideational forces shaping post-war trajectories of this state, without taking any responsibility away from domestic political elites. For European security analysts and policymakers, the book provides a space to imagine a more meaningful peace for BiH and demonstrates how different civil society actors and activists are providing small but notable changes to that end. Because the book uses examples from BiH to reflect on the broader matters of global governance and prevention, it draws lessons for ongoing and future contexts of transitional justice. The claims, reflections, and imaginings presented in this book can speak to people and struggles of dealing with the past in ongoing conflicts, societies recovering from authoritarianism, those rebuilding after civil conflicts, and even societies eager to address historical injustices, as they all at different points may become the subjects of transitional justice governance.

1.6 Transitional Justice, Security, and Non-recurrence: A Brief History

The travels and transformations of the principle of non-recurrence into and through transitional justice can be understood effectively only in relation to transitional justice as a project born out of neoliberal legalist thinking, different from but complementary to human rights, and a vehicle of peace as much as of security. Different genealogical accounts of transitional justice-like processes start with different events,[39] but generally, the notable early developments of transitional justice as we know it today were shaped by political transitions from oppressive regimes across Latin America.[40] Both non-recurrence and security as concepts and sought-after values played a role in these early makings of transitional justice. In countries such as Argentina and Chile, 'Never Again' enjoyed a prominent position and was utilised by many activists as a slogan shaping their calls for action. It was also in these countries that some staple mechanisms of transitional justice, namely truth commissions and criminal trials, were developed and trusted with the potential to contribute to the fulfilment of the 'Never Again' promise in practice. To be more precise, the ideas of 'Never Again' being more than a moral obligation and instead becoming an action-filled obligation which states owed to individuals were first developed here. The emphasis, in these early transitional justice interventions, was first and foremost on state security[41] and, secondly and relatedly, on human security, as the 'long-term human fulfilment'.[42]

In Argentina, during its transition from dictatorship, the National Commission on Disappeared People published a report entitled *Nunca Más = Never Again* in 1986. The name of the report was inspired by the activism and slogans used by groups of victims' families such as the Mothers of the Plaza de Mayo who had sought the truth about the children forcibly disappeared by the Argentine dictatorial regime since the late 1970s, and, later on, by other human rights organisations and exiles groups.[43] These activists, who were often simultaneously victims of the regime, sought to highlight the connections between the dictatorship and the crimes that had been perpetrated, contextualising the atrocities within the cycle of military interventions in Argentina.[44] The moral

39 Teitel begins her genealogy in the immediate post-WWII period, with the Nuremberg Tribunal. See Ruti Teitel, 'Transitional Justice Genealogy' (2003) 16 Harvard Human Rights Journal 69. Elster, on the other hand, seeks the roots of the first 'negotiated transition' in ancient Greece. Elster, *Closing the Books.*

40 Paige Arthur, 'How "Transitions" Reshaped Human Rights: A Conceptual History of Transitional Justice' (2009) 31 Human Rights Quarterly 321.

41 Iavor Rangelov and Ruti Teitel, 'Transitional Justice' in Mary Kaldor and Iavor Rangelov (eds.), *The Handbook of Global Security Policy* (Wiley 2014) pp. 338–51.

42 Lauren Marie Balasco, 'The Transitions of Transitional Justice: Mapping the Waves from Promise to Practice' (2013) 12 Journal of Human Rights 198, p. 208.

43 Emilio Crenzel, 'Genesis, Uses, and Significations of the Nunca Más Report in Argentina' (2015) 42 Latin American Perspectives 20.

44 ibid, pp. 22–3.

imperative of 'Never Again' became associated with the state and its institutions, as calls were made by the activists to investigate 'state terrorism' and, eventually, cleanse the state of its violence in order to prevent recurrence.[45] In the final report, the president of the Commission declared that 'only with democracy' can society be certain that these atrocities will be repeated 'never again'.[46] The *Nunca Más* report gained further importance for the Argentine public once it was offered and accepted as court evidence in the trials of military juntas and eventually reached the status of a bestseller, with translations in several other languages.[47] Secure and non-violent futures were linked to the state and its democratic values, principles, and structures.

The truth commission model and the resulting report carried the 'Never Again' promise with them into the very fabric of transitional justice as they were subsequently exported to various countries in Latin America, such as Guatemala and Paraguay, developing the project of 'justice in transition'.[48] The ultimate goal of the emerging interventions of 'justice in transition' in Latin America, be it a truth commission or a criminal trial, was to never experience such grave violations again and therefore to protect the citizens against further state oppression. The institutions of criminal tribunals and truth and reconciliation commissions became the most notable markers of the increasingly universalised platform for 'dealing' with the past. This made dealing with the past, and consequently the goals of such an intervention, both more tangible and actionable. The values enshrined in these mechanisms are reflected in the normative development of 'transitional justice' as a concept, as the early stages of such development demonstrate a focus on security of the state as well as on human security. While the state is being reformed into a 'better', more law-abiding, and effective formation, the relationship between the state and its citizens is restored, evidenced in state recognition of the citizens' dignity, values of accountability and transparency, and a more general reconstitution of the state security

[45] ibid, p. 23.

[46] Marcos Zunino, *Justice Framed: A Genealogy of Transitional Justice* (Cambridge University Press 2019) p. 74.

[47] Crenzel, 'Genesis, Uses, and Significations', p. 20.

[48] Daniel Rothenberg (ed.), *Memory of Silence: The Guatemalan Truth Commission Report* (Palgrave Macmillan 2012); Fernando Cruz Artunduaga and Vera Podbornaya (eds.), *Comisiones de la Memoria, Verdad y Reconciliación* (Centro de Investigación por la Paz IDEASUR 2012).

structure so that it is no longer a threat, and therefore a source of insecurity, for its own population.[49]

These links between transitional justice, security, and non-recurrence remained evident as transitional justice became globalised. The making of 'transitional justice' as a distinct and necessary accomplice to peaceful and secure transitions to democracy was facilitated through planned and purposeful interactions of different actors such as human rights activists, legal scholars, journalists, donors, and policymakers who provided an 'intellectual framework' for the project,[50] making an inseparable link between it and the promise of 'Never Again' at the global level. These actors gathered, among others, at several 'justice in transition'-themed conferences in the late 1980s.[51] Already at one of these first conferences, Jose Zalaquett, a Chilean lawyer and later a commissioner at the Chilean National Commission on Truth and Reconciliation (TRC), began to advocate for concrete measures such as the state security reform to be undertaken for the purposes of 'guaranteeing to victims that violations would not be repeated'.[52] This is the language that, at that time, had only been used by the activists in Latin America and the Human Rights Committee.[53] Until then, the language of guaranteeing non-recurrence was reserved for diplomatic interstate disputes, by and large practised as a right of states.[54] But in 'justice in transition' developments, non-recurrence began to be conceptualised as a right of victims and an obligation of states towards their subjects. While shaping the field's boundaries, the promoted measures also gave normative content to the principle of 'Never Again' that was quickly conceptualised as an overarching objective of 'justice in transition' in Latin America.

In 1990, around the time these conferences were taking place, Zalaquett published a key piece on confronting human rights violations.[55] This article was not only important for its influence on the

49 Balasco, 'The Transitions of Transitional Justice'.

50 Arthur, 'How "Transitions" Reshaped Human Rights', p. 327.

51 ibid.

52 ibid, p. 358.

53 'Ensuring that violations are not repeated' was the phrase typically used in the Human Rights Committee's recommendations issued to the violating state.

54 Maja Davidovic, 'The Law of "Never Again": Transitional Justice and the Transformation of the Norm of Non-Recurrence' (2021) 15 International Journal of Transitional Justice 386.

55 Jose Zalaquett, 'Confronting Human Rights Violations Committed by Former Governments: Applicable Principles and Political Constraints' (1990) 13 Hamline Law Review 623.

setting of the intellectual framework for transitional justice but also for feeding content into the norm of non-recurrence in both transitional justice and IHRL, as human rights lawyers were developing 'GNRs' as a form of reparations for human rights violations throughout the 1990s and into the early 2000s. In this article, Zalaquett outlined nearly all measures today known as 'GNRs' in core human rights documents on GNRs such as the UN Basic Principles of the Right to Remedy and Reparations.[56] He then saw 'dealing with transitional political situations' as 'a new area of human rights practice'.[57] Up until that point, Zalaquett observed, human rights organisations had dealt with these complex questions in the same way they responded to human rights violations committed by governments currently in place. Due to the myriad of (at the time) unanswered questions such as what international legal responsibilities governments have with respect to past human rights violations, Zalaquett found such efforts 'inadequate'.[58] He aspired to design a policy that would deal with past human rights violations in a more effective way.

Such a policy would have two general objectives: 'to prevent the recurrence of such abuses; and ... repair the damage they have caused'.[59] Here we can also see the birth of the idea that transitional justice is both backward- and forward-looking.[60] The proof of Zalaquett's pioneering work lies in his discussion of the concrete contents of these policies. In support of his arguments, Zalaquett used examples from domestic practices in Guatemala, the Philippines, Spain, and Panama. Admitting that 'there exists no single formula for how best to prevent human rights violations', Zalaquett outlined the following new measures for preventing recurrence: (1) reinforcement of the legal system's protection of human rights (e.g., amending constitutions and signing human rights treaties); (2) reforming/strengthening institutions to reinforce the protection of human rights (judicial reform, human rights education, etc.).[61]

In the year after the article was published, Zalaquett sat on the Chilean TRC. The Commission's lengthy final report included a set of

[56] ibid.
[57] ibid, p. 625.
[58] ibid.
[59] ibid, p. 628.
[60] Ruti Teitel, *Transitional Justice* (Oxford University Press 2000).
[61] Zalaquett, 'Confronting Human Rights Violations', p. 635.

recommendations regarding the prevention of human rights violations in this country, in line with its mandate.[62] In the introductory remarks written for the English language version of the report, Zalaquett repeated the two ultimate objectives of a 'justice in transition' policy from his 1990 article, preventing repetition of atrocities being one of them. In Zalaquett's words, the Commission's mission was to decide how such an objective could be achieved. The prevention recommendations stressed the 'significant flaws and shortcomings' of the domestic legal system that disabled it from effectively protecting human rights.[63] To that end, the Commission recommended a series of measures of institutional and legal reforms: aligning Chile's legal framework into line with IHRL, reforming the judicial branch (including legal training), ensuring that armed forces, security forces, and the police exercise their functions in complete accordance with the obligation to respect human rights, creating an institution to protect human rights, and making changes in the legal order in constitutional, criminal, and procedural matters to better protect human rights. These elaborate measures were an extension to the 1990 article by Zalaquett, although ideologically identical.

Zalaquett's interpretation of these various measures of *institutional* and *legal* reform as measures best preventing renewed human rights violations, and the subsequent practices of 'justice in transition', helped give content to the otherwise content ambiguous norm of GNRs in IHRL, forever tying the concept of non-recurrence, legally speaking, to the reforms of the state and its structures.[64] This is, in the briefest sense, how the principle of non-recurrence in IHRL became identified with and equated to a non-exhaustive list of measures of legal and institutional reform. The 'Never Again' promise became concrete, actionable, and achievable (as much as any promise can be) through better, reformed, human rights-friendly structures of the state. What transitional justice can do for security on the ground is reform the core structures of the state and improve the relationship between those structures and the people who survived mass violence and oppression from the former state structures, allowing the society to function and prosper as a democracy.

[62] Center for Civil and Human Rights, *Report of the Chilean National Commission on Truth and Reconciliation* (University of Notre Dame Press 1993).

[63] ibid, p. 1075.

[64] Davidovic, 'The Law of "Never Again"'.

These promoted measures of non-recurrence in Latin America are unsurprising, for they are well-placed within the global end-of-the-Cold-War context. Arthur argues that the transfer of local-level advocacy against impunity, such as, for instance, in Chile and Argentina, to the international level was marked by a focus on the political change, thereby prioritising legal and institutional reforms over, for example, social justice issues. Such a deliberate preference shaped 'the initial conceptual boundaries for the field'.[65] Indeed, the Chilean TRC itself saw measures of legal and institutional reform as necessary but insufficient to ensure non-recurrence of violations and advocated for a consolidation of a culture truly respectful of human rights through education (formal, non-formal, and informal) and symbolic measures.[66] In particular, the TRC found it 'absolutely necessary that a space for broad public debate on human rights is open' by, for instance, organising public forums and carrying out cultural activities.[67] Yet these recommendations were not picked up and decontextualised as measures of non-recurrence at the level of IHRL or transitional justice policy, at least not until very recently. Instead, the links between institutional and legal reform and non-recurrence were preferred. These are characteristic of the overarching post-Cold War focus of the Western international community on security and the rule of law. In Eastern Europe at that time, reforming and controlling the security sector by new regimes became integral to the desired democratic and economic transformations of countries in transition. In broader international politics, 'good institutions' and 'good governance' emerged as the most sought-after values in aid-receiving, developing states, defining how successes of state- and peacebuilding, and therefore sustainable peace and ultimately non-recurrence, are measured.[68]

Soon after, however, transitional justice began to be conceptualised as a mechanism of international peace and security, making transitional justice processes important not solely for state–society relations in former autocracies but also for the seemingly global pledges to sustainable peace and prevention of mass atrocities of the international community, as the guarantor of peace and security. The ad hoc international

[65] Arthur, 'How "Transitions" Reshaped Human Rights', p. 326.

[66] Davidovic, 'The Law of "Never Again"'.

[67] Center for Civil and Human Rights, *Report of the Chilean National Commission*, p. 1111.

[68] Padraig McAuliffe, *Transformative Transitional Justice and the Malleability of Post-Conflict States* (Edward Elgar 2017) pp. 26–8.

tribunals for Rwanda and the former Yugoslavia established in the 1990s made the link between transitional justice and international security very clear as their very foundations required evoking UNSC resolutions and positioning these tribunals as responses to conflicts essentially perceived as threats to international peace and security.[69] Crucially, since 2004, transitional justice has been included on the UN's agenda, often presented hand-in-hand with the rule of law objectives of the organisation.[70] Here, transitional justice is established as a crucial element in the UN's post-conflict security framework and, as Teitel asserts, 'the relevant questions of transitional justice are now considered part of the broader international commitment to human security'.[71]

At the UN, the two imperatives of non-recurrence and transitional justice have been connected from the very beginning of its positioning of transitional justice as a project of relevance for maintaining international peace and security. In the first major transitional justice report, in 2004, Secretary-General Kofi Annan wrote that it was the horrendous events of the 1990s that showed that there can be no immediate or long-term peace without appropriate redress for grievances and fair administration of justice.[72] In this report, it was believed that 'the root causes of conflict have often been left unaddressed' and that using legitimate and just approaches to address the causes of conflict can help societies avoid returning to conflict.[73] Ultimately, the UN wanted to draw lessons from former Yugoslavia, Rwanda, and other then-recent cases, claiming that *prevention* was one of the United Nations' main objectives in its transitional justice involvements.

Around the same time, high importance was given to transitional justice and the rule of law by the High Commissioner for Human Rights, Louise Arbour. In 2005, the Commission on Human Rights requested Arbour's office to conduct a study on transitional justice and human rights activities that had been done by agencies of the UN, hoping to learn from best practices and assist countries in their transitional

[69] United Nations Security Council Resolution 827 (25 May 1993) UN Doc. S/RES/827; United Nations Security Council Resolution 955 (8 November 1994) UN Doc. S/RES/955.

[70] In the 2004 report, Kofi Annan stated that transitional justice had in fact been on the agenda of the General Assembly since 1993 as a concept entitled 'strengthening the rule of law'. See United Nations Secretary-General, 'The Rule of Law and Transitional Justice'.

[71] Ruti Teitel, 'Editorial Note-Transitional Justice Globalized' (2008) 2 International Journal of Transitional Justice 1, p. 3.

[72] United Nations Secretary-General, 'The Rule of Law and Transitional Justice'.

[73] ibid, para 4.

justice trajectories.[74] The Commission placed emphasis on prevention of further violations to which the totality of transitional justice processes and mechanisms contribute, stating that:

> exposing the truth regarding violations of human rights and international humanitarian law . . .; holding the perpetrators . . . accountable; obtaining justice and an effective remedy . . .; as well as preserving historical records of such violations and restoring the dignity of victims through public acknowledgement and commemoration of their suffering are integral to . . . the prevention of future violations.[75]

Moreover, in 2009, an analytical study on human rights and transitional justice was submitted to the Human Rights Council within the annual report of the Office of the High Commissioner for Human Rights.[76] Preventing recurrence of human rights violations, in comparison with previous reports by other UN organs, was more generally attached to institutional reform, on the hypothesis that fair and efficient public institutions allow governments to ensure non-recurrence.[77] In 2010, the Secretary-General published a guidance note on transitional justice in which the duty of prevention was discussed.[78] Importantly, this guidance note highlighted that transitional justice processes should 'ensure the right of victims to reparations, the right of victims and societies to know the truth about violations, and GNRs of violations, in accordance with international law'.[79]

While subsequent developments in both research and practice fixated on both trials and truth commissions, scholars and policymakers were less interested in understanding non-recurrence either qualitatively or quantitatively. In other words, the 'Never Again' promise was present simply as the backdrop of the most prominent mechanisms of transitional justice. This remained so until the UN revamped the 'Never Again' promise as 'GNRs', adding this otherwise developing legal norm more forcefully into the package of transitional justice tools. The UN's agenda

[74] United Nations Commission on Human Rights, 'Human Rights and Transitional Justice. Human Rights Resolution 2005/70' (2005) UN Doc. E/CN.4/2005/L.10/Add.17.

[75] United Nations Commission on Human Rights, 'Human Rights Resolution 2005/81: Impunity' (21 April 2005) UN Doc. E/CN.4/RES/2005/81.

[76] United Nations Human Rights Council, 'Analytical Study on Human Rights and Transitional Justice' (2009) UN Doc. A/HRC/12/18.

[77] ibid.

[78] United Nations Secretary-General, *Guidance Note of the Secretary-General: United Nations Approach to Transitional Justice* (United Nations 2010).

[79] ibid, p. 4.

on transitional justice culminated with the establishment of the mandate of the Special Rapporteur on the promotion of truth, justice, reparation, and guarantees of non-repetition in 2011 by the Human Rights Council.[80] The Special Rapporteur is widely regarded as the 'transitional justice' rapporteur and truth, justice, reparations, and guarantees of non-repetition as the four pillars of the field.[81]

As a result, the ideas of non-recurrence are currently integrated into the transitional justice in several different forms. As explained earlier, consisting of a non-exhaustive list of measures of legal and institutional reform in international law, GNRs became a specific tool for ensuring non-recurrence, which confirmed that this promise could be fulfilled through law and its institutions. Simultaneously however, as this book will demonstrate, scholars and practitioners found that other tools in the transitional justice repertoire also have the potential to contribute to meaningful non-recurrence, while still maintaining the idea of ensuring non-recurrence of past violence as an actionable goal. Others continued to propose that transitional justice in toto aids non-recurrence.[82] It follows that the 'Never Again' promise is instrumentalised in contexts of mass violence around the world through all individual parts of the transitional justice project, whether working in isolation or harmony. In other words, while what about transitional justice exactly contributes to meaningful assurances of 'Never Again' is debated, there is a general acceptance among scholars and practitioners alike that something does. Therefore, the application of a combination of these measures of transitional justice, which give substance to the basic human rights norms, is believed to help make affected populations more secure; with that, it contributes, or so is believed, to a long-lasting 'Never Again'.

With its relevance for security, stability, reconstruction, as well as justice, transitional justice has become an urgent matter, one of the shiniest tools the international community led by the UN seems to have for fulfilling its prevention promises. It has been packaged in a multi-pillar model of solutions and subsequently exported across the world. Since the initial conferences on 'justice in transition' in the late 1980s, the

[80] UN Human Rights Council, 'Special Rapporteur on the Promotion of Truth, Justice, Reparation and Guarantees of Non-Recurrence' (13 October 2011) UN Doc. A/HRC/RES/18/7.

[81] For a recent such conceptualisation at the United Nations, see Rebecca Brubaker, *The UN Security Council and Transitional Justice: A Preliminary Look* (United Nations University Centre for Policy Research 2021).

[82] Duthie, *Transitional Justice and Prevention*, p. 1.

field has expanded vertically to include different kinds of actors other than the state, all of whom are seen as relevant and capable of practising transitional justice.[83] As a result of the professionalisation of the field, numerous specialist NGOs, projects, and even university courses on transitional justice followed, and transitional justice provisions have found a way into multiple peace agreements.[84] In addition, transitional justice has also stretched horizontally from originally being an area of research and practice in transitions from authoritarianism to democracy, to being applicable to a variety of different contexts around the world.[85] In its short lifespan, transitional justice has seemingly become 'the only legitimate response to conflict'.[86] From transitions from authoritarianism in Latin America to transitions from socialism in Eastern Europe and the Balkans; from civil conflicts in Sierra Leone, Uganda, and Mali to post-Arab Spring contexts in Tunisia and Libya; from neglected Cold War-era atrocities in Cambodia and Mexico to historical injustices towards Indigenous peoples in Canada and Australia; from ongoing wars in Ukraine and Syria to slavery legacies in the US – the global project of transitional justice is everywhere.[87]

1.7 Outline and Chapter Summaries

This book proceeds in seven chapters, each interweaving academic debates, and the formation of scholarly knowledge with illustrations, stories, and observations. Chapter 2 is a theoretical chapter; it serves to frame the book and provide it with its theoretical underpinnings, drawing on structuration theory and ontological security studies. This chapter invites the reader to become intrigued and think about the questions of this book in relation to the broader political world. I explore in more depth the claims of positive influence of different tools of the global project on non-recurrence, proposing that both scholars and

[83] Thomas Obel Hansen, 'The Vertical and Horizontal Expansion of Transitional Justice' in Susanne Buckley-Zistel and others (eds.), *Transitional Justice Theories* (Routledge 2014) pp. 105–124.

[84] Christine Bell, *On the Law of Peace: Peace Agreements and the Lex Pacificatoria* (Oxford University Press 2008).

[85] Hansen, 'The Vertical and Horizontal Expansion'.

[86] Turner, *Violence, Law and the Impossibility of Transitional Justice*, p. 22.

[87] An illustrative example of this global reach is the International Center of Transitional Justice which has thus far worked in more than fifty countries. International Center for Transitional Justice, *Where We Work*, www.ictj.org/where-we-work accessed 8 June 2023.

practitioners remain unsure of what 'works' while retaining their faith that something surely does; that some transitional justice is better than none. I delineate some common threads from these multiple promises of non-recurrence to reflect on the characteristics of transitional justice as a structure. The chapter proceeds to theoretically complicate the existing position of non-recurrence in transitional justice scholarship by asking questions about temporality, security, and the purpose of the transitional justice project. The chapter provides a new outlook on the ontological security/transitional justice nexus and discusses where non-recurrence fits within it.

Chapter 3 is a critical genealogy. This chapter rests on a history of the global project's trajectories in BiH to reevaluate contemporary conceptions of 'Never Again'. Its aim is to paint the picture of the material and ideational aspects of the transitional justice project in BiH, from the establishment of the ICTY in 1993, to the myriads of measures of institutional and legal reform advocated for or straightforwardly implemented by different actors of the international community present in transitional BiH. The chapter opens with brief background information about the dissolution of Yugoslavia and the war in BiH 1992–5. It illustrates the conflict resolution process and explains what kind of BiH was imagined in the 1995 Dayton Peace Agreement. In providing a skeleton of transitional justice in this country, it shows that certain areas of transitional justice, such as criminal justice and institutional reform, have been significantly more developed and invested in than others, putting these developments in the context of the promises of neoliberal legalism. Finally, this chapter poses questions about the end of the transitional justice project in BiH and muses on what remains of transitional justice in this country.

Chapters 4, 5, and 6 should be read as a triptych. They return the reader to the present day and narrate a story about what 'Never Again' means for the people of BiH and why, in response to the key questions set in the chapter. Drawing on interviews, observations, and life stories from BiH, each chapter in isolation tells an important part of this story, formulating a claim of transitional justice's complicity in the construction of conflict recurrence anxieties. Yet together, they complicate the images and illuminate the lived experiences of both 'Never Again' and transitional justice. Chapter 4 proposes that the lack of truth recovery, that is, a state-sponsored, state-wide consensus or even dialogue about the characteristics, dynamics, and consequences of the war, creates anxieties about potential conflict repetition. It further demonstrates how the global project of transitional justice is complicit in creating and sustaining these anxieties. In particular, the chapter shows how the normative hierarchies of transitional justice and the positioning of the ICTY as a key source of the historical status quo helped enhance the building of multiple, competing, and often parallel biographical narratives about the war, many of which engage in historical revisionism.

In Chapter 5, I suggest that education more broadly, and history education in particular, can make or break meaningful assurances of conflict non-recurrence. In this chapter, I show that ethnically segregated history teaching in BiH plays a key role in the maintenance of a post-conflict status quo which has, for many people, frozen the anxiety around the uncertain future of peace in the country. The chapter further posits that the global project of transitional justice, while not responsible for the burgeoning ethnonationalism, has actively made bad situations worse with its short-sighted security priorities and general misunderstanding of security as lived experience. In particular, the chapter discusses how and why the ICTY undertook a role of an educator of the BiH youth and public and how the advocates of the transitional justice project have continued to ignore the complexity of the prevention needs of the BiH society.

Chapter 6 concludes the three-partite discussion about what hampers meaningful assurances of 'Never Again' in BiH and what transitional justice has to do with that. I identify the widespread glorification of war criminals and denial of atrocity crimes as key sources of anxiety about potential renewed conflict in BiH. The chapter explains these behaviours as responses to the perceived threats to different political communities' ontological securities. It analytically links these practices to the global project and discusses how past practices of legal and institutional reform such as vetting led to a legal structure that did not regulate convicted war criminals' access to power. The resulting widespread practices of glorification and the culture of denialism are framed by the international community as a 'civilisational issue' which serves to prolong the relevance and presence of the external actors in BiH and stigmatise actors in international society.

Like the preceding three chapters, Chapter 7 is an empirical chapter in the sense that it is grounded in field research in BiH and is about experiences and observations in and of BiH. It is different from the triptych in its outlook. While the preceding three chapters are critical, Chapter 7 can be described as hopeful. It asks the question of 'what now', having identified numerous sources of anxieties around a potential renewed conflict in BiH, as helped or fully created by the global project of transitional justice. Here I am interested in changes *for* 'Never Again'. As such I explore how activists and practitioners in BiH resist and challenge the practices seen as harmful for non-recurrence, pushing different political communities towards a place of enhanced ontological security *with*, *despite*, and perhaps even *against* transitional justice. In this chapter, there are numerous illustrations of what people can do to challenge and change the post-conflict status quo across different aspects of action at the intersection of truth recovery, memorialisation, and education. I conceptualise and imagine non-recurrence beyond governance as not only resistance but also coexistence, binding, and healing.

Finally, Chapter 8 aims to draw wider conclusions about prevention of conflict repetition in and after transitional justice as a field of research, policy, and practice. I summarise where non-recurrence stands theoretically and practically in relation to the book's findings and stories of 'Never Again' as lived experience. Furthermore, I invite the reader to imagine the futures of prevention of conflict repetition and transitional justice, together as well as apart. The chapter ends by signalling how pertinent the 'Never Again' promise continues to be in the lives of millions of people and invites further research on the topic that will enrich the discipline with new contexts and perspectives.

2

The Promise of Non-Recurrence

On Governing Uncertainty and Transitional Justice as a Structure

2.1 Introduction

Transitions are deeply uncertain times. While the transitions which transitional justice deals with come full of hope for a better, more peaceful future, they represent significant changes in the political, legal, economic, and social landscape as the threats of immediate mass violence and/or state abuse are removed, often after many years or even decades. Peace advocates and practitioners step in to jointly create an image of the future the society is transitioning to, often even before the transition can begin, yet the successes and final forms of such transitions remain doubted in the years to come. Many wars end up recurring as transitional societies witness renewed violence, violent regime changes, a rise of non-state armed groups, and growing economic instabilities.[1]

The global project of transitional justice, although not branded as such in character, essentially seeks to manage some of these uncertainties by promising to address the grievances, facilitate the attainment of justice, truth recovery, and reconciliation, and repair past harms, even those seemingly beyond repair, all for a long-lasting 'Never Again'. At least in its traditional form of intervention in post-conflict and post-authoritarian contexts,[2] the project seeks to support structures which can re-establish some sense of normality and routine. For instance, courts

[1] Scott Gates, Håvard Mokleiv Nygård, and Esther Trappeniers, 'Conflict Recurrence' (2016) 2 Conflict Trends PRIO 1. www.prio.org/publications/9056#:~:text=Recurring%20conflict%20is%20symptomatic%20of,the%20years%20immediately%20following%20war.

[2] Here I do not include transitional justice in non-transitional contexts such as established democracies. For more information on these cases, see, for instance, Stephen Winter, *Transitional Justice in Established Democracies: A Political Theory* (Palgrave Macmillan 2014).

are reformed so that people can trust them to effectively solve their future problems while truth and fact-finding commissions uncover information that helps people make sense of what happened by building and simplifying the narrative and creating 'perpetrators', 'victims', and other such categories. While burgeoning research exists on transitional justice as a force for peace, justice, reconciliation, truth, and other values, transitional justice as a force against insecurities and uncertainties about both the self and others, as well as the future, has been less explored. It is therefore necessary, I posit, to take a further step of linking the sought values of truth and justice, among others, to managing uncertainty for meaningful non-recurrence. It is here, I propose, that the nexus between non-recurrence and transitional justice can be more effectively interrogated, showing both a fuller picture of meaningful 'Never Again' beyond material state structures and the impacts of the global project of transitional justice on perceptions, attitudes, and experiences of the (un)certain future and one's own position in it.

In this chapter, I seek to retheorise the relationship between 'Never Again' and the global project of transitional justice. I start with the question of 'what' is non-recurrence in and for transitional justice. In Section 2.2, I examine why non-recurrence is conceptualised in seemingly contradicting ways in both scholarship and international policies on transitional justice. In doing so, in Section 2.3 I also rethink transitional justice itself not merely as a set of normative standards but as a structure characterised by purposeful and simultaneous rigidity and ambiguity and embedded into the deeper structures of neoliberalism and legalism. I situate the theoretical foundations of my claims in structuration theory, proposing that a look into the longue durée of institutional time suggests that the structure of transitional justice, while short-lived in individual contexts, has survival, permanence, and legitimacy needs on a global scale in order to sustain itself as a global project over time and space. Lastly, in Section 2.4, I seek to theoretically underpin the core claims of the book which I will continue to explore empirically in forthcoming chapters. I propose a novel outlook to interrogating non-recurrence in transitional justice and, by extension, transitional justice itself. I reorient scholarly debates about what transitional justice is for from values such as justice, truth, and reconciliation to governance of uncertainty. There, I link transitional justice with ontological (and not merely physical) (in)securities of political communities and discuss non-recurrence in relation to anxieties about potential renewed conflict. Ultimately, I identify three core characteristics of transitional justice as a global project due to which the 'Never Again' promise remains questionable despite wide applications of the project's tools and mechanisms.

2.2 The 'Promise': Transitional Justice as a Positive Force on Non-recurrence

As a normative expectation, non-recurrence is positioned within transitional justice interventions as an objective towards which all distinct solutions, that is, prescribed and proscribed behaviours in the transitional justice repertoire, might be able to contribute. There is little disagreement that ensuring non-recurrence of violations is the organising telos of transitional justice. The global project of transitional justice exists, inter alia, to put 'Never Again' to practice. In the words of Lykes and van der Merwe, 'most (scholars) recognise transitional justice as a set of processes and mechanisms, including accountability, justice, and reparations, operationalised by those seeking to come to terms with the multiple legacies of large-scale past abuses and *to ensure non-recurrence*'.[3]

Ensuring non-recurrence of violations is framed as a tangible goal and often one stripped of context and subjective values. If an intervention aims to ensure non-recurrence, it is quite clear where it is heading – to a society free from mass violations and injustices and conflict – 'the society' here being painted with a broad brush. This is a state of affairs all transitional justice enthusiasts are on board with. Because non-recurrence in transitional justice is both the organising telos and a goal underpinning the pillar of 'guarantees of non-recurrence' (GNRs), it is conceptualised as achievable through concrete actions. To be more precise, 'dealing with the past' becomes a necessity in order to ensure 'Never Again', which can be achieved, it is said, through all or a combination of tools in the global project's repertoire. Transitional justice, in that sense, is a self-fulfilling prophecy.

In transitional justice scholarship and policy, therefore, links have been drawn between the objective of non-recurrence and just about every known transitional justice mechanism. The objective of non-recurrence therefore frames transitional justice pillars and various practices found within these pillars. At the same, GNRs, measures aimed at preventing repeated violations of human rights and humanitarian law, are a stand-

[3] M Brinton Lykes and Hugo van der Merwe, 'Exploring/Expanding the Reach of Transitional Justice' (2017) 11 International Journal of Transitional Justice 371, p. 372 (my emphasis).

alone pillar of transitional justice, often but not always equated with institutional reform. To make sense of these conceptual conundrums, I explore six key claims of how different elements of the transitional justice project positively contribute to 'Never Again'.

2.2.1 *Criminal Trials*

Criminal trials, as institutional enforcement of (international) criminal law, are a core, if not the most prominent mechanism of transitional justice, due to which transitional justice is in practice often straightforwardly equated with international criminal justice. The arguments made for retributive justice are numerous and commonly linked to the objective of ensuring non-recurrence of violations. International and national trials are often exercised on the premise of their forward-looking potential to achieve deterrence and guarantee non-recurrence of violations in doing so.[4] In ordinary times, typical attributes of a trial would be their potential to enforce general and specific deterrence and prevent recidivism as well as increased crime rates.[5] Yet, the alleged potential of criminal justice in transitional times exceeds its usual influences. According to Teitel, trials 'play the leading foundational role in the transformation to a more liberal political order'.[6] Because past violations are often committed or sponsored by state officials, holding these high-ranking officials accountable is seen as the best way to promote a normative transformation to the new system that upholds the rule of law. Teitel even goes so far as to say that criminal law is not solely 'an instrument of stability but also one of social change'.[7] Others have argued that obliging the new regime to obey the international rules against impunity promotes the rule of law, offers incentives to rebuild the judiciary, and draws a final line between the old and the new regimes.[8] Osiel, for instance, asserts that criminal trials in transition are 'moments of truth' in and out of themselves as they highlight state officials' violence and complicity and,

[4] Padraig McAuliffe, 'Transitional Justice and the Rule of Law: The Perfect Couple or Awkward Bedfellows?' (2010) 2 Hague Journal on the Rule of Law 127.

[5] See, for instance, Jack P Gibbs, *Crime, Punishment, and Deterrence* (Elsevier 1975).

[6] Ruti Teitel, *Transitional Justice* (Oxford University Press 2000) p. 7.

[7] ibid, p. 67.

[8] See Oskar NT Thoms, James Ron, and Roland Paris, 'State-Level Effects of Transitional Justice: What Do We Know?' (2010) 4 International Journal of Transitional Justice 329.

therefore, inspire people to 'reassess their foundational beliefs'.[9] The opposing action of not prosecuting those responsible for grave violations of human rights and humanitarian law is seen as an omission to uphold a state's legal obligation which is claimed to have a direct link to further renewed violence.[10]

2.2.2 Truth Commissions

The pinnacle of truth recovery efforts in transitional justice has been the non-judicial institution of truth commission. Ad hoc and short-term, truth commissions are defined as bodies created 'to investigate, document, and report upon human rights abuses within a country over a specific period of time'.[11] Unlike criminal trials, which are focused on individual criminal responsibility, truth commissions are valued for their potential to include both victims and perpetrators and provide broader historical narratives, elaborating on the role of state institutions as well as non-state actors.[12] While dealing with the past, truth commissions have future-oriented aspirations linked to the prevention of non-recurrence. As explained in Chapter 1, the moral imperative of 'Never Again' became 'a central rallying cry of' the early truth commissions in Latin America, showing commissions' dual preventive and restorative role.[13] In addition to entitling their reports 'Never Again', commissions around the world also took it upon themselves to make the truth known *in order to* prevent repetition of future violations, as a part of their mandates. For example, the South African TRC stated that the hearings held before the commission would establish the truth about 'the motives and circumstances' in which violations happened and 'make the findings known in order to prevent a repetition of such acts in [the] future'.[14] Scholars have echoed

9 Mark Osiel, *Mass Atrocity, Collective Memory, and the Law* (Transaction Publishers 1999) p. 2.

10 Mattia Pinto, 'Historical Trends of Human Rights Gone Criminal' (2020) 42 Human Rights Quarterly 729, p. 748.

11 Ruti Teitel, 'Transitional Justice Genealogy' (2003) 16 Harvard Human Rights Journal 69, p. 78; Priscilla B Hayner, *Unspeakable Truths: Transitional Justice and the Challenge of Truth Commissions* (2nd ed., Routledge 2011).

12 Teitel, 'Transitional Justice Genealogy'.

13 Robert I Rotberg, 'Truth Commissions and the Provision of Truth, Justice, and Reconciliation' in Robert I Rotberg and Dennis F Thompson (eds.), *Truth v. Justice: The Morality of Truth Commissions* (Princeton University Press 2000) p. 3.

14 Promotion of National Unity and Reconciliation Act (Government Gazette, Act No. 34) enacted 26 July 1995.

these sentiments. Roht-Arriaza argues truth commissions have the mandate to 'at a minimum' elaborate on a common narrative about past violence in order to recommend reparations and therein prevent repetition of the violence.[15] Urban Walker similarly asserts that truth commissions' findings are a necessary condition for effective prevention of recurrence.[16] Provided that the findings of truth commissions are disseminated and included in school curricula, media outputs, and public dialogues, it is claimed that the work of a truth commission can decrease the public's resistance to acknowledging human rights violations.[17]

2.2.3 Reparations

Reparations have weak links to prevention of recurrence in transitional justice. Traditionally reparations are understood as responses to violations that seek to *restore* the post-violation conditions to those that existed prior to the violation, with the exception of GNRs, which reform the status quo as a form of reparation in international human rights law. In the light of this seeming normative incompatibility, reparations are also claimed to have a more general task of deterrence and advancing transformative goals such as reconciliation.[18] Whereas it is not claimed that reparations could single-handedly prevent repetition, their non-recurrence-relating potential rather concerns creating a social and political climate in which recurrence would be less likely. Such claims are made on the account of reparations' prioritisation of victims,[19] potential publicisation of the structural conditions that led to violence,[20] and

[15] Naomi Roht-Arriaza, 'The New Landscape of Transitional Justice' in Naomi Roht-Arriaza (ed.), *Transitional Justice in the Twenty-First Century: Beyond Truth and Justice* (Cambridge University Press 2006) p. 3.

[16] Margaret Urban Walker, 'Nunca Más' in Larry May and Elizabeth Edenberg (eds.), *Jus Post Bellum and Transitional Justice* (Cambridge University Press 2013).

[17] ibid.

[18] Dinah Shelton, *Remedies in International Human Rights Law* (2nd ed., Oxford University Press 2005); Teitel, *Transitional Justice.*

[19] Jemima Garcia-Godos, 'Reparations' in Olivera Simić (ed.), *An Introduction to Transitional Justice* (Routledge 2017); Luke Moffett, 'Transitional Justice and Reparations: Remedying the Past?' in Cheryl Lawther, Luke Moffett, and Dov Jacobs (eds.), *Research Handbook on Transitional Justice* (Edward Elgar 2017); Rodrigo Uprimny Yepes, 'Transformative Reparations of Massive Gross Human Rights Violations: Between Corrective and Distributive Justice' (2009) 27 Netherlands Quarterly of Human Rights 625.

[20] Moffett, 'Transitional Justice and Reparations'.

fortifying political transformation by publicly condemning past regime's actions.[21]

Transitional societies have resorted to reparations such as compensation (e.g., a monetary contribution to those who qualify as victims of conflict),[22] restitution (e.g., returning the property taken away during conflict),[23] rehabilitation (e.g., providing survivors of conflict with medical and psychological services free of charge),[24] and measures of satisfaction that include symbolic reparations such as apologies.[25] In the literature, these individual types of reparations are not typically expected or required to achieve the goal of non-recurrence. However, there has been some discussion about symbolic reparations such as apologies, with their collective element, having strong links to 'Never Again' due to their potential to repair group harm, memorialise victims' suffering,[26] and promote efforts to reform institutions.[27]

2.2.4 *Institutional Reform*

As previously explained, measures of institutional reform are most fervently linked to the promise of 'Never Again' in transitional justice. Because GNRs are simultaneously a pillar of transitional justice and a stand-alone type of reparations in international human rights law linked to institutional reform, in scholarship as well as policy, the concepts of 'institutional reform' and 'GNRs' are often used interchangeably. For instance, in the 2015 European Union's Policy Framework on support to transitional justice, the fourth pillar of transitional justice is listed as 'GNRs/institutional reform', thereby making the two equal and inseparable.[28] For this reason, measures of institutional reform are almost by default given the quality of preventing future violations and are treated as

21 Teitel, *Transitional Justice*.

22 Ruben Carranza, *Relief, Reparations and the Root Causes of Conflict in Nepal* (International Center for Transitional Justice 2012).

23 Nicole Summers, 'Colombia's Victims' Law: Transitional Justice in a Time of Violent Conflict?' (2012) 25 Harvard Human Rights Journal 219.

24 Clara Sandoval-Villalba, *Rehabilitation as a Form of Reparation under International Law* (REDRESS 2009).

25 Ruben Carranza, Cristian Corre, and Elena Naughton, *More than Words: Apologies as a Form of Reparation* (International Center for Transitional Justice 2015).

26 Moffett, 'Transitional Justice and Reparations'.

27 Carranza and others, *More than Words*.

28 The Council of the European Union, *The EU's Policy Framework on Support to Transitional Justice*, https://shorturl.at/lAVZ1 accessed 3 June 2024.

key forms of action towards the actionable goal of non-recurrence in transitional justice.

Public institutions such as the police, the army, the judiciary, and the security sector are often seen as instruments of repression and violence and as such, it is claimed, need to be reformed and cleansed in the light of the transitional justice project. Institutional reform is seen as a more long-term solution to the problems of the violent past, affecting not only victims and perpetrators but also entire transitional societies.[29] Preventative measures tied to institutional reform are vast and range from individual measures such as banning perpetrators from reassuming power to those targeting broader reconstruction, for example, building a justice system where violation claims can be adequately accommodated.[30] Certain widespread measures of institutional reform target specific individuals, most prominently vetting, which is more administrative than criminal in nature as it relies on more relaxed evidentiary and procedural rules.[31] Most practices in this regard, however, have to do with state accountability and a larger transformation of state structures, such as the police or armed forces.[32]

The idea is that through institutional reform, the rule of law is reasserted and there is a blanket political confirmation that some constitutional and political structures played a role in conflict and are now stripped of their power.[33] Practices of institutional reform hence unequivocally seek to challenge and transform some of the structures of power that would otherwise help maintain the status quo if kept in their original form. In that sense, public institutions such as the security sector and judiciary are reformed both to eliminate past abusers and to improve the effectiveness and accountability of the sectors in future prosecutions and prevention of potential future atrocities.

[29] Alexander L Boraine, 'Transitional Justice: A Holistic Interpretation' (2006) 60 Journal of International Affairs 17.

[30] Ellen Lutz, 'Transitional Justice: Lessons Learned and the Road Ahead' in Naomi Roht-Arriaza (ed.), *Transitional Justice in the Twenty-First Century: Beyond Truth and Justice* (Cambridge University Press 2006).

[31] Pablo De Greiff, 'Articulating the Links between Transitional Justice and Development: Justice and Social Integration' in Pablo De Greiff and Roger Duthie (eds.), *Transitional Justice and Development* (Social Science Research Council 2009) p. 38.

[32] Laurel E Fletcher, 'Editorial Note' (2015) 9 International Journal of Transitional Justice 193.

[33] Christine Bell, Colm Campbell, and Fionnuala Ní Aoláin, 'Justice Discourses in Transition' (2004) 13 Social & Legal Studies 305.

Other interventions targeting institutions can send a clear message that the former ideology is illegitimate or significantly weakened,[34] so institutional reform is seen as contributing to the increased levels of civic trust.[35] Vetting in particular is praised for its power to break apart networks of criminal activities[36] and remove people with suspicious pasts, thus transforming institutions and people's trust in them.[37] These effects of institutional reform, most notably changing the structures of power and improving civic trust, are repeatedly claimed in international transitional justice policy and practice to be either essential for the objective of non-recurrence or, in fact, applications of GNRs, as per international human rights law.[38] They are also claimed to enable other transitional justice measures, for instance, by removing parts of the structure obstructing criminal prosecutions or truth-seeking.[39]

2.2.5 Memorialisation

The rhetoric of 'Never Again' itself gives a framework to discuss different aspects of memorialisation and its usefulness.[40] The general idea, as Clark describes it, is that '[o]nly by remembering ... can we learn from the past'.[41] Scholars offer numerous examples of mnemonic practices seemingly beneficial for non-recurrence that encompass a combination of institutionalised and non-institutionalised practices such as museum visits and art making. As such, this scholarship introduces venues and

[34] Clara Sandoval, 'Transitional Justice and Social Change' (2014) 20 SUR – International Journal on Human Rights 181.

[35] De Greiff, 'Articulating the Links between Transitional Justice and Development'.

[36] Pablo De Greiff, 'Vetting and Other Transitional Reforms' in Alexander Mayer-Rieckh and Pablo De Greiff (eds.), *Justice as Prevention: Vetting Public Employees in Transitional Justice* (Social Science Research Council 2007) p. 522.

[37] Roger Duthie, 'Introduction' in Alexander Mayer-Rieckh and Pablo De Greiff (eds.), *Justice as Prevention: Vetting Public Employees in Transitional Justice* (Social Science Research Council 2007) p. 16.

[38] For example, the United Nations Office of the High Commissioner for Human Rights, *Rule-of-Law Tools for Post-Conflict States: Vetting: An Operational Framework* (United Nations 2006).

[39] Alexander Mayer-Rieckh, 'Vetting to Prevent Future Abuses: Reforming the Police, Courts, Prosecutor's Offices in Bosnia and Herzegovina' in Alexander Mayer-Rieckh and Pablo De Greiff (eds.), *Justice as Prevention: Vetting Public Employees in Transitional Justice* (Social Science Research Council 2007).

[40] Janine Natalya Clark, 'Reconciliation through Remembrance? War Memorials and the Victims of Vukovar' (2013) 7 International Journal of Transitional Justice 116.

[41] ibid, p. 117.

processes otherwise not ordinarily encompassed in the paradigmatic transitional justice such as art and informal education, both of which carry with them values that seemingly impact non-recurrence.

To illustrate, museums that depict the struggle of victims/survivors of oppression are portrayed as educational sites where audiences can be introduced to the horrors of violence.[42] Such spaces are believed to help ensure that the new generations will not resort to the same forms of abuse in the future by exposing past abuses. For instance, Hamber and colleagues track the intersections between memorialisation and art for the purpose of non-recurrence in Bangladesh's Liberation War Museum and their mobile museum that travels around the country with a photo exhibition of the history of the Liberation War.[43] This minibus museum visits rural areas where the youth are considered to be more susceptible to radicalisation and religious violence. Combining oral history and art, the museum engages with participants for effective, experiential learning and, ultimately, deterrence from resorting to violence. Similarly, numerous other initiatives organised by non-governmental sectors in transitional societies are discussed as showing that visiting and engaging with sites of memory impact young people in numerous ways, including changing their opinions and encouraging civic engagement.[44] In this way, memorials and commemorations done by the grassroots can also be seen as struggles against forgetting as well as against repetition.[45]

2.2.6 Prevention as Everything

Lastly, recent policy developments which seek to reconceptualise 'GNRs' as more than institutional reform and/or something entirely different from it provide illuminating insights into the idea that the totality of transitional justice tools and mechanisms is beneficial for non-recurrence. In the scarce theorisation of GNRs in transitional justice, there are competing understandings of GNRs as measures of legal and

[42] Nayanika Mookherjee, '"Never Again": Aesthetics of "Genocidal" Cosmopolitanism and the Bangladesh Liberation War Museum' (2011) 17 Journal of the Royal Anthropological Institute 571.

[43] Brandon Hamber, Liz Sevcenko, and Ereshnee Naidu, 'Utopian Dreams or Practical Possibilities? The Challenges of Evaluating the Impact of Memorialization in Societies in Transition' (2010) 4 International Journal of Transitional Justice 397.

[44] ibid.

[45] Lia Kent, 'Local Memory Practices in East Timor: Disrupting Transitional Justice Narrative' (2011) 5 International Journal of Transitional Justice 434.

institutional reform or 'something else', a magical norm with transformative potential, 'a bridge' between different mechanisms of transitional justice as well as different streams of research–policy–practice in transitional justice, the legalist and the more transformative ones. On that note, GNRs' potential to prevent further violations is magnified where there is an understanding that criminal trials, truth commissions, or reparations are not 'enough' but are nevertheless essential. GNRs are both distinct from and complementary to other pillars of transitional justice. Where they are not conceptually limited to measures of institutional reform, GNRs, it is claimed, should be informed by systemic analyses of the root causes of violence and patterns of exclusion.[46] GNRs beyond institutional reform can trigger fundamental changes by transforming the old regime's ideology that supported or allowed violence to be committed.[47]

These ideas about GNRs are reflected at the level of international policy, particularly in the work of the UN Special Rapporteur on truth, justice, reparation, and guarantees of non-repetition. In the first and most elaborate report on GNRs, Special Rapporteur De Greiff defined a guarantee of non-recurrence as a *function* performed through a variety of measures to which previously victimised societies as a whole are entitled and where state institutions are duty bearers.[48] In that sense, guaranteeing non-recurrence of violations becomes 'an object of rational policy-making'.[49] In De Greiff's view, once the basic preconditions for institutional interventions such as ensuring security and access to legal identity are met, there exist three fields of intervention through which policies relating to GNRs should be structured: at the level of official state institutions, civil society, and cultural/personal dispositions. For each of the interventions, a series of measures were proposed, such as ratification of treaties and legal reforms, judicial reforms, constitutional reforms, removing legal and practical obstacles imposed on civil society, community-level programmes for those who previously lacked legal rights, educational reforms, trauma counselling, and psychosocial

[46] Naomi Roht-Arriaza, 'Measures of Non-Repetition in Transitional Justice: The Missing Link?' in Simon Robins and Paul Gready (eds.), *From Transitional to Transformative Justice* (Cambridge University Press 2019) p. 124.

[47] Sandoval-Villalba, 'Transitional Justice and Social Change'.

[48] United Nations Human Rights Council, 'Report of the Special Rapporteur on the Promotion of Truth, Justice, Reparation and Guarantees of Non-Recurrence, Pablo de Greiff' (7 September 2015) UN Doc. A/HRC/30/42.

[49] ibid, para 22.

support. Cultural and personal dispositions are seen as sources of stability and as a means to allow for continuing social relations.

The key idea stemming from this report is that ensuring non-recurrence is a complex function cutting across sectors of society, with multiple potential measures that could be achievable through transitional justice institutions, mechanisms, and processes, and which generally require the mobilisation of the entire society. The Special Rapporteur stated,

> The core function of guarantees of non-recurrence is preventive in nature. It is one to which truth, justice and reparations are themselves supposed to contribute: criminal justice mainly through deterrence; truth commissions through disclosure, clarification and formulation of recommendations with a preventive intent; and reparations by strengthening the hand of victims to claim redress for the past and future violations and to enforce their rights more assertively.[50]

There is, therefore, an emerging understanding that GNRs are flexible, open for re-contextualisation and qualitatively different in transitional justice than in international law.[51] Yet there is also a veil of ambiguity in these scholarly assertions as to what GNRs are – if a function, why/how is this different from prevention? How do these transformations occur and why are these specific transformations connected to prevention of renewed violence? To sustain this malleability, GNRs continue to be largely undefined and understudied empirically, while advocates of the global project of transitional justice continue to claim that it possesses some transformative, status quo-changing function called 'GNRs' in its repertoire.

2.3 Rigid and Ambiguous: Transitional Justice as a Structure

Across these six claims, some common threads can be identified. First, all claims of positive influences of different core elements of the transitional justice project on non-recurrence share the view that non-recurrence requires some transformation of the status quo. It is held that there must have been some structural conditions in place that helped, supported, or actively triggered the past violations and,

[50] ibid, para 24.

[51] Maja Davidovic, 'The Law of "Never Again": Transitional Justice and the Transformation of the Norm of Non-Recurrence' (2021) 15 International Journal of Transitional Justice 386.

although these structural conditions are not always identified, they comprise the status quo that needs to be reformed under the premise that the existence of the same conditions would lead to the same, or similar, violent outcomes. The transitional justice project typically comes with a regime change and proceeds with transformations of public institutions, the principles held valuable by key political actors, and the behaviours they perform publicly. Jointly these processes create a transformed climate different from the status quo that preceded the conflict. However, very little space is left for debating who defines and experiences the said status quo, whether any status quo can be reduced to the state and its organs as well as how the new status quo affects non-recurrence.

Second, there is a conscious process of linking certain modes of being characteristic of neoliberalism and legalism, such as good governance, the rule of law, transparency, and public acknowledgement, to the absence of mass atrocities. The very premise that prevention and commission of mass atrocities can be governed in the first place should be debated, but it is unsurprising considering the nature of transitional justice as a project. However, this linking practice suggests, wrongly, that neoliberal legal and institutional structures are the antithesis of conflict and implies, wrongly, that the most horrendous atrocities are not committed or are very unlikely to be committed in and by liberal states. Because the project of transitional justice is born within the specificities of the end of the Cold War and dominant values and ideals of this era, imaginaries of life, peace, and conflict in and after the neoliberal legalistic mode of being play no role in its operations.

Third, these claims can be read as a continuous and rather undeserved trust in the state to be transformed. There is an acknowledgement that just about every state organ or institution can be violent and complicit in the atrocities, yet at the same time, each can be 'corrected' with a little help from friends. In that sense, the state in transitional justice is often both the problem and the solution to the problem. None of these claims examine whether the modern state itself can be an inherently violent creation, or that there are global, regional, and transnational factors that could prompt abuses of power across different forms of neoliberal governance the transitioning state might practice.

Needless to say, each claim of positive influence on non-recurrence has been debated and challenged in context-based practices and experiences of transitional justice. As numerous countries transitioned from communist and authoritarian regimes to democracies, they faced dilemmas over the alleged appropriateness of criminal trials.[52] First, the contexts of transitions in Latin America and Central and Eastern Europe were different from that of, for instance, the former Yugoslavia and very distinct from each other. Second, the complex political realities of criminally prosecuting individuals from the past regime became apparent.[53] Leaders of certain new regimes in these contexts questioned selective prosecutorial policies and whether they would diminish public trust in the new regime's institutions.

Elsewhere, debates were had on whether truth commissions should be preferred over criminal prosecutions and if amnesties should be offered in exchange for 'the truth' like it was the case in South Africa, or whether such actions were acts of injustice and immorality that consequently weaken truth commissions' role in preventing future abuses.[54] Further discussion followed about the morality and practicality of establishing, interpreting, and enforcing a single narrative about the past onto people. In this line of critique, the construction of any 'truth' narrative is seen as a political act, an exercise of control.

In a similar vein, reparations, institutional reform, and memorialisation processes have been exposed for their exclusions and how they could potentially harm the prospects of sustainable peace. Compensation schemes in particular are very costly, placing hard, political choices in front of transitional societies which must balance between monetary reparations and deeper socio-economic inequalities, with or without external support and often at the expense of potential beneficiaries or the chosen benefits.[55] As a result, comprehensive reparations schemes are typically lacking in transitional societies and unrealised reparations claims continue to be made decades after the violations took place. For this reason, scholars express concern about the exclusion of certain types of victims[56] and reparations laws' limited ability to do

[52] Teitel, 'Transitional Justice Genealogy'.

[53] ibid.

[54] Rotberg, 'Truth Commissions and the Provision of Truth, Justice, and Reconciliation'; Kent Greenawalt, 'Amnesty's Justice' in Robert I Rotberg and Dennis F Thompson (eds.), *Truth v. Justice: The Morality of Truth Commissions* (Princeton University Press 2000) p. 191.

[55] Uprimny Yepes, 'Transformative Reparations of Massive Gross Human Rights Violations'.

[56] On how women tend to fall under the cracks of reparation schemes, see Ruth Rubio-Marin (ed.), *What Happened to the Women? Gender and Reparations for Human Rights Violations* (Columbia/SSRC 2006).

justice,[57] both of which weaken the already ambiguous links made between reparations and the objective of non-recurrence. Measures of institutional reform are rarely exercised as planned, failing to achieve the envisaged goals of the international community.[58] Other criticism includes allegations of the failure of institutional reform to redistribute wealth and power, therefore reinforcing, rather than transforming, the status quo.[59] Memorials are used for mourning as well as for 'making politics'.[60] State-led commemorative practices in particular can produce new victims, perpetrators, and ideologies and reinforce certain patterns of historical interpretation over others.[61]

Why then, do we remain confident about the utility of transitional justice as a global project? Jointly, these threads tell us something about transitional justice as a mode of global governance and as a structure, 'a set of internally related elements'.[62] The internally related elements of transitional justice include its objects, such as mechanisms, and tools enshrined in the pillar-like model and the situations the project examines. Nevertheless, I propose that as a structure, transitional justice is also bound by its own *characteristics* evident in the claims around non-recurrence. The tendency towards determinacy, predictability, and set outcomes arises out of the field's initial positioning as a subset of international law, a prominent way to enforce developing and feeble state obligations around 'dealing' with their violent pasts. The attachment to legalism, as a process where law 'regulates behaviour' while also shaping 'political relations, . . . language [and] . . . the way we think',[63] has brought certain values into transitional justice which have subsequently been transformed into its inherent characteristics. Zunino, for

57 Moffett, 'Transitional Justice and Reparations'.

58 Padraig McAuliffe, 'Weighing Domestic and International Impediments to Transformative Justice in Transition' (2015) 3 London Review of International Law 169.

59 See Dustin N Sharp, 'What Would Satisfy Us? Taking Stock of Critical Approaches to Transitional Justice' (2019) 13 International Journal of Transitional Justice 570.

60 Johanna Mannergren Selimovic, 'Making Peace, Making Memory: Peacebuilding and Politics of Remembrance at Memorials of Mass Atrocities' (2013) 1 Peacebuilding 334, p. 334.

61 Jelena Đureinović, *The Politics of Memory of the Second World War in Contemporary Serbia: Collaboration, Resistance and Retribution* (Routledge 2020).

62 'Internally related' means that the elements are defined through their position in the structure. Alexander E Wendt, 'The Agent-Structure Problem in International Relations Theory' (1987) 41 International Organisation 335, p. 357.

63 Kieran McEvoy, 'Beyond Legalism: Towards a Thicker Understanding of Transitional Justice' (2007) 34 Journal of Law and Society 411, p. 416.

instance, explains that transitional justice is 'comparative, technical . . . teleological, liberal . . . multilevel and state-centric'.[64] These characteristics are rooted in field-defining developments in specific contexts discussed so far in the book and are exclusive of many other Cold War-era transitions that were non-liberal, non-legalistic, or otherwise did not fit into the emerging discourse.[65] Over time, the characteristics became its inherent values: legalism, state-centralism, and liberalism,[66] exported to numerous countries dealing with their violent past. The values of predictability, objectivity, and certainty have been particularly valued in the context of turbulent political transitions across contexts where the rule of law is prioritised as necessary for successful transitions, often hand-in-hand with physical security assurances achieved through measures such as disarmament, demobilisation, and reintegration, characteristic of liberal peace- and state-building projects. Having been transferred to courts as the most representative institutions of law, as well as other institutions of transitional justice such as truth commissions, these characteristics set transitional justice as a global project well suited to ensure transformations of new regimes.

It follows that the global project of transitional justice can be interpreted as a set of 'rules of the game' in which actions, that is, practices of non-recurrence, ought to take place.[67] As explained in Chapter 1, there is a 'settled consensus' and a growing sense of inevitability that some kind of transitional justice is necessary to deal with the past – the question only remains what.[68] At the same time, there is also 'uneasiness' about the means, results, and efficacy of the project. Yet, its objectives, including non-recurrence, remain certain. As Miller contends, transitional justice is organised around specific social justice goals where practitioners understand the limits of what she calls the 'enterprise' but have faith in its utility.[69] To further quote Miller, '[o]ne of the greatest successes of transitional justice as a governing enterprise was to manifest

[64] Marcos Zunino, *Justice Framed: A Genealogy of Transitional Justice* (Cambridge University Press 2019) p. 229.
[65] For example, Russell's tribunal with respect to the atrocities committed in Vietnam. See ibid.
[66] ibid, p. 231.
[67] Wendt, 'The Agent-Structure Problem', p. 338.
[68] Rosemary Nagy, 'Transitional Justice as Global Project: Critical Reflections' (2008) 29 Third World Quarterly 276, p. 276.
[69] Zinaida Miller, 'Embedded Ambivalence: Ungoverning Global Justice' (2020) 11 Transnational Legal Theory 353.

increasing uniformity, predictability, and expertise while at the same time maintaining the fundamental need for difference, contingency and participation'.[70]

The simultaneous certainty and ambiguity are not natural or accidental; they are essential to the success of transitional justice as a project. The ambiguity of the project accounts for its rapid success and migration to incredibly different contexts, allowing different actors to interpret core ideas differently while faithful to the progressive goals and non-negotiable elements of the project. This is not unheard of for global projects; in fact, it is part and parcel of deeper structures[71] transitional justice is a part of, namely legalism and neoliberalism. For instance, it has been argued that the adaptability and mutability of neoliberalism are key reasons for its global success.[72] Similarly, the trope of 'civilisation' continues to persist, arguably, on account of its adaptability as conceptualisations of 'civilisation' shift while the overarching structure remains constant.[73] As such, both certainty and ambiguity require constant and deliberate work to be maintained. For the global project of transitional justice to survive, it must sustain a degree of flexibility, adaptability, and context-dependence, of which transitional justice has lots. Simultaneously, the core 'rules of the game' we have come to know as 'dealing with the past' must keep a level of rigidity, fixity, and consistency. These characteristics and the efforts to maintain them, I propose, should be studied not as an interesting anomaly but as a part and parcel of the 'project' of transitional justice and its effects on the socio-economic, political, and cultural lives of people and phenomena in contexts where transitional justice travels. The structure, with all its structural properties, thus shapes not only the limits of transitional justice as a 'project' or 'enterprise', as per these previous theorisations,[74] but also how the *internal elements* of the structure, such as norms and mechanisms, are created and recreated at all levels where transitional justice exists – local, national, regional, and global.

[70] ibid, p. 355.

[71] On deep and surface structures, see Adriana Sinclair, 'Why We Should See International Law as a Structure: Unpicking International Law's Ontology and Agency' (2021) 35 International Relations 216.

[72] Vivien A Schmidt and Mark Thatcher, *Resilient Liberalism in Europe's Political Economy* (Cambridge University Press 2013).

[73] Ntina Tzouvala, *Capitalism as Civilisation: A History of International Law* (Cambridge University Press 2020).

[74] Nagy, 'Transitional Justice as Global Project'; Miller, 'Embedded Ambivalence'.

Needless to say, no structure is ever fully fixed or static. Key sociological theorising on structure and agency suggests that the two opposites are in interplay and that therefore the agents of transitional justice and their practices are shaped by the structure of transitional justice while simultaneously shaping it.[75] Both structure and agency are 'simultaneously involved' and have the power to shape 'the production of social phenomena' including meaningful assurances of non-recurrence.[76] In Giddens' structure–agency duality, structures become both the medium and outcome of practices' reproduction and power relations are inevitably conceptualised as two-way. In Giddens' view, therefore, it is not social systems that reason, think, or have a purpose but rather human agents who can do these things. Furthermore, it is not institutions that operate and conspire against agents but rather agents who produce them. In fact, in *The Constitution of Society*, Giddens argues that structures 'have no existence independent of the knowledge that agents have about what they do'.[77] Hence, when I speak of transitional justice having its own survival needs, I do not see it as an invisible floating body, living and breathing on its own, but as sustained by practitioners, bureaucrats, policymakers, and others.

In structuration theory, the duality of structure and agency suggests that structures are both 'enabling and constraining' for human agency, meaning that structure is ultimately involved in the production of action in some capacity.[78] But the structure of transitional justice is not an omnipotent force. Instead, agents are equipped with different kinds and levels of power which shapes the capacity to act as well as the outcome of their actions. Although power is integral to the constitution of social practices and structures that are powerful enough to enable or constrain, they are not sufficiently powerful to entirely block actions by wilful agents.[79] That said, when proposing that the transitional justice project is complicit in making bad situations worse, it should be noted that

[75] Anthony Giddens, *Central Problems in Social Theory: Action, Structure and Contradiction in Social Analysis* (The Macmillan Press 1979); Anthony Giddens, *The Constitution of Society: Outline of the Theory of Structuration* (Polity Press 1984); Margaret S Archer, *Structure, Agency and the Internal Conversation* (Cambridge University Press 2003).

[76] Wendt, 'The Agent-Structure Problem', p. 361.

[77] Giddens, *The Constitution of Society*, p. 26.

[78] Giddens, *Central Problems in Social Theory*, p. 69.

[79] Kathleen E Hull and Robert L Nelson, 'Gender Inequality in Law: Problems of Structure and Agency in Recent Studies of Gender in Anglo-American Legal Professions' (1998) 23 Law & Social Inquiry 681, p. 695.

actors are too. Similarly, in Chapter 7, I show how actors seek to improve meaningful assurances of 'Never Again' both with and despite transitional justice. Not just any action counts, instead I am interested in activities or series of activities conducted over time to alter some of the existing socio-economic/political situations out of an understanding that these situations presently contribute to (the increased risk of) renewed violence in the near or far future.

What about the temporality of transitional justice? The global project of transitional justice, one might argue, is by default time limited. While it might not always have a clear beginning, it is supposed to end. The conceptions of transitional justice as a radical shift from the past to the future, from the old and the new, a simultaneously backward- and forward-oriented process support a dominant linear time-bound view.[80] Linear conceptions of time are characteristic of Western industrial societies as, through the invention of the mechanical clock, time became measurable and objective and the future became 'something that could be predicted and expected based on a steady repetition of the same events'.[81] On this linear path, transitional justice benefits from a 'two-way gaze' whereby it seeks to repair the past and ensure a peaceful future.[82] As previously explained, the project is largely outcome-oriented which makes the objectives of transitional justice achievable and therefore the project 'completable'.

Yet, while transitional justice as a project in a specific context might have a beginning and end, as a structure, it needs permanence over time. Giddens posits that temporality and time–space intersections more generally are essential for understanding any social practices. Structure is composed of '*patterning elements of interaction* . . . and the *continuity of interaction* in time', that is, rules and resources that bind time and space in social reproduction.[83] Giddens differentiates between the durée of daily life (as a duration that does not lead anywhere, instead it is repetitive); the life span of the individual (finite and irreversible) and the longue durée of institutional time, which lasts for generations and can also include some elements of repetition or routinisation of practice.[84]

80 Teitel, *Transitional Justice.*
81 Maja Davidović, 'Reconciling Complexities of Time in Criminal Justice and Transitional Justice' (2021) 21 International Criminal Law Review 935.
82 Lynn Davies, 'Justice-Sensitive Education: The Implications of Transitional Justice Mechanisms for Teaching and Learning' (2017) 53 Comparative Education 333, p. 333.
83 Giddens, *Central Problems in Social Theory*, pp. 62–4.
84 Giddens, *The Constitution of Society.*

As a structure, therefore, transitional justice, both as an imperative and a set of institutions, needs to survive and remain consistent across and despite contexts in the *long durée*. From Rwanda to Cambodia, from Sierra Leone to Iraq, we see a certain kind of transitional justice routine, with certain non-negotiable elements that persist while maintaining an overall welcoming tone towards context-specific approaches and practices. That said, everyday practices in contexts such as Bosnia and Herzegovina relating to justice, peace, truth, and non-recurrence are integral for understanding how institutionalised practices endure.[85]

2.4 Governing Uncertainty

Although transitional justice as a project in a specific context might have a beginning and end, as a structure, it needs permanence over time. Rather than proposing that the impacts of transitional justice on perceptions of meaningful assurances of non-recurrence can be examined in isolation through individual mechanisms or pillars, I here contribute to the emerging idea that transitional justice in toto impacts non-recurrence to demonstrate how it may do so negatively.

In my proposition, there are no vague causal links, ambiguous hypothesising, or self-prophesising about the potential of transitional justice. Instead, I argue that answering the question about the impacts of transitional justice on non-recurrence requires scholars to rethink what the transitional justice project is for. In addition to seeking to 'achieve' values such as truth, justice, peace, and reconciliation, the project is first and foremost there to manage the *uncertainty* that characterises periods of rupture as well as the overall historical period in which the project of transitional justice was born. The end of the Cold War and the collapses of authoritarian and/or socialist regimes across the world brought uncertainty about what the world would look like in a no longer (or so it seemed) bipolar climate. Institutions and principles of the rule of law and good governance were a part of the response to such unsettling uncertainty and creating a new world order. In concrete situations where the past needed to be dealt with, the questions about the future persisted and transitional justice lurked on the horizon as a form of hope. As an overarching telos of transitional justice, ensuring 'Never Again' requires providing assurances about this uncertain future – that

[85] ibid, p. 282.

all will be well and that the regimes of international law which underpin transitional justice are not utopian. Accepting that nobody can predict the future to the fullest, the goal is to control it, in the sense of ensuring that there is no renewed conflict, to the extent possible, by governing the past.

This is an element of the transitional justice project thus far neglected by scholars and policymakers alike. As shown in Section 2.2, scholarly and policy works have focused on the material elements through which non-recurrence could be guaranteed, whether trials, commissions, or memorials. That is the 'how' of transitional justice as a positive force on non-recurrence. The 'why' has also been explored in some depth – because it recovers the truth, promotes accountability and the rule of law, and develops a culture of remembrance. However, the very fundamental question of 'what' is neglected – what does recovering the truth or promoting accountability or developing a culture of remembrance do for the non-recurrence of conflict?

To expand the purposes of the transitional justice project to this sphere, I propose an interrogation into other forms of security beyond the physical. The answer, I propose, is not merely that these processes decrease the likelihood of violence by managing the state and its institutions, or through objective assessments of when a status quo is reformed or not. It is also that, to make meaningful assurances of non-recurrence, actors of transitional justice ought to mitigate the kind of behaviours that cause *anxieties* around renewed conflict. Definitions of anxiety vary, but in studies of ontological security, there is a general agreement that anxiety is experienced internally and is linked to uncertainty, that is, anxiety arises in relation to some feeling or state of uncertainty about own existence, others' actions, and the future more generally.[86] While states, global projects, and other political communities do not experience anxiety as individuals do, anxiety can be contained by individuals through mechanisms that are both socially and politically produced.[87] The anxieties experienced within those entities 'produce aggregate behavioural outcomes ... analogous to ... the individual

[86] Nina C Krickel-Choi, 'The Concept of Anxiety in Ontological Security Studies' (2022) 24 International Studies Review 1.

[87] Bahar Rumelili, 'Ontological (In)Security and Peace Anxieties: A Framework for Conflict Resolution' in Bahar Rumelili (ed.), *Conflict Resolution and Ontological Security: Peace Anxieties* (Routledge 2015) p. 13.

level'.[88] Furthermore, Rumelili proposes that whether or not a situation causes anxiety in an individual is also determined by collective attunement, whereby being in a collective 'attuned to the world in anxiety' can make even milder situations as anxiety-inducing.[89] These collective senses of living in anxious times are politically produced for 'anxious subjects … are in continuous demand for a politics of reassurance'.[90] The physical absence of armed conflict is crucial, but it means less in people's everyday lives if they are anxious about the longevity and strength of such absence in ways that cause them discomfort, worry, and dread. Importantly, however, anxiety about renewed conflict can be paralysing and detrimental to action, but it can also bring new possibilities for creativity and social and political change.[91]

If transitional justice flourishes in periods of rupture, between the old and the new, the violent and peaceful, then it flourishes in periods of crises. It is here that I propose that the transitional justice project is designed to govern both the physical and the more neglected, ontological insecurities of different actors. I understand ontological security as 'security not of the body but of the self, the subjective sense of who one is, which enables and motivates action and choice'.[92] Ontological security is 'a basic need' of individual and collective actors, sought and maintained through routinised, stable relationships[93] and a sense of predictability and order in the international system.[94] In Giddens' words, routine is 'linked to the minimizing of unconscious sources of anxiety' through the enactment of which 'agents sustain a sense of ontological security'.[95] All actors engage in routines of different kinds, including

88 ibid, p. 17.

89 Bahar Rumelili, '[Our] Age of Anxiety: Existentialism and the Current State of International Relations' (2021) 24 Journal of International Relations and Development 1020, pp. 1025–6.

90 ibid.

91 Catarina Kinnvall and Jennifer Mitzen, 'Anxiety, Fear, and Ontological Security in World Politics: Thinking with and beyond Giddens' (2020) 12 International Theory 240. On the distinction between neurotic and normal anxiety in relation to change and creativity, see Karl Gustafsson and Nina C Krickel-Choi, 'Returning to the Roots of Ontological Security: Insights from the Existentialist Anxiety Literature' (2020) 26 European Journal of International Relations 875.

92 Jennifer Mitzen, 'Ontological Security in World Politics: State Identity and the Security Dilemma' (2006) 12 European Journal of International Relations 341, p. 344.

93 ibid, p. 343.

94 Jelena Subotic, 'Political Memory, Ontological Security, and Holocaust Remembrance in Post-Communist Europe' (2018) 27 European Security 296.

95 Giddens, *The Constitution of Society,* p. 282.

routines and relationships with significant others as ways to construct and sustain one's identity and, in doing so, they create relationships of attachment to the routines.[96] Routines, in other words, 'make the world knowable' and help actors feel secure about their sense of self.[97] In that sense, certainty, too, is a basic need. Uncertainty, on the other hand, is largely treated in ontological security studies as a threat to the security of self and self-identities.[98] As Mitzen posits, '[w]here an actor has no idea what to expect, she cannot systematically relate ends to means, and it becomes unclear how to pursue her ends'.[99] The *unknown* and *unknowable* are deemed undesirable for actors who crave knowledge about the self and the world. When political and social processes can no longer contain anxieties, ontological insecurities occur.

It follows that uncertainty is triggered when routines and routinised relationships are ruptured through situations that can be described as 'critical'[100] and 'unpredictable'.[101] These situations are critical and unpredictable because they defy the routinised behavioural frames. In these situations, actors lose 'their stabilising anchor' and ability to 'answer questions about doing, acting, and being', becoming ontologically insecure.[102] All critical situations meaningful to an actor will invite a re-examination of one's identity. Ejdus proposes that critical situations disrupt actors' responses to four fundamental questions of existence, finitude, relations, and autobiography, bringing these questions 'to the level of discursive consciousness', that is, actors' ability 'to express their actions verbally'.[103] Upon crisis, ontologically insecure actors thus proceed to restore certainty and ability to answer these fundamental questions. They do so in different ways by, for instance, rewriting one's biography, or securitising the national identity. As Subotic argues, something becomes a 'crisis' when an actor perceives it as such, so any situation can be labelled as 'critical' for the relevant actor, even if it is

[96] Mitzen, 'Ontological Security in World Politics'; Subotic, 'Political Memory, Ontological Security, and Holocaust Remembrance'.
[97] Mitzen, 'Ontological Security in World Politics', p. 347.
[98] ibid, p. 345.
[99] ibid, p. 342.
[100] Filip Ejdus, 'Critical Situations, Fundamental Questions and Ontological Insecurity in World Politics' (2018) 21 Journal of International Relations and Development 883.
[101] Eun A Jo, 'Memory, Institutions, and the Domestic Politics of South Korean–Japanese Relations' (2022) 76 International Organisation 767, p. 771.
[102] Kinnvall and Mitzen, 'Anxiety, Fear and Ontological Security', p. 246.
[103] Ejdus, 'Critical Situations', p. 884.

seemingly irrelevant globally.[104] Equally, situations perceived as crises by the outside actors can in fact provide certainty for the actors being affected by them. Conflict, for instance, can under different circumstances provide both a sense of normality and a sense of crisis while seemingly positive developments such as peace agreements can be sources of ontological insecurity. Conflict can be a source of certainty (of action, roles, relationships, and conditions), informing shared experiences necessary for collective identities and allowing actors to meet their ontological security needs.[105] As such, it can be preferred by actors over 'the unsettling condition of deep uncertainty' that might await in peacetime.[106] It follows that conflict resolution and peace processes can in fact trigger 'political and social processes that reproduce and reactivate conflict'.[107]

The advocates of the transitional justice project aim to manage uncertainty in deeply uncertain times of transition in recipient communities, through or together with local structures such as governments. This is done through numerous processes characteristic of global projects such as making promises (of justice, peace, and democracy); collecting and establishing authoritative information (through, for instance, truth and reconciliation and fact-finding commissions but also trials); restoring roles, positions, and conditions (which existed prior to violations); and undertaking multiple solutions at the same time.[108] In that sense, the transitional justice project has capacity to act – and therefore should be ascribed responsibility for such actions – as 'an anxiety controlling mechanism'.[109]

However, the project in and out of itself can rupture the routines of different actors and bring with it new or aggravated uncertainties. Because of what the global project does and promises to do, it comes with certain normative commitments which, as Mälksoo argues, provide

104 Subotic, 'Political Memory, Ontological Security, and Holocaust Remembrance'.

105 Rumelili, *Conflict Resolution and Ontological Security.*

106 Mitzen, 'Ontological Security in World Politics', p. 342; Bahar Rumelili, 'Breaking with Europe's Pasts: Memory, Reconciliation, and Ontological (In)Security' (2018) 27 European Security 280.

107 Bahar Rumelili, 'Introduction' in Bahar Rumelili (ed.), *Conflict Resolution and Ontological Security: Peace Anxieties* (Routledge 2015) p. 2.

108 Ryan J Orr, Raymond E Levitt, and Richard W Scott, *Global Project: Institutional and Political Challenges* (Cambridge University Press 2011).

109 Felix Berenskötter, 'Anxiety and the Biographical Gestalt of Political Leaders' (2021) 24 Journal of International Relations and Development 1057, p. 1058.

'specific challenges to a state's continuous sense of self'.[110] Transitions, Mälksoo proposes, bring about state identity disjuncture, whereas the transitional justice project brings pressures on the continuity of state identity as the state is pressured to 'diagnose' the transition.[111] Although not even the most powerful states are immune to ontological uncertainties of power transitions, in general scholars have suggested that states on the margins of the Western international community tend to be more vulnerable.[112] Collective, or in this case state identities, rest on political memories, what Subotic describes as 'careful curating of select events, setbacks and triumphs, myths and symbols'.[113] Political memories help create the identity of the relevant political community, a sense of who it is, what it has been through, and where it is going.[114] States recipients of transitional justice resort to different approaches to it, that is, more comprehensive adoption of different tools and mechanisms offered by the project or more hostile ones which seek to fix certain meanings of the past in social memory.[115] Often, these reactions come at material or reputational costs or even at the expense of physical security. Here an ontological security lens helps observe the values and prescribed behaviours of the transitional justice project as dependent on states' sense and security of self, their status-related anxieties, historical sensitivities, and routine-seeking.[116] It proposes that there could be certain elements of the transitional justice project that states can interpret as attacks or challenges on political memories which need to be rethought, updated, or revised in the light of transitional justice mechanisms and therefore are a strain on collective identities. The transitional justice project can hence trigger ontological insecurities in situations deemed as critical from the outside but otherwise are comforting to the involved actors or worsen existing insecurities triggered by creating situations perceived as critical by these actors.

110 Maria Mälksoo, 'The Transitional Justice and Foreign Policy Nexus: The Inefficient Causation of State Ontological Security-Seeking' (2019) 21 International Studies Review 373, p. 374.

111 ibid, pp. 374–5.

112 Ayşe Zarakol, 'Ontological (In)Security and State Denial of Historical Crimes: Turkey and Japan' (2010) 24 International Relations 3; Ejdus, 'Critical Situations'.

113 Subotic, 'Political Memory, Ontological Security, and Holocaust Remembrance', p. 298.

114 ibid.

115 Mälksoo, 'The Transitional Justice and Foreign Policy Nexus'.

116 ibid, p. 377.

Yet, the issue at stake here is not only what the project does for domestic and foreign policies of a specific state, for 'the state', or the recipient community is never homogenous or passive and both identities and memories of and within the state are multiple. The transitional environment to which transitional justice has travelled is one where multiple different political communities (former belligerent parties, victims, marginalised groups, etc.) seek to make sense of the uncertainties pertaining to the conflict in a reflexive reconstruction of self-identities as well as new uncertainties and questions about the self arising from and in relation to the interactions with the transitional justice project itself as they go on to engage in truth-, justice-, and reparations-seeking processes. In the case of Bosnia and Herzegovina, the issue therefore is not *one* of security, stability, and certainty of Bosnia and Herzegovina, but of at least three different political communities who draw their political powers based on ethnicity: Bosniak, Croat, and Serb and their interactions with the imperative of dealing with the past. Security, as Croft and Vaughan-Williams effectively summarise, 'means different things to different people in different places and at different times'.[117] The environment to which the transitional justice project travels is one with multiple ongoing and often competing claims and requests for certainty, routine, stability, and continuity, including the project's own pursuits, as established in the previous section. This is an environment in which non-recurrence can be studied qualitatively.

Stability, certainty, and continuity are not the opposite of change. Instead, in critical situations, each requires renegotiations of the knowledgebases of collective identities of both self and others, as well as biographical narratives through, as this book shows, history teaching, fact-finding, and denial revisionism. In the long run, different political communities can exhibit both comprehensive and hostile approaches to transitional justice, being more accepting of transitional justice measures in the early years of transition when there is a wide range of material incentives and pressures (internal as well as external) to do so and growing more hostile over time as the elements of the transitional justice project trigger new anxieties or worsen existing ones. Similarly, as Chapter 7 will show, a quest to alleviate anxieties around potential new

[117] Stuart Croft and Nick Vaughan-Williams, 'Fit for Purpose? Fitting Ontological Security Studies "into" the Discipline of International Relations' (2017) 52 Cooperation and Conflict 12, p. 22.

conflict can lead to creative action, occasionally independent from the global project itself.

I have established the importance of (un)certainty, identities, and ontological (in)securities for the project of transitional justice, arguing that the successes and failures of the latter can only effectively be examined through the former. Yet, I have also overall claimed that the transitional justice project worsens ontological insecurities of different political communities and can ultimately make societies more anxious about potential renewed conflict. This requires further elaboration before being demonstrated through practice. At least three interrelated characteristics of the structure, inseparable from its embeddedness in deeper structures of neoliberalism and legalism, are at play. These characteristics of the project are manifested together or apart at different times and serve to sustain the legitimacy and longevity of transitional justice and its institutions.

First, the global project of transitional justice relies on institutions for its survival and legitimacy. As such, it engages in an exercise of linking local transitional justice needs to those institutions, such as courts or commissions. More precisely, local needs and urgencies become validated in relation to and within the bounds of the institutions of the project. The linking practice confirms and maintains the structure of transitional justice itself. As Giddens asserts, 'the most important aspects of structure are rules and resources recursively involved in institutions'.[118] Institutions and all the norms and ideas enshrined in them are among the more enduring elements of social life, and they give structures form through time and space.[119] For transitional justice, this means that as a global project, it can only exist through the legal frameworks and norms that underpin it and as long as the institutions which enforce those norms exist. In doing so, the advocates of transitional justice exhibit a misunderstanding of security as a lived experience as they propose that uncertainty can only effectively be governed through institutional structures, suppressing, or ignoring the everyday dynamics and complexities of managing uncertainties after a conflict.

Second, the transitional justice project, like other global projects, breeds hierarchies. Structures organise relations in hierarchical ways by

[118] Giddens, *The Constitution of Society*, p. 24.
[119] ibid.

allocating different capacities, positions, and benefits.[120] In the forthcoming chapters, I show how normative hierarchies in transitional justice are formed to prioritise certain prescribed and proscribed behaviours akin to the institutionalised forms of the anti-impunity norm. In particular, in this normative hierarchy, institutions of criminal justice arise as authoritative sources of truth and history in a process that is violent and exclusionary towards other complementary truth recovery and history-making processes. In Bosnia and Herzegovina, the global project of transitional justice positions institutions of criminal justice as sources of authoritative truth/historical status quo upon which different political communities are expected to revise and adjust their autobiographies, as they normally would in critical situations. Not only does this practice trigger further ontological insecurities as actors try to fit court judgements in their narrative about the self, but it also resists the impulse to debate, discuss, negotiate, and in doing so truly 'come to terms' with the past presenting the truth as exhaustive, and fixed.

Third, the project and its institutions are positioned as an inevitable source of good, a necessary force of progress, betterment, and therefore civilisation. Transitional justice as civilisation cannot be detached from the deep structures of neoliberalism and legalism in which transitional justice is embedded. Tzouvala suggests that one of the underpinning logics of civilisation is improvement. In *Capitalism as Civilisation*, Tzouvala clearly demonstrates that reform is not opposite to civilisation but that the very standard of civilisation operates on a conundrum between exclusion and conditional inclusion, the latter meaning that non-white political communities can be included in the structure of international law on the condition that they reform to align with the tenets of capitalist modernity.[121] The project of transitional justice and its mechanisms such as criminal trials and institutional reform are fruits of this kind of labour. This is not all transitional justice can be or is, but it is what the specific institutional arrangements of the transitional justice project and the discourse around them exhibit. If and when the project or its institutions fail to deliver, the responsibility is shifted onto the subject and the problem becomes a civilisational issue. In such discourse, it is implied that the proponents of the project seemingly tried their best to integrate, reform, and include the 'uncivilised' but the recipients

[120] Michael Barnett and Raymond Duvall, *Power in Global Governance* (Cambridge University Press 2005); Sinclair, 'Why We Should See International Law as a Structure'.
[121] Tzouvala, *Capitalism as Civilisation*.

seemingly choose to continue to be uncivilised in their behaviour. This narrative is further stigmatising for actors on the receiving end of the 'civilised' vs 'uncivilised' binary who develop awareness that, in the eyes of others in the international system, they are perceived as different and 'deviant'. The positioning of institutions of law as a 'standard' of civilisation can also be internalised by the subjects, posing questions about the collective self's ability to ever join the club of the civilised. This is opportunistic for domestic political elites who sustain success based on the politics of fear, humiliation, and injustice towards one ethnic group over others.

Through interactions of these three core characteristics of the structure, the transitional justice project triggers, supports, or otherwise inspires practices that could be understood as ontological security-seeking or maintaining by different political communities: historical revisionism, genocide and atrocity crimes denial, and ethnic segregation in education. In this changing space of physical securities and ontological insecurities carved by the proponents of the project and domestic political elites in interaction and over time, anxieties around potential new conflict fester.

2.5 Conclusion

This chapter has served as a theoretical and contextual foundation for investigating the nexus between the two imperatives of 'Never Again' and transitional justice. Building on my brief history of non-recurrence in transitional justice from Chapter 1, I have sought to explain how, over time, the proponents of the project made the imperative of 'Never Again' more fervently attached to all core mechanisms of the global project including truth commissions, criminal trials, and even memorialisation. The outcome, where non-recurrence is both enshrined in the pillar of 'GNRs' and presented as an overall objective of transitional justice, may sound conflicting and confusing but is in fact characteristic of the project itself as it rests on simultaneous ambiguity and rigidity. Almost anything within the project of transitional justice is claimed to potentially benefit meaningful assurances of non-recurrence depending on the context. At the same time, whatever benefits it must remain certain of the non-negotiable elements of the project such as its deep belief in reformative potentials of state agencies and neoliberalism as a force of peace. This duality is what defines transitional justice as a neoliberal and legalist project. Building my claims based on structuration theory, I have proposed that transitional justice as a structure, while time-limited in a given context, globally speaking needs permanence in space and time. It has its own needs of survival, legitimacy, and relevance. As such, transitional justice cannot be inherently benevolent, nor a necessarily positive force on non-recurrence, or other sought-after values for that matter.

To further my claims of detrimental influences of the transitional justice project on meaningful assurances of non-recurrence and at times seeming incompatibility between the two, I have called for a rethinking of what transitional justice is for and with that, what non-recurrence might mean in and for the global project. In my rethinking of transitional justice, I have stepped away from the state and from physical security assurances and invited the reader to enter the sphere of the ontological, as an addition to, and not separate from the physical. In these latter parts of the chapter, I have positioned transitional justice as a project which seeks to govern uncertainty but, in and out of itself, represents a period of rupture, and one whose success essentially depends on multiple political communities' securities of self, and managing historical sensitivities, routine, and anxieties. Furthermore, I have discussed non-recurrence not as an objective assessment of whether or not status quo has been reformed but as mitigation of behaviours that cause anxieties around potential renewed conflict in different political communities, particularly the kinds of anxieties that bring worry, discomfort, or even dread about the uncertain futures of peace.

In seeking its own legitimacy, relevance, and, ultimately, survival, the global project of transitional justice exhibits certain characteristics that trigger or worsen political communities' ontological insecurities. In these interactions between the structure and agency, I have argued, anxieties around potential renewed conflict fester. This is not all they can do, as anxieties about the future of peace have also, I intend to show, offered opportunities for novel ways of dealing with the past outside of or in cooperation with the global project. What proceeds are empirical investigations of these claims and a journey through thirty years of the transitional justice project in Bosnia and Herzegovina, with all anxieties and activism that have come with it.

3

Peace and Justice Hand-in-Hand

Global Transitional Justice in Bosnia and Herzegovina

3.1 A Lion's Den

I met Gordon outside a coffee shop, no more than thirty metres down the road from my flat in Durham, England. In my internet search of transitional justice-related actors in Bosnia and Herzegovina (BiH), Gordon's name popped up several times. For over four years, he had been the Chief of Staff of the International Commission on Missing Persons (ICMP) in BiH, now a world-leading international organisation for the identification of missing persons in conflict. He was also a member of the 2004 Republika Srpska's (RS) Commission on Srebrenica, the only post-war fact-finding commission in BiH to complete its mandate. For these two reasons, I was interested in interviewing Gordon for my research. Little did I know that Gordon not only was from Durham, which is where I studied at that time, but also in fact lived only a mile or so away from where I was. Because no other participant was ever going to be physically closer, Gordon became the very first person I interviewed for this book.

When we met, Gordon was in his mid-seventies. Retired (twice), he was travelling the world as a cricket tour manager. I didn't know much about his background, but I had assumed that Gordon must have led a high-profile international aid life to land such seemingly important positions, shaping the early days of transitional justice in BiH. Very early in our conversation, it became clear that Gordon's humanitarian path in Bosnia was unexpected and that he went there for altruistic and not so much career-related reasons. In 1992, when the war broke out, he had been working for a national security company, having retired as an Inspector with Durham Constabulary four years before. Understanding that he was going to be made redundant due to a recession, Gordon started to look for new ways to be useful. An item about an aid organisation called Feed the Children played on the radio, and a few weeks later, he was in a truck on his way to Split to help them out. Initially, Gordon moved between Split in Croatia and Vitez in central Bosnia. This was in October 1992. 'It was the worst cold I had ever experienced in my life', Gordon recounted in 2019.[1]

Gordon kept working for aid agencies in BiH throughout the war, and when the war ended, after a short deployment to Georgia, he proceeded to work for the International Rescue Committee (IRC) in Sarajevo. 'It was from there, after about two years with the IRC, [that] I was asked to be the Head of the ICMP by someone who knew me during the war, an American guy who was the head of USAID during the war'.[2] The issue of missing persons then was grave, with over 40,000 missing in BiH alone. Numerous lists were being produced by different organisations with varying names and numbers. Search and identification were fragmented. The ICMP aspired to become a single centralised mechanism for identifying missing persons, which it did, accompanied by a national Missing Persons Institute (MPI), which was established in 2005. The subsequent successes of the ICMP and MPI in identifying so many of the wartime missing persons could only happen after a period of negotiations among different parties interested in the 'job'. Gordon recalled

> I didn't know at the time that there had been a big fallout, between the Office of the High Representative (OHR) and ICMP on one side, and on the other side, the International Committee of the Red Cross (ICRC) and Physicians for Human Rights. And what caused that, I am not sure, but what I do know is that the ICRC felt like *the missing were theirs* . . . And I actually went to Geneva. Me, a former police officer and aid worker . . . and it was like going to *a lion's den*. These guys were sitting around. I said 'Look, I am a former police officer, I am an aid worker, I am here to help the people, I was there during the war, I am here to work with you, not against you.' I persuaded them to go and see the ICMP facilities . . . and the technical work that was going on to help to recover bodies and the laboratory work. I got them on our side. They realized that the ICMP was doing what the ICRC couldn't do.[3]

I wanted to know more about any coordination efforts among different actors sharing a piece of post-war recovery cake in BiH. Gordon stated

> you know what, instead of coming and saying, 'this is who I am, the organisation I represent, this is what my organisation can do, the expertise

[1] Interview with Gordon Bacon, 3 October 2019.
[2] ibid.
[3] ibid (my emphasis).

> I bring in and the people I work with,' people were coming and saying, 'that's ours, we are doing that.' They were not prepared to share. What they were doing was ring-fenced. And I just found it sad to the point of being very angry.[4]

Gordon's great regret was that, as this chapter will show, there wasn't any state-wide truth commission for BiH, despite some quite promising initiatives. 'I think it would have been fantastic, a major step along the pathway to reconciliation', Gordon said, but 'some of the international organisations sitting at that table were trying to persuade us that, you know, you need justice first'.[5]

Some truth recovery was pushed for by the Western international community involved in the post-conflict space in BiH, but only regarding Srebrenica. Gordon's appointment to the 2004 Srebrenica Commission, as a representative of the said international community, came after a call by one of the deputies of the then-High Representative Paddy Ashdown. 'I think it was partly because of the work I was doing with the ICMP and also because I was a former policeman or maybe also because I was in Bosnia for so long', Gordon told me.[6] Despite a few hiccups due to which the first president of the Commission left, the Commission did 'a thoroughly professional job', Gordon thought, in producing a report indicating that around 8,000 men and boys had been killed in and around Srebrenica in July 1995.[7] Its report eventually resulted in an official apology of the then-President of RS Dragan Čavić, for the crimes committed in Srebrenica. These were the hopeful days of transitional justice in BiH. It could and will be argued in the later chapters of this book that it all went downhill for transitional justice from there on.

This chapter rests on a history of the global project's trajectory in BiH, both its ascents and descents, in order to reevaluate contemporary conceptions of 'Never Again'. It aims to paint the picture of the material and ideational aspects of the transitional justice project in BiH, from 'justice first' and the establishment of the ICTY in 1993 to 'peace and justice hand-in-hand' and the myriad of measures of institutional and legal reform advocated for or straightforwardly implemented by

4 ibid.
5 ibid.
6 ibid.
7 ibid.

different actors of the international community present in transitional BiH and the promises made in relation to these practices. Methodologically, this chapter is written with the intent of presenting a critical genealogy (a la Foucault) of the global transitional justice project in BiH. This chapter is genealogical in the sense that it provides a descriptive account of the 'dispositif' of transitional justice within which the phenomenon of 'Never Again' is constructed and experienced and how it emerged and developed in BiH.[8] This line of inquiry uncovers a complex, contested, and continuously evolving process of 'doing' and 'sustaining' transitional justice. As such, it is also interested in errors, failed projects, and accidents,[9] some of which Gordon's story effectively illustrates. It further adds to the present problematisation of transitional justice as a global project by linking the practices and initiatives of transitional justice in BiH to how they are constituted in and within neoliberalism and legalism, reevaluating their meaning, purpose, and linearity in the present.[10]

This chapter opens with brief background information about the dissolution of Yugoslavia and the war in BiH 1992–5 in Section 3.2. In Section 3.3, I then explain the conflict resolution process and illustrate what kind of BiH and what kind of peace were imagined in the 1995 Dayton Peace Agreement. The main focus of the chapter is on sketching a detailed structure of the institutionalised transitional justice in BiH between 1993 and 2022, which I do in Section 3.4 in three parts. This skeleton of transitional justice in BiH shows that certain areas of transitional justice, such as criminal justice and institutional reform, have been significantly more developed and invested in than others, putting these developments in the context of the promises of neoliberal legalism. I furthermore examine both what is there and what is not, elaborating on multiple neglected, weakened, or straightforwardly failed initiatives of the project, primarily in areas of truth recovery, reparations, and memorialisation, and make sense of what and who was left behind. Finally, I provide brief remarks on the time of transitional justice and propose why it is still not passed.

8 David Garland, 'What Is a "History of the Present"? On Foucault's Genealogies and Their Critical Preconditions' (2014) 16 Punishment & Society 365, p. 367.

9 Michel Foucault, *Language, Counter-Memory and Practice* (Donald F Bouchard ed., Cornell University Press 1977) p. 146.

10 Gary Gutting, *Foucault: A Very Short Introduction* (Oxford University Press 2005).

3.2 The War 1992–1995

On account of its scope and brevity, this book cannot do justice to the historical, political, social, and economic roots and consequences of the war in Bosnia. However, I outline here what I consider to be basic tenets of both the war and its background to set up a context in which the global project of transitional justice, with its different elements, began to intervene already in 1993, during wartime. The Socialist Federal Republic of Yugoslavia (SFRY) was formed in 1945 under the leadership of its President-for-life Josip Broz Tito. The federation consisted of six republics: Serbia, Croatia, Slovenia, BiH, Montenegro, and Macedonia, all of which are now sovereign states, with the addition of the now sovereign state of Kosovo which, in Yugoslavia, used to be an autonomous province of Serbia. A socialist, multi-ethnic, non-aligned country, where nationalist tendencies were suppressed for the values of brotherhood and unity, for many, Yugoslavia was a utopian idea that was never meant to last. Some foreign commentators even say it was destined 'to disintegrate sooner or later'.[11]

Signs of the weakening of the unity of the SFRY became apparent after Tito died in 1980.[12] Economically, the country was not doing well, although in retrospect it did adopt quite a liberal economic stance in comparison with the Eastern Bloc countries in a mix of socialist and market mechanisms across sectors.[13] The foreign debt of the country increased significantly in the 1970s as the IMF became involved in the SFRY's domestic affairs through a programme of structural adjustment.[14] After Tito's death, the country witnessed both economic decline and political turmoil among opposing forces. Throughout the 1980s, these exacerbating political and economic issues and relative weakness contributed to the decline of the SFRY itself[15] as nationalist secession tendencies spread as wildfire.[16] In 1989, a speech by the Serb President Slobodan Milošević at the 600th anniversary of the Battle of Kosovo signalled

[11] Magnus Bjarnason, *The War and War-Games in Bosnia and Herzegovina from 1992 to 1995* (Mimir 2007) p. 10.

[12] Andy Aitchison, *Making the Transition: International Intervention, State-Building and Criminal Justice Reform in Bosnia and Herzegovina* (Intersentia 2011) pp. 40–2.

[13] Daniela Lai, *Socioeconomic Justice: International Intervention and Transition in Post-War Bosnia and Herzegovina* (Cambridge University Press 2020) p. 46.

[14] ibid.

[15] ibid.

[16] Marie E Berry, *War, Women, and Power: From Violence to Mobilization in Rwanda and Bosnia-Herzegovina* (Cambridge University Press 2018) p. 115.

territorial aggression. In the subsequent multiparty elections, nationalist political parties emerged as victorious.[17] That the dissolution of the country was inevitable was signalled by Slovenia and Croatia's declarations of independence in 1991, as these two of the most developed republics objected to continuous subsidising of the lesser developed areas, among other grievances.[18] While these declarations of independence were recognised by the international community, they triggered armed conflicts in Croatia (and a short, often neglected conflict in Slovenia) involving the Yugoslav People's Army, controlled by Belgrade, the local Serb population, and the Croatian independent army. Unlike in Slovenia, the Serb population was significant in Croatia, and so the independence faced more resistance from the Yugoslav People's Army.

But the bloodshed was most intensive in BiH, an otherwise ethnically diverse republic. There, the war[19] started in April 1992 after BiH's declaration of independence from the SFRY through a popular vote and bled on for four years. During the war, BiH witnessed the longest modern-day siege of its capital city of Sarajevo, lasting 1,425 days, and resulting in at least 10,000 deaths.[20] Elsewhere in BiH, more than 1,350 detention camps and centres were established for torture, rape, starvation, and execution, where most victims were civilians.[21] Overall, the conflict resulted in an estimated 100,000 deaths, an estimated 20,000 raped women and men, great displacement of the local population both within and outside the country, and vast destruction of property and social, cultural, and economic life.[22]

Three key armies were involved in the conflict: the Army of RS (VRS), the Army of the Republic of BiH (ARBIH), and the Croatian Defence

[17] ibid.

[18] For an overview of the academic work on the dissolution of Yugoslavia, see Sabrina P Ramet, *Thinking about Yugoslavia: Scholarly Debates about the Yugoslav Breakup and the Wars in Bosnia and Kosovo* (Cambridge University Press 2005).

[19] I use two terms, war and conflict, interchangeably throughout the book, acknowledging the international dimensions.

[20] Berry, *War, Women, and Power*.

[21] See Centre for Democracy and Transitional Justice, *Dokumentovanje logora i drugih zatočeničkih objekata u BiH*, https://cdtp.org/dokumentovanje-logora-drugih-zatocenickih-objekata-u-bih/ accessed 8 April 2021.

[22] Jessie Hronešová, 'Might Makes Right: War-Related Payments in Bosnia and Herzegovina' (2016) 10 Journal of Intervention and Statebuilding 339; Berry, *War, Women, and Power*.

Council (HVO). While the armies were ethnically organised and ethnically divided, some diversity existed, particularly in the ARBIH.[23] In addition, multiple Serb paramilitaries, most prominently funded by different political parties in what was then left of Yugoslavia (now Serbia, Montenegro, and Kosovo, separately), were actively involved in the conflict and complicit in committing atrocities. The paramilitaries from Yugoslavia were in particular led by an agenda of ethnic cleansing and 'driving non-Serbs from Serb-controlled land'.[24] The involvement and support of the sovereign states of Yugoslavia and Croatia, although evident to many, are denied by their officials to date. During the four-year war, civilian and military casualties were found among all ethnic groups, yet it is unequivocal that the vast majority were of Bosniak[25] ethnicity.

In the West, the responses to the war were overwhelmingly in support of independence but against concrete military involvement in the conflict. Germany was the first country to recognise independent Croatia in 1991, while the US and the European Economic Community recognised BiH as an independent state in April 1992. Beyond acts of recognition, the international community also provided humanitarian aid, but in general, there was little support in terms of resources such as weapons and any concrete military interventions were absent until the very end of the war. In fact, with the UNSC Resolution 713 of September 1992, an arms embargo on the BiH and other former Yugoslav governments was put in place. Already in May 1992, the UN imposed economic sanctions on the Federal Republic of Yugoslavia, prohibiting trade and financial transactions with Yugoslavia but allowing for some humanitarian exceptions.[26] Both the arms embargo and the economic sanctions were in place until November 1995.[27] The EU arms embargo on the former Yugoslavia,

[23] Ibrahim Sofić, 'Priča o Srbima u Armiji RBiH: Sahranite me kod Čede' (*AlJazeera Balkans*, 8 January 2019) https://shorturl.at/ckorF accessed 5 April 2021.

[24] Berry, *War, Women, and Power*, p. 118.

[25] The term 'Bosniak' is used to refer to ethnic Bosnians of the Muslim faith.

[26] U.S. Department of State, 'Bosnia Fact Sheet: Economic Sanctions against the Federal Republic of Yugoslavia (Serbia and Montenegro)' (13 November 1995) https://shorturl.at/aboyF accessed 19 July 2023.

[27] United Nations Security Council, 'Security Council Decides on Phased Lifting of Arms Embargo against Former Yugoslavia by Vote of 14 to None, with Russian Federation Abstaining' (22 November 1995) UN Doc. SC/6127, https://press.un.org/en/1995/19951122.sc6127.html accessed 19 July 2023.

on the other hand, remained in some shape or form until January 2006.[28]

As for positive action, the UN primarily resorted to wartime peacekeeping. In 1993, the United Nations Security Council determined six 'safe zones' in BiH protected by the UN peacekeeping forces, the most notable of which was in a small town in eastern BiH called Srebrenica.[29] By 1995, when the VRS began their military action to capture the territory of the enclave, the Srebrenica enclave was protected by a single, lightly armed Dutch battalion (Dutchbat-3). The politics of ethnic cleansing by the VRS culminated with the genocide the Bosnian Serb forces committed in and around Srebrenica when they finally penetrated the 'safe zone' in July 1995, killing more than 8,000 Bosniak men and boys. Most executions were committed while the UN peacekeeping battalion was still present in the area, unable – and/or unwilling – to prevent the atrocities from being committed. The UN personnel eventually retreated entirely from the Srebrenica area on 21 July, leaving for Zagreb.[30]

The failure to prevent the Srebrenica genocide despite being present on the ground remains one of the most significant failures of UN peacekeeping which, alongside Rwanda, resulted in significant reforms and rebranding of this branch of the UN's international security work. It is also an event which triggered changes in other states' foreign policies towards BiH. While there were some limited air strikes by NATO in May 1995, most European allies opposed more widespread NATO action on the account that it would be harmful to their own peacekeepers on the ground.[31] Once the Srebrenica genocide unravelled before the West's very eyes, leaders pushed for more decisive air campaigns by NATO in any remaining 'safe areas'. Subsequently, the US unilaterally lifted the arms embargo on the BiH government while NATO proceeded with a prolonged bombing campaign.[32]

[28] Stockholm International Peace Research Institute, *EU Arms Embargo on the Former SFR of Yugoslavia (Bosnia and Herzegovina)*, www.sipri.org/databases/embargoes/eu_arms_embargoes/bosnia accessed 19 July 2023.

[29] For an overview of the different UNSC resolutions establishing these 'safe areas', see United Nations General Assembly, 'Report of the Secretary-General Pursuant to General Assembly Resolution 53/55. The Fall of Srebrenica' (15 November 1999) UN Doc. A/54/549.

[30] ibid.

[31] Ivo H Daalder, 'Decision to Intervene: How the War in Bosnia Ended' (*Brookings Institute*, 1 December 1998) www.brookings.edu/articles/decision-to-intervene-how-the-war-in-bosnia-ended/ accessed 7 May 2024.

[32] ibid.

3.3 'The Peace': BiH Imagined

The war shattered BiH on all levels. Demographically, half of BiH's pre-war population was displaced from their homes.[33] One million of them were displaced internally. Another million fled across the border, settling in neighbouring countries of Croatia and Serbia, while others sought refugee status in places such as the UK or the US. The human cost was grave. The war took some 100,000 lives, at least 8,000 of which we now know were killed in a genocide. Many others who survived had been subjected to concentration camps, rape, and/or torture. The war also caused extensive material damage which crippled the country's economy. Close to two-thirds of all houses were damaged, and some 20 per cent were destroyed, along with 30 per cent of all hospitals and 40 per cent of the industrial facilities.[34] By 1994, unemployment reached 90 per cent.[35]

The end of official armed hostilities was concluded with the signing of the General Framework Agreement for Peace, commonly referred to as the Dayton Peace Agreement (DPA), in December 1995.[36] The peace agreement was signed by representatives of Yugoslavia and the independent states of Croatia and BiH and brokered by the US. At the time of the signing, the nascent peace in BiH was being enforced by 60,000 US and NATO troops.[37] At first, these troops worked within a NATO mission Implementation Force and later under the Stabilisation Force, both of which had been approved under Chapter VII powers of the UN Charter.[38] After the signing of the peace agreement, these forces patrolled the borders between BiH's new entities, established largely along wartime boundaries and as a result of wartime territorial gains.[39] The Stabilisation Force stayed in Bosnia until 2004 when it was replaced by European Union's Force, which remains in the country at the time of writing this book.

33 Berry, *War, Women, and Power*, p. 134.

34 Daniela Lai, 'Transitional Justice and Its Discontents: Socioeconomic Justice in Bosnia and Herzegovina and the Limits of International Intervention' (2016) 10 Journal of Intervention and Statebuilding 361, p. 369.

35 Lai, *Socioeconomic Justice*.

36 General Framework Agreement for Peace in Bosnia and Herzegovina (Dayton Peace Agreement), Dayton, OH, initiated 21 November 1995, signed in Paris 14 December 1995, UN Doc. A/50/79C, S/1995/999.

37 Daalder, 'Decision to Intervene'.

38 Lai, *Socioeconomic Justice*, p. 53.

39 ibid.

Externally negotiated, the peace agreement was meant to represent a compromise between wartime enemies, suggesting that there were no clear victors and no clear losers.[40] Instead, even though some might have won more than others, everyone won a little something they desired during the war. The treaty first and foremost served to end the hostilities and once and for all legally confirm BiH's territorial integrity and political independence.[41] Yet, inevitably, with this treaty, the international community also put forward a specific view of the future of both BiH and the broader post-Yugoslav space. In that sense, the DPA served to create a new vision for independent BiH as well as to establish it by becoming a foundational document on which the political order of the country rests. Different tools of transitional justice such as the ICTY were one but crucial part of exercising this vision.

What kind of BiH was imagined by the actors who brokered the treaty? The treaty, among others, put forward a new Constitution of BiH which the three signatory parties welcomed and endorsed.[42] The new, post-war BiH, it was said, was going to be multi-ethnic but also ethnicity-led, as ethnic identities became key in all spheres of political life in BiH seemingly for the sake of equality and recognition. In that sense, the post-war BiH was to adopt identity politics entirely different from the SFRY. While Yugoslavia suppressed, violently, some minority identities (such as Albanian) in the interest of a single common Yugoslav identity, the new BiH was to operate on the basis of equal and different ethnic identities but seemingly without a common Bosnian Herzegovinian identity. This principle of ordering life on ethnic bases replicates the ordering of the war and oversimplifies its causes.

It follows that the DPA sought to establish a decentralised state of BiH and multilevel governance that would give a voice to different ethnic groups across the country whose armies had been fighting for four years and would, over time, it was argued, overcome ethnic divisions.[43] To that end, the Constitution of BiH recognises 'Bosniaks, Croats, and Serbs as constituent peoples', along with other minority ethnicities (e.g., the

[40] Roland Kostic, 'Transitional Justice and Reconciliation in Bosnia-Herzegovina: Whose Memories, Whose Justice?' (2012) 54 Sociologija 649.

[41] Article 1 of the Dayton Peace Agreement.

[42] Annex 4 of the Dayton Peace Agreement.

[43] Dženeta Karabegović, 'Aiming for Transitional Justice? Diaspora Mobilisation for Youth and Education in Bosnia and Herzegovina' (2018) 44 Journal of Ethnic and Migration Studies 1374, p. 1379.

Romani) broadly grouped as 'Others'.[44] This principle was reflected in the division of territories and political and administrative powers. As per the Constitution,[45] although a country of only three million people, BiH has a federal political system whereby the federation is divided into two political entities: the Federation of BiH (FBiH), composed of majority Bosniak and Croat ethnicities, and RS, which, as its name suggests, is predominantly ethnically Serb. As a state, BiH is run by three presidents, one of each major ethnicity or, in constitutional terms, 'constituent peoples' who rotate every eight months. In addition, the state-level political system includes a House of Representatives and a House of People (with equal ethnic representation).

Internally, each entity, FBiH and RS, has its own President, Vice President, and a government led by a Prime Minister, a National Assembly, and a House of Peoples. The Federation is further divided into ten different cantons, each with some self-governing competencies, such as its own sets of ministries. To illustrate, this means that in the FBiH alone, there are eleven ministries of health, one for each canton and one for the entity.[46] To complicate things further, in addition to the two entities, the district of Brčko has a special status according to which it does not belong to either entity and has its own government and district assembly.

Economically speaking, BiH was set to transition to market capitalism in the immediate aftermath of the ratification of the peace agreement. As Lai argues, this transition failed to take into consideration the context in which the previous socialist system failed or what it meant to people who survived the war.[47] In particular, people kept good memories of socialist times, not necessarily because they lived in economic prosperity but because they associated it with interethnic coexistence, security, common identity, and, ultimately, peace.[48] Yet, transitioning BiH from socialism to market capitalism meant fragmenting the internal market, and insisting on privatisation of firms rather than restructuring the country's economy. Eventually, these policies discouraged serious investors, left thousands of workers unemployed, triggered sales of companies

44 See the Preamble to the Constitution of Bosnia and Herzegovina, Annex 4 of the Dayton Peace Agreement.

45 See Annex 4 of the Dayton Peace Agreement.

46 World Bank Group, 'Rebalancing Bosnia and Herzegovina: A Systematic Country Diagnostic' (1 November 2015) https://shorturl.at/fRTX8 accessed 11 June 2021.

47 Lai, *Socioeconomic Justice*, pp. 56–8.

48 ibid.

for much below their nominal value accessible to a few well-connected individuals, and ultimately contained formally socially shared resources in the hands of the powerful political-economic elites.[49]

Another important vision for BiH emerged out of the DPA. BiH was going to be supported yet closely monitored by the international community. In that sense, the DPA built a version of BiH that preserves its independence only to a certain degree and under certain conditions that closely align with the standards of international society. For instance, Annex 10 of the DPA created the Office of the High Representative as an ad hoc international institution that would oversee the implementation of civilian aspects of the Agreement until the country 'is able to take full responsibility for its own affairs'.[50] The High Representative, who has thus far always been a Western European man, is appointed by the internationally led Peace Implementation Council, comprised of fifty-five countries and agencies. Fast forward to 2023, and the OHR is still there. The official website of the Office says that 'the High Representative is working with the people and institutions of BiH and the international community to ensure that BiH evolves into a peaceful and viable democracy on course for integration in Euro-Atlantic institutions'.[51] This suggests, clearly, that in the eyes of the Western international community BiH still is not a viable democracy ready to perform to the EU standards, which is true of other countries in the region such as Serbia. Yet, it is only BiH that is not allowed to be incompetent independently.

The powers granted to the OHR have expanded over the years. Initially mandated to advise on the implementation of the DPA, since 1997, the OHR has also been able to peruse the so-called Bonn powers, such as dismissing democratically elected BiH officials should they in any way hamper the implementation of the peace treaty. The OHR still maintains its law-making powers, including its mandate to establish the rule of law as a necessary condition for other reforms. Even though the OHR did not actively practise decision-making powers between 2014 and July of 2021, in the past couple of years, the appointed High Representative has been prolific in exercising its oversight of BiH domestic affairs by, among others, passing laws and overturning decisions of elected officials.

[49] ibid.

[50] The Office of the High Representative, *General Information*, www.ohr.int/?page_id=1139 accessed 19 September 2019.

[51] ibid.

Other international actors were also made relevant and involved in BiH's affairs through the DPA. According to Article 9 of the DPA, all parties shall cooperate fully with 'all entities involved in the implementation of this peace settlement, as described in the Annexes to this Agreement, or which are otherwise authorised by the United Nations Security Council, pursuant to the obligation of all Parties to cooperate in the investigation and prosecution of war crimes and other violations of international humanitarian law'.[52] This of course primarily included cooperation with the ICTY, which at that time was basically non-operational, but also organisations such as the International Committee of the Red Cross and the United Nations Development Programme (UNDP) which assisted the repatriation and relief of refugees and internally displaced persons.[53] The Organization for Security and Co-operation in Europe (OSCE), for instance, also emerged as a prominent international organisation supporting future elections and confidence-building measures in BiH. Other cooperation obligations extended to unnamed entities yet to be present in BiH. For instance, Annex 1-A on the military aspects of the peace settlement obliges signatory parties to 'cooperate fully with any international personnel including investigators, advisors, monitors, observers, or other personnel'.[54]

The signing and ratifying of the DPA as a peace-making and peace-keeping political and legal document symbolised a transitional moment, the political act of drawing the line between the old and the new. The DPA ended the four-year-long war, thereby drawing that symbolic line between war and peace and, for transitional justice, between the past and the future. In BiH, like in many other societies, the signing of the peace accord makes the transitional moment coincide with the foundational moment. Although BiH declared independence from SFRY in 1992, it is in 1995 that the new state and new structures within the state were established. Consequently, the DPA created the complex political structure that exists in BiH today. The nature of negotiations of the peace agreement, with presidents of Croatia and Yugoslavia present and active parties to the agreement, made sure that ethnic representation and equality are ensured in all spheres of life in BiH, ultimately creating a perfect system for ethnic-based divisions.

52 Article 9 of the Dayton Peace Agreement.

53 Article 3, Annex 7 of the Dayton Peace Agreement.

54 Annex 1-A of the Dayton Peace Agreement.

3.4 Making the Global Transitional Justice Project in BiH

The global project of transitional justice did not arrive in BiH as a package. In fact, some practices I will describe in the proceeding sections might simultaneously be claimed as peacekeeping or state-building projects. The whole point is, however, that these projects are so intertwined, constructed as 'international interventions' or 'engagements' with Europe's big problem that is BiH and embedded in the same deep structures that they are hard to separate. I proceed here with an overview of the past trajectories of what is today considered to be transitional justice in BiH by practitioners, academics, and ordinary people alike. I do so in three subsections by (1) paying attention to what is most visible and fervently put forward as solutions to the problems of the past for a peaceful future, (2) examining failed, incomplete, and contested practices which help answer the 'why' question behind certain presences and absences, and (3) reflecting briefly on the seemingly never-ending expiration date of the transitional justice project in BiH, showing the unpredictable but continuous flow (with ups and downs) of the project.

3.4.1 What Is in the Project

It can be argued that the first signs of institutional dealing with the past in BiH emerged before the end of the war could even be foreseen, let alone materialised. In 1993, a year or so into the war, the UN Security Council passed Resolution 827, establishing the ICTY, making it the first international criminal tribunal since Nuremberg and Tokyo and the first ever established by the UN. As such, the ICTY was a judicial response to what was perceived as a threat to international peace and security in lieu of military intervention. It was also an emblem of the wider end-of-Cold-War turbulences. First, to show that the Security Council was no longer paralysed by the Cold War splits. Second, to signal political and moral shifts to *anti-impunity*, which culminated several years later with the establishment of the International Criminal Court (ICC), and *human rights*, both of which, it was held, could and should be governed by the international community.[55] Resolution 827 expressed hope that the ICTY 'would contribute to ensuring that such violations are halted and effectively redressed', which, to put it

[55] Andrea Birdsall, 'Creating a More "Just" Order: The Ad Hoc International War Crimes Tribunal for the Former Yugoslavia' (2007) 42 Cooperation and Conflict 397, pp. 401–2.

bluntly, it did not as it remained quite powerless until the end of hostilities.[56] In that sense, almost from the very start, the ICTY was positioned as a mechanism of international justice but also international peace and reconciliation. Upon the signing of the DPA, the President and the Prosecutor of the ICTY issued a joint statement.[57] In it, they repeated the claim that justice is 'indispensable' for national reconciliation and furthermore stated that justice 'breaks the cycle of violence, hatred and extra-judicial retribution' due to which 'Peace and Justice go hand-in-hand'.[58]

Starting with 1995, the transitional moment in BiH was shaped by a range of actors operating on international, state, and domestic grassroots levels. The transitional moment in BiH coincided with the era in which transitional justice grew as a legalised field of intervention where the ideas of anti-impunity, structural reform, and ethnic representation prevailed over, for example, socioeconomic justice, reparations, and transethnic spaces. As previously discussed in this book, in the post-Cold War politics of regime change, the overwhelming emphasis in transitional countries was placed on good governance and the rule of law. In addition to shaping the field's initial conceptual boundaries,[59] this post-Cold War, security context also moulded transitional justice interventions in places such as BiH. Measures of institutional reform in particular were promoted as crucial for restarting the rule of law in transitional societies, and transitional justice and the rule of law became 'mutually reinforcing phenomena'.[60] Consequently, many implemented transitional justice provisions in BiH stem from the DPA, chiefly, obligatory cooperation with the ICTY and assorted measures of institutional reform, such as police reform (Annex XI) and elections (Annex III). The numerous international actors present in the country after the DPA was enforced, led by the High Representative, prioritised criminal prosecutions at the ICTY and security measures which meant demobilising,

[56] United Nations Security Council Resolution 827 (25 May 1993) UN Doc. S/RES/827.

[57] International Criminal Tribunal for the former Yugoslavia, 'The Tribunal Welcomes the Parties' Commitment to Justice. Joint Statement by the President and the Prosecutor' (The Hague, 24 November 1995) CC/PIO/027-E, https://shorturl.at/deoR0 accessed 8 June 2021.

[58] ibid.

[59] Paige Arthur, 'How "Transitions" Reshaped Human Rights: A Conceptual History of Transitional Justice' (2009) 31 Human Rights Quarterly 321.

[60] Padraig McAuliffe, 'Transitional Justice and the Rule of Law: The Perfect Couple or Awkward Bedfellows?' (2010) 2 Hague Journal on the Rule of Law 127.

training, and vetting state officials and revamping BiH's constitutional order. In an obvious way, the drivers of transitional justice in BiH preferred quick fixes with easily quantifiable outcomes over the 'messy' long-term aspects such as truth recovery and education.

In the first decade after the conflict, the international community was heavily invested in reforming BiH's state institutions to be more transparent, efficient, aligned with European standards, and overall 'better'. The most notable reforms took place at the levels of the judiciary, the police, and the armed forces. The court system of BiH has gone through a major restructuring phase. The reform of the judiciary was led by the Independent Judicial Commission (IJC) established by the OHR in 2001.[61] The motive behind this restructuring project was first and foremost efficiency, as according to one commentator, post-conflict BiH found itself having 'too many courts and too many judges' which accrued costs the country could not sustain.[62] As a result, the overall number of courts and prosecutors' offices drastically decreased.[63] In addition, other non-financial reasons were given in support of the reform, mainly surrounding the issues of independence and impartiality, such as the perceived vulnerability of small courts to ethnic biases and compromises, new courts' separation of ethnic communities, and institutions being tainted by judges formerly involved in the conflict.[64] Having these concerns in mind, the reform consisted of a process of vetting where all judges were asked to reapply and have their qualifications and affiliations to conflict actors assessed. Many of the old judges were re-elected due to their outstanding qualifications, but the process also brought new and young professionals. It was considered to be a general and non-controversial success story, although only made possible due to the legislative powers the High Representative exercised at that time.[65] In efforts to localise the oversight of the judiciary, the IJC ceased to exist

[61] Office of the High Representative, 'Nezavisna pravosudna komisija preuzima zadatak izgradnje pravosudnog sistema u BiH' (*OHR*, 30 November 2000) www.ohr.int/?p=56452 accessed 7 April 2021.

[62] David Pimentel, 'Restructuring the Courts: In Search of Basic Principles for the Judiciary of Post-War Bosnia and Herzegovina' (2008) 9 Chicago Journal of International Law 111, p. 124.

[63] Visoko sudsko i tužilačko vijeće BiH, *Desetljeće utemeljenja i rada Visokog sudskog i tužilačkog vijeća Bosne i Hercegovine Dostignuća pravosudne reforme* (2013) https://advokat-prnjavorac.com/zakoni/Desetljece-utemeljenja-i-rada-VSTV-BiH.pdf accessed 11 June 2021.

[64] Pimentel, 'Restructuring the Courts'.

[65] ibid.

in 2003, and a new institution called the High Judicial and Prosecutorial Council was established in 2004 through a voluntary transfer agreement between the entities.[66] To date, this independent body has the mandate to appoint all judges and prosecutors in the country, propose judicial budgets, and determine appropriate training for judicial personnel.[67]

The reform of the security sector was conducted on an even larger scale. A joint communication issued by the European Commission and the OHR, two key actors in the reform, suggests that it was believed that the security sector reform would add to the EU objectives of fostering 'peace and stability, inclusive and sustainable development, state-building and democracy, the rule of law, human rights and the principles of international law'.[68] Police reform had already been envisaged by the DPA Annex XI, and the international community quickly followed up with a Security Council Decision on 21 December 1995 establishing the UN International Police Task Force (IPTF) with competencies to conduct police reform in BiH.[69] The IPTF, an ad hoc body, eventually became in charge of issuing certificates to all practising police officers after screening them for their involvement in the conflict as well as their qualifications and competencies to work for the police.[70] Police officers' involvement in the conflict was investigated against the ICTY's archive, checking if the police officer in question was mentioned in any collected documents. This process was considered a form of vetting in the police and was followed by continuous complaints by political elites who saw vetting as outside the IPTF's mandate as per the DPA.[71] Out of the initial total of 40,000 police officers seeking recertification, only 16,000 were successful by 2002.

66 Law on High Judicial and Prosecutorial Council of Bosnia and Herzegovina (Official Gazette BiH No. 25/04).

67 Adam Fagan, 'Judicial Reform in Serbia and Bosnia-Herzegovina: Is EU Support and Assistance Augmenting Independence?' (2016) 24 Maxcap 1.

68 European Commission and High Representative for Foreign Affairs and Security Policy, 'Elements for an EU-Wide Strategic Framework to Support Security Sector Reform' (July 2016) SWD(2016)221.

69 United Nations Security Council Resolution 1035 (21 December 1995) UN Doc. S/RES/1035.

70 Dragan M Popović, *Vodič kroz tranzicijsku pravdu u Bosni i Hercegovini* (UNDP n.d.).

71 An additional Security Council resolution was passed in 1996 to give the IPTF responsibilities relating to the investigation of human rights violations by practising police officers. See United Nations Security Council Resolution 1088 (12 December 1996) UN Doc. S/RES/1088.

While the police forces are still organised separately within each entity, armed forces were centralised during the reform. A new Ministry of Defence was created at the central level and a new Law on Defence was enacted in 2005, prescribing the role of all constitutive peoples and 'Others' in the united armed forces of BiH.[72] In addition, a new Intelligence-Security Agency was established in 2004 with competencies across the state.[73] Following the reform and centralisation of armed forces, more than 400,000 soldiers grouped in three armies at the end of the conflict were demobilised and a professional army of around 10,000 soldiers was formed.[74] However, over time, mono-ethnic regiments and brigades were preserved, underlining ethnic divisions within the army.[75]

As for the ICTY, in the first few years after the war, it encountered many challenges. The Tribunal dealt with an array of practical issues concerning the lack of adequate infrastructure, such as stable funding, permanent staff, and premises.[76] Furthermore, there were significant issues with the enforcement of arrest warrants. The Tribunal struggled to get a hold of key indictees as former Yugoslav states refused to cooperate. For instance, on Serbia's end, two key figures Radovan Karadžić and Ratko Mladić, now both convicted on genocide charges, were not arrested until 2008 and 2011, respectively. During his fugitive years, Karadžić even worked as a doctor in Belgrade under a pseudonym and in disguise, seldomly speaking at public events.[77] In the interim period, NATO occasionally managed to detain the accused individuals while the EU actively conditioned former Yugoslav governments to execute the ICTY's orders for advancement on their respective EU membership paths. Other issues were of procedural nature, for instance, interpreting and applying the Rules of Procedure and Evidence without

[72] See Article 2(1) of Law on Defence of Bosnia and Herzegovina (Official Gazette BiH No. 88/05).

[73] Established by the Law on the Intelligence and Security Agency of Bosnia and Herzegovina (Official Gazette BiH No. 12/04, 20/04, 56/06, and 12/09).

[74] Marija Arnautović, 'Oružane snage BiH: Deseta godišnjica rijetkog uspjeha' (*Radio Free Europe*, 1 December 2015) https://shorturl.at/foqNO accessed 7 April 2021.

[75] Ana E Juncos, 'EU Security Sector Reform in Bosnia and Herzegovina: Reform or Resist?' (2018) 39 Contemporary Security Policy 95.

[76] Gabrielle Kirk McDonald, 'Problems, Obstacles and Achievements of the ICTY' (2004) 2 Journal of International Criminal Justice 558, p. 558.

[77] Ellie Tzortzi, 'Karadzic Arrested in Serbia, Worked as Doctor' (*Reuters*, 22 July 2008) www.reuters.com/article/us-warcrimes-karadzic-idUSL2196241820080722 accessed 19 July 2023.

any precedent.[78] The ICTY also suffered reputationally. The Tribunal's legitimacy was challenged both by defendants and international commentators. Slobodan Milošević, former president of Yugoslavia, during his trial in 2001 famously dismissed the Tribunal as 'false' and 'illegal' for not being appointed by the UN General Assembly.[79] Others raised concerns about the ICTY adopting a Western-specific view of the political and historical context of the Yugoslav wars and lacking objectivity.[80] In 1997, the tribunal even called itself 'a partial failure' although saying that this was not due to its own fault.[81]

Much has changed since the ICTY first began operating, and over time, courts and prosecutors' offices of BiH have undertaken a heavier workload than the Tribunal. In the first years of the transition, domestic prosecutions were left to the two entities, as the only central judicial institution was the Constitutional Court. The principle of territoriality on entity-level was abused to shelter suspected war criminals, and, as a result, it was nearly impossible to see a Bosnian Serb suspect brought to court in RS or a Bosniak or Bosnian Croat in one of the Federation's courts.[82] This was improved with greater engagement of the OHR in the early 2000s.[83] To start with, the State Court of BiH was established by the OHR in November 2000,[84] and in 2002 and 2004, BiH saw amendments to the Law on the State Court of BiH according to which this Court was given primary jurisdiction regarding war crimes prosecutions and a section on war crimes was created, that is, Section I of the Court, also called the War Crimes Chamber (WCC).[85] Composed of international and national judges, the WCC follows international criminal law and is designed to hear top-priority war crimes cases that do not go to the

[78] McDonald, 'Problems, Obstacles and Achievements', p. 558.

[79] Birdsall, 'Creating a More "Just" Order', p. 412.

[80] ibid, pp. 412–13.

[81] Jinú Carvajalino and Maja Davidović, 'Escaping or Reinforcing Hierarchies? Norm Relations in Transitional Justice' (2023) 25 International Studies Review 1, p. 12.

[82] Janet Manuell and Aleksandar Kontić, 'Transitional Justice: The Prosecution of War Crimes in Bosnia and Herzegovina under the "Rules of the Road"' (2002) 5 Yearbook of International Humanitarian Law 331.

[83] William W Burke-White, 'The Domestic Influence of International Criminal Tribunals: The International Criminal Tribunal for the Former Yugoslavia and the Creation of the State Court of Bosnia & Herzegovina' (2007) 46 Columbia Journal of Transnational Law 279.

[84] Manuell and Kontić, 'The Prosecution of War Crimes'.

[85] Law on State Court of Bosnia and Herzegovina (Official Gazette BiH No. 49/09, amend. 74/09, 97/09).

ICTY.[86] In academia and international practice, the WCC was welcomed as a demonstration of national ownership over crimes committed during the war and an institution that could potentially gain higher legitimacy by the local population.[87]

Due to a large number of unsolved war crimes cases in 2007, a working group was established to draft a national strategy for prosecuting war crimes cases.[88] In 2008, the National strategy for war crimes was adopted in an effort to better coordinate and speed up prosecutions. The strategy estimated that there were at least 10,000 individuals suspected to have committed atrocity crimes, only a tenth of whom were under active investigation at the time.[89] The strategy gave additional powers to local cantonal and municipal courts to hear less complex atrocity crimes cases, while the Court of BiH remained the central body adjudicating the cases referred from the ICTY. The strategy envisaged that the complex and priority cases would be processed in seven years, and the rest, usually, but not always, left to lower-level municipal and canton courts, within fifteen years. Since the most complex cases were nowhere near completion seven years later, a revised strategy was drafted, obliging state courts to process all war crimes by 2023.[90] Yet as of 2023, numerous prosecutions are still ongoing, and many others are pending. According to the War Crimes Map, created by the OSCE, at least 583 atrocity crime cases have been completed before domestic courts in BiH by July 2023.[91] The Court of BiH has processed more cases than any other court and has adjudicated on the most complex of all domestic proceedings. Between 2004 and 2022, the Court ruled on 252 cases, finding 292 people guilty of genocide, crimes against humanity, and/or war crimes.[92]

[86] Claire Garbett, 'Transitional Justice and "National Ownership": An Assessment of the Institutional Development of the War Crimes Chamber of Bosnia and Herzegovina' (2012) 13 Human Rights Review 65.

[87] ibid.

[88] Ministarstvo pravde Bosne i Hercegovine, *Državna strategija za rad na predmetima ratnih zločina* (December 2008) https://shorturl.at/GIMR8 accessed 11 June 2021.

[89] ibid.

[90] Ministarstvo pravde Bosne i Hercegovine, *Revidirana državna strategija za rad na predmetima ratnih zločina* (May 2018) www.mpr.gov.ba/web_dokumenti/default.aspx?id=10809&langTag=bs-BA accessed 22 February 2021.

[91] Organisation for Security and Cooperation in Europe, *Mapa procesurianih ratnih zločina u BiH*, https://maparz.pravosudje.ba/bhs, accessed 2 September 2021.

[92] Court of Bosnia and Herzegovina, *Statistic on Judgements of the Court of Bosnia and Herzegovina for the Period of 2004–2022*, https://sudbih.gov.ba/Content/Read/statistika-o-presudama-suda-bih accessed 19 July 2023.

Because half of all BiH people were outside their homes when the war ended, violations of property rights were one of the most common reparation claims.[93] Annex VII of the DPA acknowledged that all refugees and internally displaced persons have the right to have their property restored or be compensated for what cannot be restored. The peace agreement also created the Commission for Real Property Claims of Displaced Persons and Refugees (CRPC) to deal with such property rights claims. The CRPC had an equal representation of the three main ethnic groups. To show its understanding of the chaotic circumstances of the war, the CRPC relaxed evidentiary requirements and allowed applications from claimants who had no written evidence that property was theirs to apply.[94] Although a compensation fund was never created, claimants could generally use CRPC's decisions to sell, lease, or transfer property rights in accordance with the law.[95] The Commission seized to exist in 2009, and since then, the Ministry of Human Rights and Refugees (MHRR) coordinates realisations of Annex VII of the DPA.[96]

Lastly, because of the limitations of the initial criminal justice intervention, whereby the ICTY and the WCC could only accommodate a small number of relatively high-profile cases, thousands of victims sought redress elsewhere. The Human Rights Chamber, established in 1996 and envisaged as a European Court of Human Rights-like institution, was mandated by the DPA to hear human rights complaints.[97] The institution had the mandate to order both pecuniary and non-pecuniary damages with the goal of redressing past violations and preventing future ones.[98] Although it was empowered to only hear those claims relating to situations that happened or continued after the DPA became effective, the Chamber was very soon overwhelmed with cases beyond its capacity.[99] During its operation, the Chamber received thousands of applications, most of them relating to property and missing persons claims, as violations whose consequences extended beyond the signing of the DPA.

[93] Hans Dans, 'Restoring Property Rights in the Aftermath of War' (2004) 53 International and Comparative Law Quarterly 429.

[94] ibid.

[95] ibid.

[96] Article 21 of the Law on Refugees from BiH and Displaced Persons in BiH (Official Gazette BiH No. 23/99, 21/03, and 33/03).

[97] Annex 6 of the Dayton Peace Agreement.

[98] J David Yeager, 'The Human Rights Chamber for Bosnia and Herzegovina – A Case Study for Transitional Justice' (2004) 14 International Legal Perspectives 44.

[99] ibid.

As a result, more victims have been involved in the cases heard before the Human Rights Chamber than the ICTY and WCC and the Chamber was able to accommodate some of the claims overlooked by the criminal justice institutions. The Chamber was eventually merged with the Constitutional Court of BiH as a Human Rights Commission and today remains largely forgotten among the BiH public.

3.4.2 *What (and Who) Is Left Behind*

Unlike criminal justice, non-judicial truth recovery interventions have received significantly less attention in BiH's transitional justice circles. Most non-judicial truth recovery initiatives have not fully materialised, and to date, there has been no state-wide fact-finding commission or any similar body. Any successes in this regard are highly limited. Pressured by the High Representative, RS authorities formed the Commission for the Investigation of the Events in and around Srebrenica between 10 and 19 July 1995 (Srebrenica Commission) in 2003.[100] The Srebrenica Commission, composed of five Bosnian Serbs (one withdrew during the process), one Bosniak, and Gordon, the main protagonist of my introduction to this chapter, as the foreign commissioner, published its report in 2004, establishing that 7,779 Bosniaks perished in Srebrenica.[101] This was the first time that an official report settled on the number of those killed in Srebrenica in the hope that minimisation and trivialisation of the figures, most frequently coming from the RS officials, would decrease.[102] The report shied away from categorising the events of Srebrenica as 'genocide', but it did recommend that an apology is offered by RS authorities to the victims and their families. Following the publication of the report, the then-President of RS President Dragan Čavić issued a public apology for the 'killings' in Srebrenica.[103]

[100] Daniela Mehler, 'The Last "Never Again"? Srebrenica and the Making of a Memory Imperative' (2017) 24 European Review of History: Revue européenne d'histoire 606.

[101] Radio Slobodna Evropa, 'Kompletan tekst Izvještaja o Srebrenici' (*Radio Slobodna Evropa*, 19 June 2004) www.slobodnaevropa.org/a/823047.html accessed 4 October 2020.

[102] Commissioner for Human Rights, *Posleratna Pravda i Trajni Mir u Bivšoj Jugoslaviji* (Council of Europe 2012).

[103] Stanko Smoljanović, 'Čavić priznao masakr u Srebrenici' (*Deutsche Welle*, 23 June 2004) www.dw.com/bs/%C4%8Davic-priznao-masakr-u-srebrenici/a-2485548 accessed 6 April 2021.

Ongoing debates about truth-telling initiatives in the country are greatly tied to the issue of missing persons in conflict. While the ICMP's mission in BiH has been greatly successful, having excavated and identified the remains of 80 per cent of those initially declared missing, over 7,000 missing persons cases remain unresolved.[104] In efforts to localise the search for the missing, the BiH government passed a Law on Missing Persons in 2004.[105] This legislation remains the only state-level legal provision awarding rights and privileges to all victims of the BiH conflict. Following the enactment of the law, a central MPI was co-founded by the Council of Ministers of BiH and the ICMP.[106] At the time of writing this book, the search for the missing continues to be led by the MPI in close cooperation with the ICMP.

The rest of the story about non-judicial truth recovery in BiH is about failures. Like the 2003–4 Srebrenica Commission, another location-specific commission was envisaged for Sarajevo. The Commission for the Investigation of the Siege of Sarajevo was established in 2006 but ceased to exist in 2007 without concrete results.[107] Talks were held about state-wide truth commissions without any concrete political steps or commitment. There has even been an initiative for a regional truth commission, RECOM, originally started by Nataša Kandić of the Serbian Humanitarian Law Centre. Today, RECOM is a largely dormant regional coalition of 2,050 non-governmental organisations, associations, and individuals from the former.[108] According to the initiative's draft statute, former Yugoslav states are asked to create an official, independent commission that will investigate the human rights abuses committed during Yugoslav wars. The main outputs envisaged would be a report with clear recommendations regarding reparations and measures of non-recurrence as well as creating a publicly accessible archive.[109] Several former Yugoslav governments showed official support for the commission so that 'the future generations would have an understanding about

[104] J Sarkin and others, *Bosnia and Herzegovina: Missing Persons from the Armed Conflict of the 1990s: A Stocktaking* (International Commission on Missing Persons 2014).

[105] Law on missing persons in Bosnia and Herzegovina (Official Gazette BiH No. 50/04).

[106] As per Article 7 of the Law on missing persons at ibid.

[107] Commissioner for Human Rights, *Posleratna Pravda.*

[108] Koalicija za REKOM, *What Is the Coalition for RECOM?*, www.recom.link/en/what-is-the-coalition-for-recom-2/ accessed 9 May 2024.

[109] Commissioner for Human Rights, *Posleratna Pravda.*

the ugly part of our past and never repeat it', but no concrete action as to its establishment has been taken yet.[110]

Bar restoration of property, reparations, too, are an ongoing struggle for many survivors and victims' families. By and large, the reparations process can be described as being held hostage by ethnonationalist politics.[111] When it comes to reparations to the families of the missing, the above-mentioned Law on Missing Persons envisages the creation of a compensation fund.[112] Nevertheless, this fund is yet to be realised due to the two entities' inability to agree on its financing.[113] This remains the only state-level law that could compensate the victims, while other reparations schemes are organised at the entity level and separately in Brčko. More precisely, both entities have created separate legislation on the rights of veterans, disabled war veterans, and fallen soldiers[114] and the rights of civilian victims of war.[115] These laws tend to discriminate between beneficiaries based on their ethnicity and/or residence. RS's laws in particular exclude any victim/veteran and their families who live in other parts of BiH or who live in RS but were in any way involved in the conflict supporting one of the 'opposing' sides.

In this piecemeal approach to reparations, many victims and survivors are left behind in seeking redress either due to eligibility criteria or the lack of funding. Among all reparation schemes, veterans, especially those who served any of the three armies for a long time, are singled out as the group most deserving of reparations. On the other hand, victims of sexual and gender-based violence in conflict are particularly unprotected. RS, while it acknowledges the act of rape as a violation that deserves

110 Koalicija za REKOM, 'Vlada Crne Gore podržala inicijativu za REKOM' (*Koaliicija za REKOM*, 28 June 2018) www.recom.link/sr/timeline/vlada-crne-gore-podrzala-inicija tivu-za-rekom/ accessed 20 September 2019.

111 Hronešová, 'Might Makes Right'.

112 Law on missing persons.

113 Jessie Hronešová, 'Bones and Recognition: Compensating Families of Missing Persons in Post-War Bosnia and Herzegovina' (2018) 13 Journal of Peacebuilding & Development 47.

114 Law on Rights of Demobilized Defenders and Members of Their Families in the Federation of Bosnia and Herzegovina (FBiH Official Gazette No. 61/06, 27/07, and 32/08); Law on Rights of War Veterans, Disabled Veterans, Families of Fallen Soldiers in Republika Srpska (Official Gazette of RS No. 134/11 and 9/12).

115 Law on Basics of Social Protection, Protection of Civilian Victims of War and Families with Children of the Federation of Bosnia and Herzegovina (FBiH Official Gazette No. 36/99, 54/04, 39/06, and 14/09); Law on Protection of Civilian War Victims of Republika Srpska (Official Gazette of RS No. 25/93, 32/94, 37/07, 60/07, 111/09, and 118/09).

reparations in the above-mentioned law, offers monetary compensation only for the damages caused through rapes committed by 'enemy forces' and not its own army, therefore excluding a vast majority of victims.[116] In more recent legislation, redress is offered to all recognised victims of torture irrespective of their ethnicity but contingent on their place of residence during the conflict, which must be in RS.[117]

For these reasons, victims of torture or civilian survivors have generally resorted to litigation on domestic, regional, and international levels to seek redress.[118] As a matter of last resort, victims of wartime sexual violence often attempt to obtain some monetary compensation through civil proceedings. However, such proceedings have been largely unsuccessful for two reasons. First, where the alleged perpetrator is known and available to the court, they are often unable to pay the settlement, leaving the victim without compensation. Second, where the alleged perpetrator is not known or otherwise unavailable to the court, the compensation claims are rendered inadmissible due to the statute of limitations, as per a 2013 decision by the Constitutional Court.[119] As a result, civilian victims of physical or psychological violence are left with very little to no options for obtaining sustainable monetary compensation.

Memorialisation too is captured by ethnonationalism.[120] Memorialisation is not organised or regulated at the central level but instead, it is governed by numerous laws and regulations at the cantonal level in FBiH, entity level in RS, and separately in Brčko. As a result, monuments, statues, memorials, memorial plaques, and such are plentiful across the country with little to no regulation about what or who they commemorate. In fact, it is estimated that, since the conflict, most monuments are built illegally without obtaining the necessary permits when such are required or after having the permit request rejected by the relevant authority.[121] According to the results of the project 'War of

116 Article 2 of the Law on Protection of Civilian War Victims.

117 Article 5 of the Law on Protection of Victims of Wartime Torture of Republika Srpska (Official Gazette RS No. 90/2018).

118 Hronešová, 'Might Makes Right'.

119 TRIAL International, 'Bosnia: Landmark Decision for a Survivor of Sexual Violence' (*TRIAL International*, 30 August 2019) https://trialinternational.org/latest-post/bosnia-landmark-decision-for-a-survivor-of-sexual-violence/ accessed 6 April 2021.

120 Janine Natalya Clark, 'Are There "Greener" Ways of Doing Transitional Justice? Some Reflections on Srebrenica, Nature and Memorialisation' (2016) 20 The International Journal of Human Rights 1199.

121 Dzana Brkanic, 'Bosnian War Memorials Become Political Battleground' (*BIRN*, 8 August 2016) https://shorturl.at/buHRX accessed 7 April 2021.

Memories' in which the Centre for Non-Violent Action documented sites memorialising the 1992–5 conflict in BiH, at least eighty-five such sites had been established by 2015.[122]

When it comes to official monuments established by whatever form of local authority, the majority of them honour fallen combatants of a singular army and not civilian victims.[123] The only city where monuments to soldiers of all three key armies, the VRS, ARBiH, and HVO, can be found in close proximity is Brčko, which, as stated before, is a separate non-entity district with its own Law on Monuments and Symbols.[124] In addition to the memorialisation efforts made by state officials, civil society organisations, veteran and victim groups conduct their own informal memorialisation, temporary and symbolic or otherwise physical and longer-lasting. Occasionally, such initiatives seek to memorialise opposing or contested memories not included in the official narrative led by political elites.[125] In a rare regulation that refers to memorialisation, the Law on Missing Persons grants the families of victims the right to mark the exhumation or burial sites of their loved ones.[126] These sites of memory are not set in stone, and memorialisation sites are known to have been changed over the years to include, for example, a list of victims' names or an updated number of casualties according to any new truth recovery developments.

The site of memory most representative of the involvement of the international community is the Srebrenica Memorial Centre. Possibly the most recognisable memorial in BiH is based in Potočari outside Srebrenica where genocide was committed in July 1995. Potočari, a site of mourning for Bosniaks, is located on the territory of what is today RS. This made the process of establishing a memorial politically challenging, seeing how no official recognition that the killings in Srebrenica constitute a 'genocide' has come from the political top of RS.[127] In 2000, a

122 Excluding commemorations, memorial events, and street names. Centar za nenasilnu akciju, *Rat Sjećanja. Istraživanje o Mjestima Stradanja i Sjećanja Na Rat u BiH* (Centar za nenasilnu akciju 2018).

123 Dzana Brkanic and Lamija Grebo, 'Bosnia Spends €2 Million on "Divisive" War Memorials' (*BIRN*, 3 January 2020) https://shorturl.at/jquGU accessed 7 April 2021.

124 Centar za nenasilnu akciju, *Rat Sjećanja.*

125 ibid.

126 Article 20 of the Law on Missing Persons.

127 In fact, while all other former Yugoslav states adopted some sort of resolution or declaration on Srebrenica, BiH was legally and politically unable to do so due to strong opposition from Republika Srpska. See Commissioner for Human Rights, *Posleratna Pravda.*

committee of two Serbs and two Bosniaks was tasked to allocate appropriate sites for the memorial, which the committee could not agree on.[128] Eventually, it was the High Representative Ashdown who allocated a plot of land in the Srebrenica municipality, in his view, to ensure that the crimes are not forgotten and to keep 'the memory of the dead'.[129] To ensure the sustainability of the memorial, such a symbolic measure had to be codified in the form of a law, and the Law on the Centre of the Srebrenica-Potočari Memorial and Cemetery for the Victims of the 1995 Genocide was enacted in 2007, giving the State of BiH authority to manage the memorial, despite it being on the RS territory.[130]

Finally, the economic aspects of BiH transitions can most effectively be observed through an investigation of both what is there and what is not. Like elsewhere in Eastern Europe, BiH's transition has been one to neoliberalism and could be, like in many other places, characterised by 'aid dependency, lack of sustainable FDI, corruption, unemployment, and gender inequalities'.[131] As evident through widespread poverty, depressing youth unemployment, and repeated socioeconomic grievances, the transition of BiH did not mitigate socioeconomic injustices.[132] Even in the largely successful restoration of property, one can see significant gaps. Returnees obtained secured housing but were not provided stable employment or welfare provisions they were accustomed to before the war, affecting their perceptions of both justice and security.[133] Furthermore, local communities were rarely consulted and even more seldomly allowed to meaningfully influence the politics of the economy in transitional BiH.[134] In many ways, the economic well-being of Bosnian Herzegovinian society was separated from transitional justice initiatives

[128] Olivera Simić, 'Remembering, Visiting and Placing the Dead: Law, Authority and Genocide in Srebrenica' (2009) 13 Law Text Culture 279.

[129] The Office of the High Representative, 'Decision on the Location of a Cemetery and a Monument for the Victims of Srebrenica' (25 October 2000) https://shorturl.at/gAIV2 accessed 11 June 2021.

[130] The Office of the High Representative, 'Decision Enacting the Law on the Center for the Srebrenica-Potocari Memorial and Cemetery for the Victims of the 1995 Genocide' (25 June 2007) https://shorturl.at/qwFT8 accessed 11 June 2021.

[131] Lai, *Socioeconomic Justice*, p. 44.

[132] Lai, 'Transitional Justice and Its Discontents', p. 362.

[133] ibid, p. 368.

[134] Kostic, 'Transitional Justice and Reconciliation'; Lai, 'Transitional Justice and Its Discontents'.

which in many ways is typical for and only serves to further reinforce the neoliberal reign.[135]

3.4.3 *What Remains*

The transitional justice project, by no means a coherent unit but rather a fragmented set of practices intertwined with peace- and state-building, has served to facilitate the version of the peace created by the DPA. As explained in previous sections, this version of peace was very particular and was supplemented by a range of transitional justice tools and supported by a range of actors. In fact, when it comes to the international community's involvement, what BiH lacked in war, it compensated for in transition. Numerous actors, sometimes in cooperation and often in direct tension, passed through BiH since 1995 with their projects, decrees, funds, and ultimatums, and some, like the OHR, stayed and are showing no signs of ever leaving. Thousands of NGOs, both local and international, have risen and fallen in the humanitarian circles in BiH since 1995. Although the time of transition has seemingly passed, for BiH has clear tenets of a peaceful democracy, the transitional justice project is still work-in-progress. With the closure of the ICTY in 2017, it might seem like the former Yugoslavia has dealt with its past. Over the course of its long twenty-four years of operation, the ICTY charged 160 people, convicted ninety with, in their own words, the goal of deterring future crimes, providing justice to victims, and therein aiding lasting peace in the region.[136] Although officially closed, the ICTY's 'essential functions' including retrials and appeals, and maintaining legacy through outreach and archives,[137] are kept in the International Residual Mechanism for Criminal Tribunals.[138] Furthermore, domestic atrocity crime trials are ongoing both at the Court of BiH and smaller regional courts. Thousands of people have returned to their homes, yet many others have sold theirs or lost them forever. Truth recovery, identification of the missing, vetting, reparations, and memorialisation are still everyday topics in the

[135] Alex Jeffrey, 'The Political Geographies of Transitional Justice' (2011) 36 Transactions of the Institute of British Geographers 344, p. 348.

[136] The International Criminal Tribunal for former Yugoslavia, *About the ICTY*, www.icty.org/en/about accessed 25 June 2021.

[137] International Residual Mechanism for Criminal Tribunals, *About*, www.irmct.org/en/about accessed 8 July 2020.

[138] United Nations Security Council Resolution 1966 (22 December 2010) UN Doc. S/RES/1966.

news and, for many people, open wounds. As Kostic argued in 2012, 'the debate over the recent conflict' has been transformed 'from a transitional process of coming to terms with the past to *a permanent state of affairs*'.[139] It is with what remains of, after, and because of the transitional justice project that I grapple with in the next four chapters, asking in my examinations the big question of '(N)ever again?'.

3.5 Conclusion

This short, yet critical genealogy of transitional justice in BiH paints a picture of some of the myriad institutional and legal efforts to *build* a long-lasting peace in this country. It adds to my earlier points about the ideational embeddedness of transitional justice in neoliberalism and legalism and illustrates what materially comprises and sustains transitional justice as a project. Prioritisation of and unconditional faith in law and institutions to address deeply complex and historically, socially, politically, and economically specific and delicate problems demonstrates (neo)liberalism at work and illustrates the Western international community's obsession with the rule of law as a means to ensure respect for human rights and sustainable peace.[140] I have argued that the DPA and subsequent projects envisaged the future of BiH in a certain way that promoted ethnicity as a trait with the most purchase power and a tool for peace, neglecting the fact that it was also a tool for war. Transitional justice, like most public life in post-war BiH, has subsequently been structured along these lines. Moreover, I have also proposed that the peace process has created a relationship of dependency between Bosnia and the Western international community, keeping the country in a seemingly permanent state of political infancy.

By focusing on implemented projects as well as failed, non-existent, or incomplete ones, in this chapter, I have sought to highlight the turbulences, contestations, and sometimes very pragmatic and detached decisions that characterise justice in transition. All in all, both peace and transitional justice, together with peace- and state-building projects, have since 1995 symbolised clear priorities of the international community for the future of BiH, which bypassed entire aspects of human life. Peace assurances were entrenched in institutional ethnicity-based set-ups with

[139] Kostic, 'Transitional Justice and Reconciliation', p. 664 (my emphasis).

[140] Kerstin Bree Carlson, *Modeling Justice* (Cambridge University Press 2018) p. 57.

very little regard for human relations and the everyday struggles of Bosnian Herzegovinians, across and beyond ethnic divides, in transition.

This chapter has set a contextual and factual foundation for the next four chapters, having introduced key actors, institutions, laws, demands, and disputes. My hope is that this chapter has helped the reader imagine the material and ideational post-war environment in which subjects of transitional justice as well as its practitioners such as Gordon lived, and many continue to live, their everyday lives, experiencing, requesting, and hoping for 'Never Again'. In the following four chapters, I transport the reader back to the present day to take stock of what the transitional justice project has meant for the promises of preventing renewed conflict in BiH.

4

'If We Do Not Talk About These Issues Now . . .'

Fragmented Truths and the Negotiation of Biographical Narratives

4.1 'You Think You Will Find the Truth on Facebook?'

It was my second time visiting Sarajevo's City Hall. The building was restored and given a new purpose more than two decades after being bombarded with flammable artillery missiles which destroyed the two million books it used to host in its former capacity as the National University Library.[1] I was there to attend a presentation about the Women's Court, a feminist contribution to transitional justice and dealing with the past. The Women's Court is a mechanism of public testifying created by the Women in Black, a civil society organisation from Belgrade, and several other women's organisations across the region. Thirty-six women from all seven former Yugoslav states participated in this court when the testimonies originally took place in Sarajevo in 2015. The purpose of the Court and subsequent presentations such as the one I attended was to allow women to become subjects of justice and bring to light topics, experiences, and insecurities during and after the war which otherwise were not of political and public interest. Among others, the witnesses testified about the continuity of violence against women, economic violence, forced mobilisation of their young sons, and displacement.

The day I attended the presentation about the Court, the audience was greeted by women from Bosnia and Herzegovina (BiH), Croatia, Serbia, and Montenegro. 'Why wouldn't women of Srebrenica or Zvornik be more important for this process than Judith Butler?' a member of Women in Black asked, and I nodded fervently. We proceeded with a

[1] Gradska vijećnica Sarajevo, *War Suffering*, www.vijecnica.ba/bs/ratno-stradanje accessed 9 May 2024.

video presentation of the Women's Court, followed by short testimonies from the present women, stories about rape, murder, displacement, pain, sorrow, but also life and hope. There were lots of hugs, and words of support, but also a sense of uncomfortable silence in the audience mostly comprised of university students. Then it was time for questions. No hands were raised apart from mine. Some might have received the silence from the audience as a sign of shyness, sleepiness, or anxiety around public speaking. Yet others understood it as passivity and therefore complicity in potential further conflict in BiH. One woman from a women's organisation in Foča looked at the youth in the audience and said, and I paraphrase, 'the youth need to be more active. Ask questions and learn so that the same [war] is not repeated for you, too. We are speaking so that young people could learn ... because they do not learn this stuff through formal education, not all families speak about this'.

Another woman joined in, quite angrily, asking the audience, 'Do you think you will find the truth on Facebook?' No response. 'You must learn in order to save yourselves tomorrow', she added. The woman then shared how her own father was burned alive by his neighbour, yet even though she knew who killed her father, this was not enough for justice. 'In addition to your own eyes and ears, you still need to prove something to some court', she concluded. Somehow, the most obvious of truths were being questioned, denied, and silenced. What 'we', the audience, and 'we', the former Yugoslav societies, knew about the war on that cold January morning twenty-five years after the war ended was fragmented and limited as the desire and willingness to know were seemingly diminishing.

This chapter is the first of the three empirical chapters to discuss the lived experiences of 'Never Again' in BiH and what shapes them. It is a chapter about how different political communities (re-)write their autobiographies after war and how, in doing so, they interact with courts as the main sources of the historical status quo, that is, the widely accepted and shared understanding of historical events, in and after transitional justice. This chapter seeks to establish why and how truth recovery – or a lack thereof – creates these insecurities and to demonstrate how the global project of transitional justice is complicit in this. The normative hierarchies of the global project and positioning of the International Criminal Tribunal for the former Yugoslavia (ICTY) as the key source of the historical status quo have left BiH without any state-sponsored, state-wide consensus or even dialogue about the characteristics, dynamics, and consequences of the war. The ICTY judgements are used and abused to deduct claims about the war broader than what is within the limits of a criminal case. This is a role that the ICTY actively carved for itself and was essential to the specific form of governance asserted over the pasts of Bosnians and Herzegovinians. However, judicial truths can be a source of security for many individuals while simultaneously being experienced as major triggers of ontological insecurities for other political communities who find themselves having to interrogate and reconsider their sense of selves in the world in the light of the metanarrative arising from the judgements. Rather than producing an 'objective' truth, as originally planned, what this has done is enhance the building of multiple, competing, and often entirely parallel biographical narratives about the war, many of which engage in revisions of this very status quo. I identify these fractured and false 'truths' about the war, its causes, dynamics, actors, and consequences as the main sources of anxiety around conflict recurrence.

Section 4.2 discusses how the numerous missing and incomplete truths about the conflict affect the lives of individuals, communities, and states and shape the perceptions of 'Never Again' and what threatens it. In Section 4.3, I explore how we got there and what the global project has to do with it. I identify that the transitional project in BiH has operated on the basis of a normative hierarchy which elevates the institutionalised form of the anti-impunity norm above other potential sources of 'truth' and simultaneously fuels political communities' ontological insecurities. In Section 4.4, I elaborate on historical revisionism and multiple, often parallel truths in and about the past of BiH as competing and simultaneous ontological security-seeking endeavours. In particular, I highlight the ongoing efforts to revise judicial truths established by the ICTY and domestic courts in BiH by different entity-based research institutions in attempts to move certain political communities to more ontologically secure positions which in turn serve to further the anxieties around potential conflict repetition. In Section 4.5, I conclude by reflecting on the implications for truth recovery and non-recurrence in transitional justice.

4.2 Home-Baked, Half-Baked Truths

As the introduction to this chapter illustrates, there are many missing truths about the war still out there, affecting individuals, families, communities, and relationships. As previously explained, there continues to be no information about approximately 7,000 wartime missing people in

BiH, and several more thousands who are missing throughout the region. The International Commission on Missing Persons (ICMP), with its Sarajevo office, is considered to have been largely successful in its work, having identified over 80 per cent of the originally 40,000 missing persons after the war in BiH alone. Yet, the fact that there are still 7,000 missing people continues to shape the lives of thousands of families who never have and likely never will know the truth about the whereabouts of their loved ones and the circumstances in which they died.

It can be presumed that the people who might know the information about the whereabouts of the remains of those missing are still alive. They are encouraged to report the location of the grave and are given an opportunity to do so anonymously on the ICMP's website. However, the representatives of the ICMP and its state-sponsored companion, the Missing Persons Institute (MPI), both expressed concerns about the number of received anonymous tips being on a steady decline. 'Witnesses die, people move, there is no more interest', the representative of the ICMP told me.[2] Furthermore, when people do make reports, this information almost always proves to be false. The ICMP representative explained how before, out of ten new exhumations, they would have had only one miss, a false clue due to fading memories. 'Nowadays, it is reversed. You would have sixty exhumations and no single remain found'.[3] One of the three members of the Board of Directors of the MPI shared these concerns. 'We often deal with cases where people take us to an alleged grave location and, after twenty years, they cannot orient themselves on that field; the vegetation has changed, perhaps new trees have grown in the meantime', he explained.[4]

Missing persons cases are only one yet illustrative example of how unknown truths about the war continue to shape private and public lives in BiH and throughout the former Yugoslavia. Beyond providing thousands of people with perpetual grief and inability to properly mourn their killed loved ones, the ongoing searches for and often unsuccessful excavations of human remains keep the conversations about victimhood, sacrifice, loss, and responsibility ongoing in public discourse. Numbers matter, not the least because behind them are actual people with actual

[2] Interview with representative of the International Commission on Missing Persons, 6 December 2019.

[3] Maja Davidović, 'Reconciling Complexities of Time in Criminal Justice and Transitional Justice' (2021) 21 International Criminal Law Review 935, p. 947.

[4] Interview with representative of the Missing Persons Institute, 17 December 2019.

families who grieve them but also because they play key roles in the construction of different groups' narratives about their own victimhood and sacrifice in the war. The metrics assigned to this particular demographic tend to be used and abused for political gains and perpetuation of inter-ethnic animosities, whereby different political elites count how many of those still missing belong to their proclaimed ethnic group. 'All sides now are engaging in a war of victims ... of numbers', one practitioner told me.[5] In particular, politicians and the media in both Republika Srpska and Serbia are using the low numbers of identified missing Serbs to discredit the ICMP and the MPI, labelling them as institutions aimed at identifying only 'Bosniak victims', while failing to acknowledge that overall, ethnic Bosniak victims of war by far outnumber ethnic Serb victims.[6] Finally, missing persons cases shape inter-state relations among the former Yugoslav states, as regional leaders have long been urged by the likes of the EU Commission to cooperate and coordinate on the matter in order to advance on their respective EU accession paths.[7]

Beyond this, the very character of the war in BiH and therefore its causes, actors, and responsibilities continue to be disputed and crafted along ethnic and political lines among different parties. For the ICTY, this was an 'international armed conflict', while for many in BiH today, it was an aggression on BiH. For Republika Srpska, it was a defensive-patriotic war or aggression on Srpska, and for an inexperienced foreign eye, for instance, it might as well look like a civil war. A typical post-positivist observation that there is no objective reality, if applied to this context, might be a harmful, destructive force.[8] Indeed, to settle on a qualification of the violent events committed in BiH between 1992 and 1995 is a political choice, but not making it means walking a thin line between war and peace in the years to come.

[5] Interview with representative of the Foundation Truth, Justice and Reconciliation, 11 November 2019.

[6] Maja Bjelajac, 'Rat rečima oko nestalih bosanskih Srba' (*Institute for War and Peace Reporting*, 2011) https://iwpr.net/sr/global-voices/rat-recima-oko-nestalih-bosanskih-srba accessed 5 April 2023.

[7] See the Joint Declaration on Missing Persons in the Framework of the Berlin Process, signed at the Western Balkans Summit in 2018 by the Heads of Government of the Western Balkans states, www.icmp.int/wp-content/uploads/2018/09/Deklaracije.pdf accessed 9 May 2024.

[8] Deborah Lipstadt, *Denying the Holocaust: The Growing Assault on Truth and Memory* (Penguin 1993).

The idea behind truth recovery as necessary for non-recurrence arises out of anxiety that without a public discussion about competing narratives between former conflict parties, and reconciliation thereof, repetition of conflict can be expected.[9] Without an openly discussed, negotiated 'metanarrative' about the war, the concern is that when those who bore witness to the war are no longer alive, future generations might fall into the traps of ethnic-based, victimhood-oriented narratives and resort to fighting.[10] As one interviewee posited, 'if we do not talk about these issues now, [repetition] will be the case in thirty, forty, fifty years. It is not the only thing one could expect but it would be a very logical situation, a totally logical course of events that there will be a repetition [of conflict]'.[11]

Insisting on truth recovery as a way to prevent recurrence of conflict is inspired by living through and remembering past conflicts and crises as well as the 1992–5 war. This interpretation of how 'Never Again' can be made meaningful for BiH thus stems from lived experiences of continuity and interrelatedness of harm, of war and peace and not merely a desire to fulfil the legal 'right to truth'. What happened or did not happen in previous wars and what is known or not known after these past wars are discovered through family and oral histories, lived experiences, as well as the teachings about the absence of what can now be known as 'transitional justice' upon the formation of what later became the Socialist Federal Republic of Yugoslavia.

The lessons learned from the past lead many people to believe that not discussing the atrocities committed during World War II (WWII) directly aided the emergence and brutality of the conflicts of the 1990s.[12]

[9] For example, Interview with representative of the Institute for research on crimes against humanity and international law, 7 November 2019; Interview with representative of the Youth Initiative for Human Rights BiH, 11 December 2019; Interview with representative 1 of the Helsinki Committee for Human Rights RS, 12 November 2019.

[10] Interview with representative 1 of the Helsinki Committee for Human Rights RS.

[11] Interview with representative of the Youth Initiative for Human Rights BiH.

[12] I am referring here to conflicts (plural) seeing how in the 1941–5 period, in addition to being occupied by Nazi Germany, Yugoslavia was also experiencing internal conflicts between Partisans, who led the National Liberation Movement against the occupiers, and Nazi collaborators predominantly Chetniks, a radical Serb Royalist group who sought to maintain the monarchy and 'cleanse' the territory of non-Serbs, and, in Croatia, Nazi collaborators Ustashe ran a puppet state with concentration camps for the extermination of Jews, Serbs, Roma, and communists. With the Partisans' eventual victory over the occupiers and their collaborators, Yugoslavia became a socialist country, and these former enemies continued to live under the same roof with no transitional justice processes as we know them today.

After WWII, former enemies lived together under the Yugoslav flag, and atrocities committed between these groups were not discussed for the sake of 'brotherhood' and 'unity', core values of socialist Yugoslavia. Forty-five years later, upon the dissolution of Yugoslavia, personal interpretations and distinct, conflicting perceptions of what had happened in WWII fuelled some seemingly unsolved inter-group tensions which re-emerged in political leaders' narratives and were used to mobilise war support. For instance, many crimes committed by ethnic Serb individuals in the wars of the 1990s are presented as crimes committed by 'Četnici', the Royalist group involved in the atrocities in WWII, while Croatian soldiers and perpetrators can often be referred to as 'Ustaše', with reference to the WWII-era regime.[13] Earlier grievances dating from the time of the Ottoman Empire also resurfaced as Bosnian Muslims were identified as 'Turks'. As a civil society activist explained,

> crimes happened in the 1940s, but they were not talked about. They were pushed under the rug for the sake of the ideas of brotherhood and unity ... Simply, they were neglected ... And then it happened that you had a general enter a [Bosnian] town [in 1995] saying 'this is revenge for 500 years of the Ottoman rule, revenge for this, revenge for that'.[14]

They were of course alluding here to Ratko Mladić's speech upon entering Srebrenica on 11 July 1995 in which he said, 'Finally, after the rebellion against the Dahis [an Ottoman-era event], the time has come to take revenge on the Turks in this region'.[15] Such rhetoric has long been employed by political elites in pursuit of nationalist agendas. The above reference to Ratko Mladić's statement upon entry into Srebrenica (referring to the Bosniak population as 'Turks') is the kind of rhetoric that strategically portrayed the existence of 'ancient dangers' posed by the other in order to accomplish a genocidal agenda.[16] Among the Serb population, in addition to the memories of the Ottoman era and particularly the Battle of Kosovo, WWII memories were also weaponised for

[13] Ben Lieberman, 'Nationalist Narratives, Violence between Neighbours and Ethnic Cleansing in Bosnia-Herzegovina: A Case of Cognitive Dissonance?' (2006) 8 Journal of Genocide Research 295.

[14] See BBC News, 'Footage of Mladic Entering Srebrenica Played at Trial' (*BBC News*, 17 May 2012) www.bbc.co.uk/news/av/world-europe-18102216 accessed 9 May 2024. Translation by the ICTY.

[15] ibid.

[16] Emir Suljagić, 'Genocide by Plebiscite: The Bosnian Serb Assembly and Social Construction of "Turks" in Bosnia and Herzegovina' (2021) 23 Journal of Genocide Research 568.

reasons such as justification of war and recruitment. Overall, in war and post-war Serbia, BiH, and Croatia, competing WWII memories are mobilised to recreate nations' autobiographies with stories of suffering, victimhood, betrayal, and grave injustices as well as biographies of the Others and othered, creating simplified and often mythical stories of continuity of both sets of identities over the years. By constructing Bosniak Muslims as 'Turks', Serb nationalists could have traced their grievances against the group back to the fourteenth century, buttressing their territorial claims and justifying the violence committed at the end of the twentieth century.

Narratives serve to build connections between one's past, present, and future.[17] In Critical Security Studies, clear links between narrative and ontological (in)security are drawn. Across contexts, different political actors rely on historical narratives, that is, a typically causal story about how certain historical events unfolded, to explain the current position and promote a specific version of their desired future.[18] As Subotic asserts, '[n]arratives are important for state ontological security seeking because they provide ... continuity with the "good past"'.[19] Being ontologically secure partly means maintaining a stable narrative about the group's self, which includes links with the past that political communities can feel good about.[20] Sustaining a particular biographical narrative requires the use of 'historical signposts', that is, 'careful curating of select events, setbacks and triumphs, myths, and symbols'.[21] As argued in Chapter 2, periods of transitions, from war to peace, from socialism to democracy, and from being a part of a federation to being an independent state, are all periods of major change and disruption that require a re-examination of one's sense of self. This re-examination of Bosniak, Croatian, Serbian, and other senses of self endured during the war and

[17] Maria Mälksoo, 'The Transitional Justice and Foreign Policy Nexus: The Inefficient Causation of State Ontological Security-Seeking' (2019) 21 International Studies Review 373.

[18] Faye Donnelly and Brent J Steele, 'Critical Security History: (De)securitisation, Ontological Security and Insecure Memories' (2019) 4 European Journal of International Security 209.

[19] Jelena Subotic, 'Narrative, Ontological Security, and Foreign Policy Change' (2015) 12 Foreign Policy Analysis 610, p. 614.

[20] Ayşe Zarakol, 'Ontological (In)Security and State Denial of Historical Crimes: Turkey and Japan' (2010) 24 International Relations 3; Subotic, 'Narrative, Ontological Security, and Foreign Policy Change'.

[21] Jelena Subotic, 'Political Memory, Ontological Security, and Holocaust Remembrance in Post-Communist Europe' (2018) 27 European Security 296.

in many ways was able to continue in the immediate post-war period with the ethnicity-centred arrangements found in the Dayton Peace Agreement.

In the light of these multiple competing narratives about the guilt, as well as the responsibility for the atrocities committed during the war, it is commonly believed in BiH that younger generations, without their own lived experiences, build their impressions and memories of the war based on home-baked stories and myths. In doing so, they also strengthen their identities, a sense of who they are in the community, in the country they found themselves in, and in the world. That identity is based on difference. However, it is not merely about the difference between 'being Bosnian-Herzegovinian' and its significant other, but also between the positions of self and the Other within BiH itself. Such family and community stories are often centred on their ethnic group's victimhood and the impossibility of cohabiting with other ethnic groups in a political, administrative, and economic system based on ethnic segregation. The lack of shared knowledge, discussion, and consensus about the metanarrative of the war and its replacement with home-baked and often half-baked truths make many people worry about the future of the youth and seemingly relative ease with which inter-ethnic tensions can be further aggravated. One practitioner stated,

> It is important to work on the preservation of the truths we already have because new generations are coming, who luckily did not live through the 90s and do not know what it means to survive war and suffering and, in fact, that is what we are afraid of . . . that these young, new generations do not know what it means to go through war but on the other hand they are growing in an environment that constantly strengthens the divisions. We do not talk about history at all . . . It is all up to subjective interpretation, 'My grandma told me this, but your father said that' . . . Large numbers of [BiH] youth are growing up in a very confused world. Precisely such young people are likely to succumb to new divisions.[22]

I have identified why fragmented, incomplete, and missing truths serve as a source of anxiety about potential conflict repetition. The next step is to explain, at least in part, how this happened and why there are so many 'truths' out there. Truth recovery is a key pillar of the global project of transitional justice. How come then the need for truth recovery in BiH remains so strong after years of this country being subject to various transitional justice projects?

[22] Interview with representative of the Post-Conflict Research Center, 6 November 2019.

4.3 No Interference, Please

As previously mentioned, to date, there have been no successful state-wide truth and reconciliation commissions or fact-finding inquiries that would investigate the causes, dynamics, and consequences of the 1992–5 war. In its place, the authority to shape the historical status quo is by and large given to the ICTY and, to a lesser degree, domestic courts adjudicating atrocity crimes. Establishing a state-wide, state-supported truth commission or inquiry was undesirable in the light of the rather specific, anti-impunity-heavy model of transitional justice that BiH was undergoing. The absence of state-wide fact-finding is thus by and large a story of a visible normative hierarchy in transitional justice in BiH whereby the institutionalised forms of anti-impunity, that is, the ICTY and domestic courts, have undertaken a wide range of social values that would otherwise be prescribed to other acceptable behaviours in this norm cluster.

In the first decade after the war, Neil Kritz from the Rule of Law Program at the US Institute of Peace and Jakob Finci, the executive director of the Open Society Foundation in BiH, launched a rather prominent initiative to create a central Truth and Reconciliation Commission (TRC) in Bosnia. In an article these two activists wrote together in 2001, it was claimed that a TRC-like non-judicial institution would help produce the ultimate, objective truth that is not tainted by ethnonationalism.[23] Kritz and Finci argued that BiH had already seen the suppression of the truth about violence in its past (i.e., after WWII) and that this only led to the recurrence of violence.[24] In their view, the TRC would serve to avoid the repetition of that 'mistake' and prevent future generations from fighting over which version of the ethnocentric truth is the correct one.[25] The TRC, Kritz and Finci wrote, 'will then be responsible for proposing specific steps which ought to be taken to restructure society, to deal with past abuses and to preclude their repetition'.[26] Acknowledging the necessity of the ICTY to address criminal responsibility, unlike criminal trials that place emphasis 'on the specific crimes of individual perpetrators', the prospective TRC would explore 'the experience of the victims' and 'the structural elements ... which made ...

[23] Neil J Kritz and Jakob Finci, 'A Truth and Reconciliation Commission in Bosnia and Herzegovina: An Idea Whose Time Has Come' (2001) 3 International Law FORUM du droit international 50.

[24] ibid.

[25] ibid.

[26] ibid, p. 52.

patterns of violations possible', producing knowledge of the conflict by way of 'painful self-examination'.[27] Essentially, it was argued that transitional justice efforts, in order to not only ensure accountability for past abuses but also transform and therefore prevent future abuses, would be incomplete without more comprehensive truth-telling practices.

Nevertheless, the initiative was never realised due to a marriage of influences from both the global project of transitional justice and the rising ethnonationalism. It was heavily contested by two perhaps least expected opposition groups – the ICTY and the victims' associations. The ICTY, having already been set up and ready to deal with the legacies of the conflict when the Dayton Peace Agreement was signed, feared that a truth commission would act as its alternative and therefore interfere with its work. The ICTY expressed 'a number of concerns about the potential effectiveness of the [Truth and Reconciliation] Commission' considering its 'proposed mandate' and 'the nature of truth commissions relative to criminal prosecutions'.[28] At the civil society conference that started off the TRC process in 2000, an ICTY representative informed the public that the Court's President and the Chief Prosecutor would not be supporting the initiative.[29] They expressed scepticism towards the possibility of obtaining 'one definite truth' through the commission and an overwhelming concern that the TRC would undermine the ICTY's investigations and decision-making.[30]

By that time, the ICTY had changed its original mandate from solely 'prosecuting persons responsible for serious violations of international humanitarian law' to contributing to the creation of a historical record and aiding truth and reconciliation.[31] Starting in 1998, clear attempts of the ICTY to undertake the task of writing an alternative history of the region and elevate itself above the 'messy' domestic political wranglings are detected. The ICTY held that the record established through judicial

[27] ibid.

[28] International Criminal Tribunal for the former Yugoslavia, 'Fifth Annual Report of the International Tribunal for the Prosecution of Persons Responsible for Serious Violations of International Humanitarian Law Committed in the Territory of the Former Yugoslavia since 1991' (10 August 1998) UN Doc. A/53/219, S/1998/737, para 225.

[29] Jasna Dragovic-Soso, 'History of a Failure: Attempts to Create a National Truth and Reconciliation Commission in Bosnia and Herzegovina, 1997–2006' (2016) 10 International Journal of Transitional Justice 292, p. 302.

[30] ibid, p. 302.

[31] Jinú Carvajalino and Maja Davidović, 'Escaping or Reinforcing Hierarchies? Norm Relations in Transitional Justice' (2023) 25 International Studies Review 1.

proceedings 'provides the basis for the long-term reconciliation and reconstruction of the region'.[32] The establishment of such a historical record was to be followed by educating local populations about it. It was stated that people of the former Yugoslavia 'have been denied access to objective information regarding the conflict' and being exposed to images of the ICTY 'as a tool of division rather than of healing'.[33] In doing so, the ICTY separated itself from the other bodies and actors in the transitional justice landscape as a neutral or as neutral as one can be with a much more expansive reach than originally envisaged, leading to the sustainment of a normative hierarchy in the transitional justice cluster in BiH.

This superiority of the ICTY as a producer of a historical record meant that other competing producers could only ever be inferior to it. The TRC could either not exist or only exist in a very limited capacity. Eventually, when it became obvious that the ICTY would have to outsource some of its tasks domestically to meet the workload demands, the Tribunal came around and expressed support for the initiative under the provision that it would only deal with those matters not prioritised by the ICTY.[34] Fulfilling such a provision would essentially prevent the TRC from enquiring about any more 'serious' crimes such as genocide, otherwise accommodated by the Tribunal. More specifically, the proposed TRC would have to hold a mandate that contributes but in no way impinges on the work of the ICTY. It could not and should not, ICTY President asserted in a speech in Sarajevo in 2001, aspire to be vested with 'real investigative powers', over which the Prosecutor has primacy, or to demand access to 'all information useful for its mission' which would, vaguely put, allegedly infringe upon the activities of the Prosecutor.[35] Even if realised, the TRC would have had a very limited and rather cosmetic mandate.

Domestically, no political support was gained for the TRC at either entity or national level. Victims' associations also rejected the idea of a TRC seemingly out of their dependence on local political parties who

[32] International Criminal Tribunal for the former Yugoslavia, 'Fifth Annual Report', para 202.
[33] ibid, para 297.
[34] Dragovic-Soso, 'History of a Failure'.
[35] President of the International Criminal Tribunal for the former Yugoslavia, 'The ICTY and the Truth and Reconciliation Commission in Bosnia and Herzegovina' (17 May 2001) JL/P.I.S./591-e, https://shorturl.at/FTY59 accessed 8 August 2022.
ibid.

essentially opposed the initiative.[36] Some of the reasons offered by victims' groups were rooted in their scepticism towards both the truth and reconciliation aspects of the TRC's work, seeing both as individual, voluntarily given, and not something achieved through 'compromise'.[37] Unable to gain enough political and public support, the TRC was never established and the initiative to found such a body on the state level was entirely abandoned.

The initiative for a textbook TRC, the crown jewel of the truth recovery pillar in transitional justice, is different from what many practitioners identify would be necessary now in order to fortify any assurances of conflict non-recurrence. As one interviewee put it bluntly, people discard TRC initiatives because such an enterprise, often associated with faith-based ideas of interpersonal reconciliation, 'could never be a part of their culture'.[38] Another interviewee, a director of a documentation-oriented NGO, explained to me that he was 'the biggest opponent' of the USIP truth commission.[39] When asked why he was opposing the establishment of a truth commission, he reflected on the short-term-ness of such institutions. 'All commissions are *ad hoc* bodies', he added, explaining how the society is rather in need of permanent institutions to deal with truth-related issues and provide explanations about the conflict that would last 'for all times'.[40]

Even the practitioners involved in the initiative to establish a regional commission, RECOM, more recently do not present the initiative as a 'truth and reconciliation' one. When I interviewed one of the drafters of the statute of the regional commission, they warned me that RECOM was explicitly never going to be 'a truth and reconciliation' but a fact-finding commission.[41] The difference is, they asserted, that RECOM would 'scientifically' and 'objectively' establish facts such as statistics about the victims. With the idea of TRC becoming a synonym for the South African model of TRC in these transitional justice circles in BiH, the truth recovery needed for non-recurrence, for these transitional justice actors, is stripped of 'reconciliation' and 'forgiveness' as sought-after values and, instead, a move is made towards 'science' and 'objectivity',

36 Dragovic-Soso, 'History of a Failure'.
37 ibid, pp. 306–7.
38 Interview with Anonymous 1, 7 February 2020.
39 Interview with representative of the Research and Documentation Center, 21 January 2020.
40 ibid.
41 Interview with representative of RECOM Coalition Working Group, 14 November 2019.

values otherwise attached to criminal justice. It is evident then that such a state-wide fact-finding commission would not only adopt the language of the ICTY but it would also have some overlapping competencies with some elements of the ICTY through which the background of a legal case is constructed, such as the ability to elaborate and decide on the characteristics of war.

That ICTY and other domestic court records are the main, if not only, sources of authoritative knowledge about the war is at the centre of debates and tensions around the gaps and imperfections of truth recovery in BiH. In the context of a lack of state-wide fact-finding, the institutionalised forms of anti-impunity are primarily valued for their truth recovery (and not only justice) potential and much more so than a prospective TRC. While courts in general are seen as legitimate vessels of knowledge about the conflict, it is the ICTY in particular that is positioned as the hub of conflict-related knowledge in BiH, and its judgements are treated as historical records. For most transitional justice actors in BiH, the ICTY and its legacy are holy. As one interviewee observed, '[w]hoever knows how the tribunal operated [can see that] there are no mistakes there'.[42] Linked to these statements is another participant's qualification of court judgements as 'the best thing that the human society could come up with' in the context of mass violence.[43] He further added that the BiH society has 'a unique opportunity to be written down in the books of humanity and civilization as [a society] that solved the worst possible situation in the correct way', this way being through court proceedings.[44] The validity of treating court records as authoritative knowledge is not questioned by this group of actors. 'Here the only truth is the adjudicated one', said one activist.[45] 'If we do not take the findings of the ICTY as the truth of what happened, then we really won't know what happened', she continued.

Criminal law and its institutions are seen as objective, or at least more objective than the alternatives, a civilisational way of addressing the grievances harmful for non-recurrence and building a shared, 'metanarrative' narrative about the war. The ICTY in particular is seen as more credible than domestic institutions. Not all practitioners negate the political power of the ICTY but see it as a more suitable option when

[42] Interview with representative of the Research and Documentation Center.
[43] Interview with representative of the High Judicial and Prosecutorial Council, 10 December 2019.
[44] ibid.
[45] Interview with representative of the Post-Conflict Research Center.

compared to domestic politics which is captured by ethnonationalism. This factual foundation is not built under a presumption that criminal justice is the only form of justice or for the appraisal of the resulting accountability. Instead, it is built on the basis of criminal justice institutions' qualifications to create 'the truth', the only truth that is not to be disputed, a historical status quo that can shape that autobiography of BiH.

Some of this belief relates to the perception that court-established facts rely on science and are therefore as objective as any truth can be and can solve disputes between multiple sources of truth. Relying on expert witnesses and forensic evidence collected by the likes of the ICMP, courts can confirm – by way of acceptance – both who died and the circumstances in which they died during the conflict. A representative of the Western Balkans Program at the ICMP gave a detailed example of this forensic and seemingly objective truth recovery process.

> There are victims buried in a small area and one party [of the conflict] says that they were civilian victims, while the other party says that there were soldiers who died in battle, which would make them legitimate targets. Then we [the ICMP] dig out the mass grave and find remains of the people whose hands and feet were tied with a wire or who had blindfolds over their eyes which means that evidently, they were captured and brought [to the execution site]. … Another thing, if you find one person in four mass graves tens of kilometres apart from one another, how could this man, if he died on the battlefield, end up in four different mass graves? This means that somebody, in an attempt to conceal the crime … put the bodies in four different trucks, drove them within a radius of 120 km and buried them in four different graves.[46]

All legal tools including courts and criminal prosecutions are forms of knowledge infused with the power to, among others, maintain the influence of both ideational and material structures such as transitional justice, giving it existence over time and space. By capturing the imagination of what truth about the war is and can be, the ideas about legitimate sources of truth simultaneously allow for the continuation of normative superiority of the anti-impunity norm and its attributes within the project of transitional justice, prolonging the idea that the model is generalisable and applicable to multiple contexts.[47] Yet, the initial idea

[46] Interview with representative of the International Commission on Missing Persons.

[47] Anthony Giddens, *The Constitution of Society: Outline of the Theory of Structuration* (Polity Press 1984) pp. 20–1.

that the ICTY establishes the truth and thus leads to reconciliation offered an oversimplified notion of the truth due to its limited capacity to hear cases and other procedural reasons such as resorting to plea bargains.[48] As Teitel argues, when the ICTY presented itself as 'advancing the aim of "deterrence" of prospective humanitarian tragedies' what was new to this assertion was 'the notion that law itself can define what constitutes peace and stability internationally', and that 'it could somehow displace politics to resolve international conflict'.[49] But more so, because criminal justice is heightened to the ultimate level of purity and formality in the project of transitional justice, the power dynamic it creates is often neglected, which allows it to prescribe what the 'good' acceptable truths are in a society. Criminal justice in that sense is promoted for both helping make sense of complex social phenomena and managing them.[50]

But here is the catch. While judicial truths can serve as a source of security, recognition, and accountability for many individuals, they are simultaneously sources of ontological insecurity for different political communities. As discussed in Chapters 1 and 2, ontological security can be understood as 'a quest for a stable narrative' about a group's sense of self, of which writing and cementing an autobiography or a story about oneself is a part and parcel.[51] Taken as historical records in this context, court judgements are promoted as a tool for rewriting and securing histories after a period of crisis, drawing boundaries between the past and the present, the guilty and the innocent, or indeed mechanisms of disrupting such processes in a political community.[52] To fully accept and internalise an international tribunal's qualifications of not only a single crime but also the entire conflict and its actors, dynamics, and consequences inevitably necessitates an interrogation and perhaps reconsideration of one's sense of self, one's collective identity and position in the

[48] Janine Natalya Clark, 'Transitional Justice, Truth and Reconciliation: An Under-Explored Relationship' (2011) 11 International Criminal Law Review 241.

[49] Ruti Teitel, 'Humanity's Law: Rule of Law for the New Global Politics' (2002) 35 Cornell International Law Journal 355, p. 385.

[50] Kevin E Davis, Benedict Kingsbury, and Sally Engle Merry, 'Introduction: The Local-Global Life of Indicators: Law, Power, and Resistance' in Kevin E Davis, Benedict Kingsbury, and Sally Engle Merry (eds.), *The Quiet Power of Indicators: Measuring Governance, Corruption, and Rule of Law* (Cambridge University Press 2015) p. 2.

[51] Zarakol, 'Ontological (In)Security and State Denial'.

[52] Donnelly and Steele, 'Critical Security History'; Maria Mälksoo, 'Militant Memocracy in International Relations: Mnemonical Status Anxiety and Memory Laws in Eastern Europe' (2021) 47 Review of International Studies 489.

world. This is, as Mälksoo argues, 'consequential for state behaviour'.[53] In that way, the hope that, in the absence of a truth recovery mechanism established by the people of BiH for the people of BiH, judicial truths can and should become the foundation of the common BiH narrative about the war and, with that, its history is, in this specific context, nigh on impossible to realise. Coated in attributes of neutrality, objectivity, science, and civilisation, the institutions of criminal justice are coercive, generating how potential conflict repetition and its prevention are conceptualised and acted upon. Instead of creating a common political narrative, a shared historical consensus about the war in political imaginaries, the global project's emphasis on judicial truths being the prioritised legitimate source of knowledge has further helped create not only multiple but also *parallel* truths which provide seemingly irreconcilable versions of reality.

Consider, for instance, the tensions around what is and what is not labelled 'genocide'. The ICTY jurisprudence suggests that genocide in BiH was location-specific and was committed in the area in and around Srebrenica in July 1995, although the genocidal ideology might have been brewing for much longer. There are two contestations of this qualification – one which seeks to minimise the decision, suggesting that what happened in Srebrenica was not a genocide (but maybe a war crime or in any case a 'terrible' crime) and one which seeks to maximise the decision, suggesting that genocide was not only committed in Srebrenica but also in the entire BiH. With the very final judgements being issued by the International Residual Mechanism for Criminal Tribunals in 2021 and 2022, much contestation remains about the Tribunal's qualification of 'genocide' being limited to a single area in and around Srebrenica. For example, in a news article, Borger, of *The Guardian*, is quoted to have said that not including 'the war crimes in [other] towns in Mladić's genocide conviction could be emotionally scarring for those whose experiences are very similar to what happened in Srebrenica'.[54] It is claimed that this is due to the powerful emotive force the term genocide carries with itself.

Yet, what is often absent from these discussions is a reminder about the legal functions of the court. The Mladić case concerns a single

[53] Mälksoo, 'The Transitional Justice and Foreign Policy Nexus', p. 374.

[54] Aleksandar Brezar, 'Not Bad Enough for Genocide? The Bosnian Towns Cheated by Mladić Verdict' (*Euronews*, 11 June 2021) https://shorturl.at/coHU0 accessed 15 June 2021.

person's criminal accountability for ordering, organising, aiding, abetting, or otherwise committing the said crimes. As per courts' operations in general, not legally qualifying a case as 'genocide' simply states that there is no sufficient evidence to do so in relation to the specific accused individual. To be more precise, just because Ratko Mladić was not convicted of genocide in the area of Brčko, for example, should not be interpreted as a definite claim that in fact genocidal agendas were not pursued in that area; yet it is. In fact, part of the reasoning in the Jelisić case, which concerned the crimes committed in the Brčko area, included not only if the said crimes constitute genocide but also if 'low-ranking perpetrators' such as Jelisić have the capacity to perpetrate a complex crime such as genocide and, if yes, whether they ought to be prosecuted for it, to which the ruling was eventually in the negative.[55] Still, 'reducing genocide to law'[56] and treating the ICTY as a history-making institution that causes disagreement about the ICTY's seemingly conclusive facts triggers fragmentation of the 'truth'. I want to make it clear that for me as the author of this book, there is no debate about the crimes committed in Srebrenica were a genocide – they were. However, other misinterpretations of legal cases influence the social and political life in BiH. At least three such options stem from the above decision alone – (a) that genocide was committed in Srebrenica and nowhere else in BiH, as per the ICTY, (b) that genocide was committed in Srebrenica, as per the ICTY, but was also committed elsewhere in BiH, and (c) that some differently qualified crime was committed in Srebrenica but not genocide. The unfamiliarity of much of the audience with how the judicial truth issued by the ICTY was arrived at and with what methods it could possibly be revised or not can make these three appear as options of equal standing, even though they are not, leaving assurances of non-recurrence on rather shaky ground.

In Section 4.4, I demonstrate the myriad ways in which court records are used to revise, widen, and broaden truth recovery about the war. In particular, I am interested here in options (b) as a form of exposing lived experiences of genocide not recognised by the ICTY and (c) as revisionist efforts which serve to reject and discredit court records as legitimate sources of the historical status quo. I illustrate with two cases of entity-supported research centres in Republika Srpska and Federation

[55] Payam Akhavan, *Reducing Genocide to Law: Definition, Meaning, and the Ultimate Crime* (Cambridge University Press 2012) p. 154.

[56] ibid, p. 10.

BiH (FBiH) as actors that build beyond or against the ICTY records. Although very different political projects, both these examples create new myths about victimhood and suffering and re-mystify some of the old ones to polish their autobiographies while interacting with the ICTY records in distinct, parallel ways to ensure the continuity of their renegotiated narratives.

4.4 What Truth Can Courts Write?

A political community's ontological security is shaken when its biographical narratives are subject to inconsistency or rupture.[57] The global project of transitional justice, with the ICTY at the forefront, provided disruptions as the truths about the roles, actions, dynamics, and characteristics of the war, which undoubtedly held a prominent place in different groups' biographies, were being written by these courts in the first two decades of the transition. These emerging truths, positioned by the ICTY itself as the authoritative 'metanarrative' about the war, needed to be situated within the pre-existing biographies which had their own metanarratives. As such, they continued to test some core aspects of these biographies by revealing information that different political communities might perceive as shameful. Situating judicial truths within the metanarratives of these political communities has involved revision, reclassification, trivialisation, and minimisation.

The most contentious legal qualification is whether the killings of over 8,000 Bosniak men and boys in and around Srebrenica in July 1995 constitute genocide, as per the ICTY and the International Court of Justice judgements,[58] a case which has been the source of much revisionism both in and outside BiH. Calling the Srebrenica events genocide is frequently outright rejected as the proper classification of the crime by ethnic Serb public figures who would rather it be called 'massacre' or simply 'a terrible crime'. For example, one such public figure is Mladen Grujičić, the mayor of the town of Srebrenica, who dismissed the ICTY's classification of the crime in an interview and furthermore held that the

[57] Maysam Behravesh, 'State Revisionism and Ontological (In)Security in International Politics: The Complicated Case of Iran and Its Nuclear Behaviour' (2018) 21 Journal of International Relations and Development 836.

[58] *Prosecutor v Krstić* (Appeals Judgment) ICTY-98-33 (19 April 2004); *Case Concerning Application of the Convention on the Prevention and Punishment of the Crime of Genocide (Bosnia and Herzegovina v Serbia and Montenegro)* [2007] ICJ GL No 91.

list of Srebrenica victims ought to be 'revised and changed'.[59] To remind the reader, Srebrenica is part of Republika Srpska, which is why it is possible to appoint such a person to the mayor office. Milorad Dodik himself, the Serb member of the BiH Presidency, has many times undertaken the role of Srebrenica genocide denial spokesperson by, for instance, calling the Srebrenica genocide 'a myth' that never happened.[60] The political elites of neighbouring Serbia and Croatia have also had their fair share of denial and trivialisation, with Serbia's Prime Minister Ana Brnabić calling Srebrenica 'a war crime'.[61] In 2021, Croatia's President Zoran Milanović argued that if Srebrenica is a genocide, other, 'graver' crimes such as the Holocaust need a new category.[62]

The normative hierarchy of transitional justice established in the previous section contributes to and often triggers the establishment of new grievances and multiple, *parallel* truths about the war which serve the purpose of re-establishing the ethnic group's ontological security but in turn sustain the discourse of – and anxiety about – potential conflict repetition. They are parallel truths because, while they might have the same starting points, they have different aims and trajectories. For some of the rewriting of the ICTY decisions, the starting point is one of *difference* and making it deeper, with more meaningful emphasis on the unique, ethnic- and religion-based suffering of their community vis-a-vis all others. '*Maybe all suffered, but we suffered the most*'. '*Maybe the atrocities committed towards your people were grave, but what happened to us was genocide and is thus the gravest*'. For the revisionists found in Republika Srpska, the starting point is also one of *difference*, but the aim is to reduce it and move towards *sameness*, making ethnic Serbs as an entity less special, singled out, and unique in their perpetration of atrocity crimes during the war. '*Maybe we committed atrocity crimes, but so did everyone*'. '*Maybe you suffered, but so did we*'.

59 Igor Spaić, 'Srebrenica's Serb Mayor Repeats Denial of Genocide' (*BIRN*, 13 April 2017) https://shorturl.at/bcdAY accessed 29 November 2020.

60 Radio Slobodna Evropa, 'Dodik: U Srebrenici nije počinjen genocid, to je mit poput kosovskog' (*Radio Slobodna Evropa*, 12 July 2019) www.slobodnaevropa.org/a/30052016.html accessed 9 May 2024.

61 Tim Sebastian, 'Ana Brnabić: "U Srebrenici nije bio genocid"' (*DW*, 15 November 2018) https://shorturl.at/gsF28 accessed 5 April 2023.

62 Radio Slobodna Evropa, 'Milanović: Srebrenica je genocid, ali onda za teže zločine treba novo ime' (*Radio Slobodna Evropa*, 6 December 2021) https://shorturl.at/jCQT2 accessed 5 April 2023.

The tensions between reducing and maximising difference are identifiable in the two key research centres on atrocity crimes, which operate at the entity level. In FBiH, such an institution is the Institute for Research on Crimes Against Humanity and International Law based in Sarajevo. Despite conducting their own research and producing their own publications about a range of topics relating to the conflict, as their name suggests, international law and the ICTY archive remain the central, always integrated body of knowledge, in the Institute's own words. Their former director explained the relationship between the Institute's fact-finding agency and the ICTY:

> Of course, we use everything that the ICTY has produced so far. We do not believe that there is some absolute justice in the world, but we have exact numbers of how many sentences were issued, for Serbs, Croats, Bosniaks. It is still the most objective thing that could happen to us. What do you think would have happened if it had been up to national courts? Who would have brought Slobodan Milošević to court? . . . Never.[63]

Among notable publications, the Federation Institute has done research on the crimes committed against children in Sarajevo under siege, the 'Greater Serbia' ideology, and the 'truth about genocide' in BiH,[64] buttressed, where applicable with ICTY's judgements. I use the phrase 'where applicable' because the Institute's body of work contains numerous summaries of ICTY judgements and completed cases but also publications that reclassify some of the crimes adjudicated by the ICTY. The reclassification is done to add to the gravity of the crimes, which results in the category 'genocide' being used to describe the crimes committed in places such as Brčko,[65] Ahmići,[66] and all of BiH.[67] This in turn aggravates the suffering, sacrifice, and victimhood of the Bosniak Muslim population as a group (and not perhaps only certain people in it) exposed

[63] Interview with representative 1 of the Institute for research on crimes against humanity and international law, 7 November 2019.

[64] Institut za istraživanje zločina protiv čovječnosti i međunarodnog prava, *Publikacije*, www.institut-genocid.unsa.ba/bs/stranica.php?idstranica=8 accessed 4 October 2020.

[65] For example, Rasim Muratović and Ermin Kuka, *Genocid u Brčkom 1992–1995* (Institut za istraživanje zločina protiv čovječnosti i međunarodnog prava 2015).

[66] Rasim Muratović, *Genocid u Ahmićima 1993* (Institut za istraživanje zločina protiv čovječnosti i međunarodnog prava 2013). See the case of Miroslav Bralo who was convicted on eight counts including persecution on political, racial, and religious grounds and torture or inhuman treatment and unlawful confinement for the crimes committed in Ahmići, *Prosecutor v. Bralo* (Judgment) ICTY-95-17 (2 April 2007).

[67] Smail Čekić, *Genocid i Istina o Genocidu u Bosni i Hercegovini* (Institut za istraživanje zločina protiv čovječnosti i međunarodnog prava 2012).

to genocidal ideology and practice in the hands of 'Great-Serbian' nationalist 'programmes' through and through. For instance, in a book about *Genocide in Sanski Most* published by the Institute, the author holds that the Bosniak Muslim population suffered due to Serbs' attempts to 'solve the Muslim question', making, implicitly, the suffering of the Bosniak people comparable to that of the Jewish people in the Holocaust as a known standard of European memory.[68] In a book about *Genocide in Brčko*, the authors emphasise the scientific method of their research concluding that 'Serb nationalists committed genocide, in addition to numerous crimes against humanity' on the basis of 'numerous documents by the ICTY and domestic courts, as well as referenced books, journals and newspapers'.[69] In doing so, they cite two ICTY cases. In the most high-profile case dealing with the crimes committed in the Brčko area, the ICTY found Goran Jelisić guilty of crimes against humanity at the gravest count but not on the count of genocide.[70] In the Milošević case, the count of genocide in Brčko was also included in the indictment; however, the former President of Yugoslavia died during the proceedings and therefore the judgement on this case was never reached. Nevertheless, the contents of the indictment were used as one of the key sources to (re)qualify the atrocities committed in Brčko as genocide.

In FBiH at least, the Institute is rather impactful as a fact-finding body that has operated as an authoritative research institution since its creation in September 1992. It was among the first ones to survey the population in Sarajevo during the siege in 1993 and 1994. The members of the Institute publish their work widely and lecture on the topic at the University of Sarajevo and public events.[71] The Institute's work is influential, and while it shapes opinions, it also reflects the growing sentiments about the legacies of the war among the Bosniak population. It is therefore not uncommon in BiH public and political discourse to hear the word genocide used to describe crimes committed outside Srebrenica. This is the new and emerging Bosniak autobiography in which all Bosniaks were victims/survivors of genocide. That this is a common

[68] Mujo Begić, *Genocid u Sanskom Mostu* (Institut za istraživanje zločina protiv čovječnosti i međunarodnog prava 2017) p. 13.

[69] Rasim Muratović and Ermin Kuka, *Genocid u Brčkom 1992–1995* (Institut za istraživanje zločina protiv čovječnosti i međunarodnog prava 2015) p. 36.

[70] See *Prosecutor v Jelisić* (Appeals Judgment) ICTY-95-10 (5 July 2001).

[71] Interview with representative 1 of the Institute for research on crimes against humanity and international law; Interview with representative 2 of the Institute for research on crimes against humanity and international law, 15 November 2019.

and understandable lived experience is a given. What interests me in this book is how the shaping of that autobiography selectively interacts with the ICTY and domestic courts as sources of the historical status quo to broaden, widen, and deepen the 'truth' about Bosniaks as a political community. While an imperfect court, the ICTY is here presented as good in its neutrality. Its potential violence through destruction or suppression of voices and lived experiences is not commonly held against it as its work by and large is seen as beneficial for the unity and identity of the collective actor this research institution undoubtedly represents.

On the other side of the coin is the Republika Srpska Institute for Research on War, War Crimes and Missing Persons from Banja Luka. The two research centres seemingly have the same mandate, but their research topics are ethnically organised and separate, and their reports produce parallel truths. The RS Institute occupies a rather controversial position in the transitional justice sector and is frequently accused, rightly, of being revisionist. Considering the officials of the RS Institute proudly call Radovan Karadžić, the former wartime President of Republika Srpska convicted of genocide, crimes against humanity, and war crimes by the ICTY, 'the first President'[72] and openly refuse to label the crimes committed in Srebrenica as genocide,[73] it is easy to see how this can be interpreted as denial of victims' grievances. While the Federation Research Institute has focused on studying the 'Greater Serbia' ideology, the RS Institute has published books regarding 'the suffering of Serbian people' in multiple areas in the region, the aggression of Croatia on Republika Srpska, and the role of Republika Srpska in what it terms 'defensive-patriotic' war.[74]

The way knowledge creation operates in the RS institute is through critiquing the ICTY and other criminal justice institutions and rejecting their work as inherently political, and therefore biased towards certain agendas. These practices are therefore not only revisionists in the historical sense, by changing the historical record with new 'facts', but also in the sense of global politics whereby they disturb the elevated status of the

[72] Republički centar za istraživanje rata, ratnih zločina i traženje nestalih lica, *Караџић – процес*, www.rcirz.org/караџић-процес accessed 12 October 2020.

[73] Republički centar za istraživanje rata, ratnih zločina i traženje nestalih lica, 'Kojić: Uvredljivo saopštenje Memorijalnog centra Srebrenica' (*RS Institute*, 27 April 2020) https://shorturl.at/eFILZ accessed 12 October 2020.

[74] Republički centar za istraživanje rata, ratnih zločina i traženje nestalih lica, *Publikacije*, www.rcirz.org/publikacije/?script=lat accessed 4 October 2020.

anti-impunity norm in the transitional justice norm cluster and the common understanding of how transitional justice should be done. The RS institute does still, by and large, embrace the policy language of transitional justice, working towards the fulfilment of the same values that the global project enshrines. On the official website, this institution reports using all its resources available 'to find the truth' because 'court proceedings and judgments cannot write the truth'.[75] The idea that tribunals can have history-making capabilities and that court records are the authoritative knowledge about the conflict is thus straightforwardly rejected. In Banja Luka, I visited the offices of the RS Institute, located in a set of government buildings they share with the National Assembly of RS. The complex is located on a square symbolically entitled 'the square of the victims of Jasenovac' commemorating those (mainly Serb) victims who perished in this WWII concentration camp in Croatia. This symbolic act buttressed the continuity of a post-Yugoslav autobiography in which the Serbs have traditionally been victims, an entity that survived despite continuous threats of extermination, scapegoating, and injustices from the outside.[76]

The representatives of the RS Institute presented me with numerous statistics aiming to prove the ethnic biases of both the ICTY and the Court of BiH due to which Serb victims were, once again, neglected. By way of example, it was stated that 'the ICTY has not fulfilled its task [to render justice], particularly if considering the fact that for the crimes committed against Serbs, the ICTY issued sentences amounting to a total of sixty-four years of imprisonment, for the whole of former Yugoslavia. At the same time, the ICTY sentenced Serb [defendants] to a total sentence of 967.5 years and six life sentences'.[77]

Similarly 'defeating' statistics were offered for the practice of the Court of BiH which, as the RS Institute calculated, issued only 13 per cent of all sentences for crimes committed towards Serbs. The overall interpretation of such court practice is that '35,000 Serbian victims of wars in Croatia and BiH' are not accounted for and probably never will be considering the passage of time.[78]

[75] Republički centar za istraživanje rata, ratnih zločina i traženje nestalih lica, *O nama*, www .rcirz.org/onama/?script=lat accessed 12 October 2020.

[76] Dubravka Stojanović, *Prošlost dolazi* (Biblioteka XX vek 2023).

[77] Written correspondence with representative of the Republika Srpska Institute for research on war, war crimes, and missing persons, 27 November 2019.

[78] ibid.

As a state institution, the RS Institute is obliged by the Dayton Peace Agreement and subsequent domestic law to cooperate with the ICTY when necessary, yet the representatives see this legal obligation as imposed and problematic. Furthermore, they were also eager to express the centralised work by the ICMP and the MPI on missing persons issues as 'manipulating science' and promoting distorted, subjective truths on the account that the number of identified missing persons of Serb ethnicity has decreased since this centralisation.[79] There is no doubt that conducting their parallel fact-finding is ethnically conditioned and serves the purpose of feeding the myths of Serbian identity with 'evidence'. The challenging practices here are directed towards institutions that are seen not as biased against justice in general, but biased against justice and truth for Serbian people, by prosecuting more ethnic Serbs, or exhuming fewer Serbian disappeared people. While some technical points (e.g., exhumation techniques) are held against these challenged institutions, the objection, and therefore reason to be proactive, is made on political and not technical arguments. More precisely, the ICTY is not problematic because it made a procedural omission but because any omissions they made were done, these actors argue, against the Serbian population, targeting the Serbian people as 'unjustly' *different*. The RS Institute's publications focusing on the 'suffering of the Serbian people' and Serbian victims exclusively seek to diminish or reverse this difference and magnify Serbian victimhood to be on par, and often greater than other people's victimhood. In addition to influencing public consciousness and discourse about the conflict through their publications, the RS Institute also establishes, suggests, and coordinates memorialisation projects in this entity, seeking to both nurture and mould a culture of remembrance.[80] These efforts jointly have 'the goal of realising the whole truth by the society, raising awareness about the horrors of war . . . out of which emerges the goal of educating the entire society in order for something like this to *never happen again*'.[81]

The statistics the RS Institute presented me with are correct but the method of arriving at the conclusion is flawed and in that sense is textbook historical revisionism.[82] The unequal party dynamics at the

[79] ibid.

[80] Republički centar za istraživanje rata, ratnih zločina i traženje nestalih lica, *Djelatnosti*, www.rcirz.org/djelatnosti/ accessed 30 April 2021.

[81] ibid.

[82] Lipstadt, *Denying the Holocaust*.

ICTY, which the RS Institute references in the statistics on imprisonment, reflect the unequal party dynamics during the conflict where the Bosnian Serb forces quantitively committed most atrocities and where ethnic Bosniaks constituted a large majority of victims. The unequal numbers therefore represent inequality in war and not necessarily in justice. But carefully crafted distortion of language and numbers is not only typical for the RS institutions. In the past couple of decades, it must be noted that such unequal party dynamics have been mistranslated into the everyday language to label Serbian people – as opposed to the Army of Republika Srpska – as aggressors. This is a label that can often be perceived as constitutive to the Bosniak autobiography of all-encompassing victims of genocide. Defending the nation against this label most gruesome of all similarly invokes the (mis)use of the language of equality among the people who were all but equal during the war. By way of example, the Sarajevo City Hall, where this chapter started, is a site where such tensions are illustratively manifested. Namely, multiple commemorative plaques placed on sites of massacres around Sarajevo and at the entrance to the City Hall all come with the same message (in Bosnian): 'At this place, *Serbian criminals* [committed a crime with certain casualties and/or damages] ... remember and warn'.[83] The text has been debated ever since it appeared for seemingly choosing not to refer to the perpetrators as 'Serbian soldiers' and instead (mis)labelling Serbian people as 'criminals'. It most recently became the subject of a discussion between the mayor of Sarajevo and the mayor of East Sarajevo, which is in the proximity of the city of Sarajevo but in the Republika Srpska territory. The mayor of Sarajevo, Benjamina Karić, refused to edit the text on the account that would represent an 'alteration of facts'.[84] The commonly accepted facts, in this case, are that Serbs, and not the Army of Republika Srpska, were the aggressors. Yet, for the mayor of East Sarajevo, this is a question of inequality. 'When you have plaques that constantly remind that one people have the qualification of "perpetrators," this definitely insults these people and puts them in some kind of unequal position' the mayor was quoted saying for Radio Free Europe.[85] 'My intention was going in the direction of equalization of the

[83] My emphasis.

[84] See Aida Đugum and Dragan Erjavec, 'Novi gradonačelnici dva Sarajeva u raspravi o spomen ploči' (*Radio Slobodna Evropa*, 13 April 2021) https://shorturl.at/dfmH6 accessed 27 April 2021.

[85] ibid.

status of peoples in that city', he further added, in order to build a multi-ethnic society.[86] When the city of Sarajevo finally, after numerous pleas by victims' associations, built a memorial to the mostly Serb civilian victims killed by an ARBiH brigade in 1992 and 1993 in the hills above the city known as Kazani, no names or ethnicities of the perpetrators were listed on it.[87]

Decades of not working on any state-wide fact-finding programmes and relying on the ICTY and domestic courts as the key sources of the historical status quo allow for such revisions that produce parallel truths with no penalty and seemingly no potential to be reconciled. Having multiple competing narratives about the war and its legacies in BiH is hence not an enrichment to the society but rather a harmful environment that serves to cement certain narratives built on a clear-cut *victim vs perpetrator* binary, confuse the audience to the point where nothing can be deemed true anymore and where all options are misinterpreted as equal when they are not, or even disassociate the audience from the past and the present, letting ethnonationalism continue to blossom.

4.5 Conclusion

In this chapter, I have discussed the practice of truth recovery and its complicated relationships with prevention of conflict recurrence and ontological security. I have offered numerous examples of why and how the lack of state-supported fact-finding or even a dialogue about the characteristics and dynamics of the war and the placeholder fragmented and parallel truths sustain anxieties about potential renewed conflict. My emphasis has been on linking truth recovery in transitional justice to the establishment and maintenance of biographical narratives of different political communities as ontological security-seeking exercises.

The point of this chapter has been not only to identify some of the key sources of anxieties around potential renewed conflict but also to reflect on *how* BiH found itself in a situation where there are seemingly multiple sources of truth, and many parallel truths compete for validity, legitimacy, and attention. It is in answering the how-question that I have argued

[86] ibid.

[87] Jasna Begic, 'Sarajevo to Build Massacre Memorial without Naming Perpetrators' (*BIRN*, 27 October 2021) https://balkaninsight.com/2021/10/27/sarajevo-to-build-massacre-memorial-without-naming-perpetrators/ accessed 30 May 2024.

that the global project of transitional justice, with its normative hierarchy which prioritised courts above other potential sources of historical status quo, should be understood as a disruption of (or a threat to) the continuity of these biographical narratives. I have claimed that judicial truths needed to be situated within political communities' narratives about the past self as they emerged, which resulted in widespread revisions, trivialisation, and minimisation of said judicial records.

These ideas reflect some of the questions raised in the transitional justice literature about the practicality as well as the morality of an 'objective' or 'scientific' single narrative about the conflict, under the presumption that truth, as well as memory, will always be multiple, contested, and negotiated and insisting on a single narrative will inevitably come at a cost of other, alternative, and marginalised narratives.[88] Similarly, in the ontological security literature, scholars dispute whether or not the convergence of different narratives about the past is necessary for peace.[89] Although a political act of truth recovery may be an exercise of control over what is officially accepted as the knowledge about the conflict,[90] it is nevertheless seen as a necessary act by many interviewed practitioners after years of fragmented, multiple, and incomplete 'truths' circulating in the society. The more important point here is that not all truths are equal in their application of the historiographic method. Some 'truths' have an overt, discriminatory political agenda aimed at perpetuating othering and presenting lies and fabrications as 'the other side' as having legitimate standing alongside all other truths.[91] The goal of truth recovery for 'Never Again' in BiH is first and foremost one of not letting grievances go unaddressed and unattended to and secondarily a reconciliation, not of individuals, but of collective narratives about the war. The goal is therefore not to suppress lived experiences which do not easily fit into the reconciled narrative but to establish benchmarks, and

[88] For an overview of these debates, see, generally, Catherine Turner and Maja Davidovic, 'Transitional Justice: An Interdisciplinary Landscape?' in Cheryl Lawther and Luke Moffett (eds.), *Research Handbook on Transitional Justice* (2nd ed., Edward Elgar 2023).

[89] Bahar Rumelili, 'Breaking with Europe's Pasts: Memory, Reconciliation, and Ontological (In)Security' (2018) 27 European Security 280; Valérie Rosoux, 'National Identity in France and Germany: From Mutual Exclusion to Negotiation' (2001) 6 International Negotiation 175.

[90] Charles S Maier, 'Doing History, Doing Justice: The Historian and the Truth Commission' in Robert I Rotberg and Dennis F Thompson (eds.), *Truth v. Justice: The Morality of Truth Commissions* (Princeton University Press 2000) pp. 261–287.

[91] Lipstadt, *Denying the Holocaust.*

boundaries of what is respected in public affairs, recognising that 'stepping over the line' will cause group or individual hurt.[92]

This chapter, the first of chapters discussing non-recurrence and transitional justice in BiH, has therefore asked the reader to learn about 'Never Again' in the wider context of transitional justice. What can be seen through the ontological security lens is that, as a project led by the value of truth recovery, transitional justice is bound to cause disruptions in political communities' desire for continuity and autobiographical projects. This chapter has shown that the project cannot afford to elevate judicial truths above other truths at the expense of truth commissions, fact-finding inquiries, and personal and individual narrations of war experiences because such a practice above all serves to enhance any existing anxieties about potential conflict repetition. Yet, not all available truths should be treated as equal options. An aspiration for the global project therefore is to recognise which alternative 'truths' are valid options, and which are perversions of reality. The idea of settling on a shared narrative is hence a violent one in the sense that it (should) suppresses alternative realities in which, for instance, tortured, handcuffed, and blindfolded men were somehow acting offensively towards those who were about to kill them as some revisionists might claim was the case in Srebrenica. What it is not is the suppression of alternative stories, experiences, and narratives. The point, therefore, is to have a discussion with a shared interest in reaching a consensus. For that discussion to happen, it is not only the case that more needs to be known, but that what is known both through and *beyond* the ICTY and domestic courts needs to be heard. Not hearing the lived experiences beyond the ICTY, I have shown in this chapter, was a part and parcel of the specific mode of governing the past exercised over BiH subjects, an element of governing producing the most harmful consequences.

92 Interview with Saliha Đuderija, 17 December 2019.

5

'Actively Preparing Children for New Conflicts'

Competing Histories and Education for (Non-) Recurrence

5.1 Bad Investments

In June 2017, a couple of hundred high school students gathered in front of the Government of the Srednjobosanski canton in a place called Travnik in central Bosnia. The students were there to protest the canton's recent decision to open a new school in their hometown of Jajce in which the students of Bosniak ethnicity would learn according to the 'Bosnian' curriculum, separately from the students of Croat ethnicity who would continue to do so according to the 'Croatian' curriculum. This move was supposed to bring the educational system in Jajce in alignment with the 'Two Schools Under One Roof' policy in the Federation of BiH (FBiH) where students of different ethnicities learn separate things in separate spaces. Up until that moment, Croat and Bosniak students in Jajce had studied together in the same schools under the 'Croatian' curriculum.

The protest was a culmination of smaller demonstrations by the students from Jajce who expressed their disagreement with the policy change and instead sent messages of unity. Young protestors in Travnik said loud and clear to the politicians: no to segregation; no to separation; abolish the 'Two Schools Under One Roof' policy. Many of the messages directed towards the canton government were warnings about the future of the country which segregates its youth on an ethnic basis, including 'Segregation is a bad investment' and 'We are here to create the future, not to repeat the past'.[1] In response to their protest, the Minister of Education in the canton said that Bosnia and Herzegovina (BiH) is a constitutionally 'divided' society, with three different languages and

[1] Ljupko Mišeljić, 'Travnički protest: Zajedničko obrazovanje protiv odvojene indoktrinacije' (*Diskriminacija*, 22 June 2017) https://shorturl.at/jrA24 accessed 31 March 2023.

histories.[2] She further stated that any children who are against segregation are 'instruments of the international community'.[3] 'They should go to a disco club', the Minister was quoted saying, 'and if they don't want to go to a disco club, then they need to start pushing for changes within the Dayton Peace Agreement itself'.[4] For the protesting students, the canton's decision, while constitutional, was 'nonsense' as they all 'went to school together' and 'hung out together' after classes.[5]

In the light of the demonstrations in Jajce, protests in Travnik, classroom walkouts, and numerous members of the international community expressing their support for the students' action, the government of the Srednjobosanski canton dropped its segregation plans by the end of June 2017.[6] These students won, yet the right to be educated together is not granted to many other students in the FBiH who continue to be segregated on an ethnic basis.

In 2019 in Sarajevo, I had a conversation with one of the civil society activists who supported this group of students before and during their protests about what this act means for prevention of conflict recurrence. 'This was probably the first true political act since BiH was founded', he observed.[7]

> [the protests] were real political processes because the kids asked to be together in a society that is made to divide. So, this was a total shift in the system's matrix . . . I am exaggerating a bit, but it was an act of destruction of the constitutional order because they [the students] took away the constitutional right of people to have classes in their mother tongue [as a basis for segregation] . . . From the legal point of view, and human rights perspective, people who asked for segregation and education in their mother tongue [Bosnian] were totally right. They wanted to attend maths classes in the Bosnian language and claimed that if they are forced to attend classes in the Croatian language and receive diplomas with *šahovnica*,[8] they would be discriminated against . . . These are children

[2] N1 BiH, 'Ministrica učenicima iz Jajca poručila: Idite u disko' (*N1 Info BiH*, 20 June 2017) https://shorturl.at/czOV2 accessed 31 March 2023.

[3] ibid.

[4] Mišeljić, 'Travnički protest'.

[5] Nezavisne novine, 'Protest učenika u Jajcu: Ne želimo podjele' (*Nezavisne novine*, 8 July 2016) https://shorturl.at/aDKXZ accessed 31 March 2023.

[6] Sarah Freeman-Woolpert, 'Bosnian Students Who Fought School Segregation Win Prestigious Award' (*Waging Nonviolence*, 24 July 2018) https://shorturl.at/ktDEG accessed 31 March 2023.

[7] Interview with Nansen Dialogue Centre, 4 November 2019.

[8] Checkerboard, a national symbol of the Republic of Croatia.

> whose parents are Bosniaks and who probably participated in the war and fought against this. From the legal point of view, and from a human rights perspective, these people asked not to be discriminated against [based on their linguistic preferences]. But then you have a group of students who say, 'alright, we are aware of the [linguistic] discrimination but that does not mean we have to be segregated' . . . And they manage to win![9]

The central message of the story of Jajce, in this activist's view, is that it creates *transethnic spaces* in a country where ethnic divisions are imposed by constitutional design. This is not to say that the protesting students wanted to abolish ethnic differences altogether; on the contrary, they wanted equality despite differences. In the demonstrations leading up to the protests, students were pictured holding three flags as a sign of unity: the flags of BiH, the Republic of Croatia, and the Republic of Serbia. It meant that the students still identified themselves through their distinct ethnic identities (as Serbs, Croats, or Bosniaks) among whom only Bosniaks expressed their belonging through the flag of the country in which they lived – BiH. Students of other ethnicities were quoted saying that they wanted to keep learning together even though they would end up receiving a diploma with *šahovnica*.[10] Yet, ethnic segregation in education continues to shape and maintain ethnic identities and links to neighbouring 'motherlands' of Croatia and Serbia and, in doing so, to benefit ethnonationalist political elites who have no common vision for the future of the country as a whole. Education in post-war BiH has therefore been a battleground for securitisation of ethnic and national identities. Despite ongoing initiatives to desegregate some of the other schools in the Federation BiH, the legal foundation of BiH as a system is 'designed well . . . for those it serves',[11] as the country speeds its way towards further homogenisation of territories. As the activist who supported the students in Jajce illustratively concluded our discussion, 'you don't need a visa to travel from one canton to another, but if you, from one canton, fall ill in another canton, this will be almost as if you fell ill in Germany. Or maybe it is even simpler to be ill in Germany!'[12]

This chapter discusses how education makes or breaks meaningful assurances of conflict non-recurrence in BiH. In this chapter, I analytically approach the current ethnically segregated formal

9 Interview with Nansen Dialogue Centre.
10 Nezavisne novine, 'Protest učenika u Jajcu'.
11 Interview with Nansen Dialogue Centre.
12 ibid.

education in BiH, demonstrating how and why it is used in ontological security-seeking exercises of different political communities in attempts to ensure the continuity of certain autobiographical narratives and secure the foundations of ethnic identities. In that sense, history teaching in BiH plays a key role in the maintenance of a post-conflict status quo which has, for many people, frozen the anxieties around the uncertain future peace in the country. My claim is that the global project of transitional justice, while not responsible for burgeoning ethnonationalism, has actively made a bad situation worse with its short-sighted security priorities and general misunderstanding of security as a lived experience. This worsening of ethnonationalism was supported by the fact that BiH never established a state-wide fact-finding inquiry, as established in Chapter 4, which enables multiple simultaneous manipulations of history teaching as political projects, as well as by creating a system of public education that operates on the basis on ethnicity and as such further aids the development of maintenance of ethnonationalist collective identities. Furthermore, I show how transitional justice institutions, most notably the International Criminal Tribunal for the former Yugoslavia (ICTY), have gradually undertaken roles of educators about the war out of concerns for their legitimacy and, ultimately, survival in the former Yugoslav region, creating a relationship of dependency of the local population on the Tribunal as a provider of objective and to some extent, exhaustive, truths about which the public need to be educated. As educators, these institutions have approached education about the war in ways that do not resonate with the prevention needs of the BiH society around plurality of collective memory and fluidity of collective identities, therefore leaving the conflict anxieties stemming from the education systems in the country largely unaddressed or even exacerbated.

This chapter proceeds in the following way. Section 5.2 discusses the policies of segregation in education and provides illustrations of how and why such education harms any meaningful assurances of conflict non-recurrence. Section 5.3 provides insights into how and why the ICTY undertook a role as an educator about the war and how such education of the BiH population was simultaneously framed as a civilising mission, furthering its relevance as a source of objective truth that needs to be disseminated through education. In Section 5.4, I use the example of the Transitional Justice Draft Strategy to demonstrate how some organic ideas about education and memorialisation for non-recurrence in BiH are recognised by international transitional justice entrepreneurs but only in relation to the ICTY and domestic courts. Finally, in the concluding section I argue that studying the sphere of education about the war in BiH shows how, due to its survival needs, the global project of transitional justice approaches prevention of further conflict in sterile, myopic, and simplified ways which are directly exclusive of the BiH's society needs relating to education for non-recurrence.

5.2 A System Meant to Divide

That education is important for prevention of conflict and its repetition should not come as a surprise to transitional justice enthusiasts. Education is increasingly praised in transitional justice literature for its perceived contributions to lasting peace.[13] In this body of literature, education is conceptualised as much broader than schooling or formal education and can underpin 'all transitional justice activities in formal, informal and non-formal ways', including, for instance, museums and memorials as educational spaces or organisations' outreach activities that aim to spread awareness about different components of transitional justice.[14] Scholars posit that education is useful in achieving the goals of transitional justice because it can facilitate dialogue, enhance remembering,[15] but also promote skills such as critical thinking and civic participation, thereby contributing to the establishment of 'thick democracy' that helps sustain peace.[16] At the same time, because history education in particular has been key in national building, citizen formations, and the forging of national identities, in post-crises periods such as transitions, it can serve its nationalist purposes in ways that foster antagonistic relations.[17]

Unsurprisingly then, many transitional justice practitioners in BiH highlighted educational reform and integration of truth narratives

[13] Michelle J Bellino, Julia Paulson, and Elizabeth Anderson Worden, 'Working through Difficult Pasts: Toward Thick Democracy and Transitional Justice in Education' (2017) 53 Comparative Education 313; Clara Ramirez-Barat and Roger Duthie, *Education and Transitional Justice: Opportunities and Challenges for Peacebuilding* (International Center for Transitional Justice 2015); Elizabeth Cole, *Teaching the Violent Past: History Education and Reconciliation* (Rowman and Littlefield 2007).

[14] Bellino and others, 'Working through Difficult Pasts', p. 317.

[15] Matilda Keynes, 'History Education for Transitional Justice? Challenges, Limitations and Possibilities for Settler Colonial Australia' (2019) 13 International Journal of Transitional Justice 113.

[16] Bellino and others, 'Working through Difficult Pasts'.

[17] Keynes, 'History Education for Transitional Justice?'.

about the war into the educational system as most meaningful for a lasting 'Never Again'. Yet, why education is important and what exactly about it mitigates some of the anxieties around conflict repetition are not well-explored topics in transitional justice literature. I propose in this chapter that education can make or break assurances of conflict non-recurrence because of its role in shaping and securitising collective identities and the longevity of a biographical narrative about the state of BiH. Education is seen as a way of taking control over the uncertain future of BiH, for better or worse. When people in BiH speak of current educational systems being sources of worry about potential conflict repetition, they do so in ways that point to a lack of hope of a common Bosnian Herzegovinian identity and a shared history of the peoples who inhabit it. What is visible is anxiety about the uncertain future of BiH in which young generations without lived experiences of the war are raised in an environment which rests on folk histories, national myths, and discriminatory teachings of history and only further strengthens ethnic divisions. One academic asserted, 'probably like any post-conflict society, what is obvious is that the education system needs to promote and create new peace builders or peace fighters, not new haters. If the opposite is happening, and there is no doubt that it is, there is no reason to be surprised that Bosnia and Herzegovina is still at war'.[18] In the political system in particular, at least formally, there seems to be a lack of a route to be constitutionally Bosnian and Herzegovinian as one establishes their political rights through belonging to one of the 'constituent peoples'.[19] The educational system, even when not segregated, succumbs to these strict divisions without as much as an opportunity for knowledge exchange, negotiations of or dialogue about the biographical narratives of BiH, Serbia, and Croatia.

The strategy of ethnic segregation known as 'Two Schools Under One Roof' was originally imposed by the OSCE under the premise of

[18] Goran Šimić, 'To Believe or Not to Believe: Current History Textbooks in Bosnia and Herzegovina' in Gorana Ognjenović and Jasna Jozelić (eds.), *Nationhood and Politicization of History in School Textbooks* (Palgrave Macmillan 2020) p. 177.

[19] Although see the Sejdić and Finci decision of the European Court of Human Rights in which it was found that the applicants' (a Roma and a Jew) inability to stand for parliamentary elections was a violation of the European Convention on Human Rights. *Sejdić and Finci v Bosnia and Herzegovina* [GC] (2009) ECHR. 27996/06 34836/06 https://hudoc.echr.coe.int/fre#{%22itemid%22:[%22002-1220%22]} accessed 31 March 2023.

maintaining security in the immediate years after the conflict.[20] This segregation in education is an indirect product of the principle of 'constituent peoples' enshrined in the Dayton Peace Agreement. However, the Dayton Peace Agreement itself was not very explicit about how education should be organised and only mentioned 'education' in the context of fundamental individual rights.[21] The OSCE, as an organisation with a mandate 'to build a stable, secure and democratic state' of BiH given directly by the Dayton Peace Agreement,[22] therefore had significant discretion to shape transitional education. In a more recent report on the policy and an attempt to wash its hands of the responsibility for it, the OSCE states that the policy was established as a temporary measure to reverse 'vast displacement and ethnic homogenization . . . and encourage the return of refugees and displaced persons'.[23] In particular, it is claimed that the policy was designed to allow returnee children to be educated in 'an extremely sensitive post-war context'.[24] To the organisation's dismay, this temporary arrangement became permanent, 'despite the efforts of the international community to ensure its transition'.[25] The policy continues to be implemented in more than fifty schools in the FBiH, where students of different ethnicities are forced to use different entrances, follow different curricula, and play in different physical spaces separated by a fence or even barbed wire.

The policy is now identified by its implementors as 'a long-term threat to stability, security and economic prosperity' which does not help 'either the process of reconciliation or the preparation of young people to prosper in the twenty-first century'.[26] Among the obstacles to solving

[20] Organisation for Security and Cooperation in Europe, '"Two Schools Under One Roof". The Most Visible Example of Discrimination in Education in Bosnia and Herzegovina' www.osce.org/mission-to-bosnia-and-herzegovina/404990 accessed 29 March 2023.

[21] Article 1, Annex 6 of the General Framework Agreement for Peace in Bosnia and Herzegovina (Dayton Peace Agreement), Dayton, OH, initiated 21 November 1995, signed in Paris 14 December 1995, UN Doc. A/50/79C, S/1995/999.

[22] The Dayton Peace Agreement establishes the OSCE's Mission to BiH as one of the actors responsible for helping secure lasting peace, and the competencies have included building 'sustainable democratic institutions' and 'strengthening good governance and human rights principles'. See OSCE Mission to Bosnia and Herzegovina, *Mandate*, www.osce.org/mission-to-bosnia-and-herzegovina/mandate accessed 4 June 2021.

[23] Organisation for Security and Cooperation in Europe, '"Two Schools Under One Roof"'.

[24] ibid, p. 8.

[25] ibid.

[26] ibid, p. 4.

this problem, the OSCE report lists a lack of political will and respect for the rule of law, and language concerns, whereby de-segregation and education in an official BiH language which is not one's non-mother tongue (Croatian, Bosnian, and Serbian are all mutually intelligible languages) would lead to deterioration of ethnonational identities.[27] The way forward, according to the OSCE, is for BiH to take ownership of the divisive educational system and end the practice of segregation.[28] One of the proposed curricula reforms includes the adoption of the common core curriculum devised by the BiH Agency for Pre-Primary, Primary and Secondary Education, with support of the OSCE Mission in BiH and other international partners, which would emphasise competency-based learning for the 'twenty-first century'.[29] With its 'rote memorisation of facts' and insufficient fostering of critical thinking and multi-perspectivity, BiH education is somehow perceived as trapped in the past century. Even a reportage about school segregation on Radio Free Europe suggested that BiH's educational system was 'backward'.[30] Some of these sentiments have been internalised, as people talk about these problems in BiH education as something that could happen 'only in the Balkans!' For instance, one BiH worker at the OSCE said, 'education is most important . . . and anywhere educated people wouldn't do things that we are doing here in the Balkans. If people have a stance to think with their own heads, things would be different . . . [It is about] the way of thinking; students need to have critical skills and they are not allowed to speak [at universities]'.[31]

Despite the OSCE's wishes for quick solutions, the way forward cannot be any imposition of textbooks that skip the fact-finding and dialogue steps about the war with a ready-made source. In particular, the problem is not only that students memorise facts in separate spaces but also which sort of facts they memorise and to what ends.

How does the current educational system in BiH break meaningful assurances of conflict non-recurrence? Schools are political institutions at the best of times, and in BiH, it is not uncommon for school principals to

[27] ibid, p. 21.
[28] ibid, p. 15.
[29] ibid, p. 24.
[30] Ajla Obradovic and others, 'Love Triumphs Over Bosnia's Segregated Schools' (*Radio Free Europe*, 25 February 2020) www.rferl.org/a/love-triumphs-over-bosnia-s-segregated-schools/30453161.html accessed 31 March 2023.
[31] Interview with OSCE representative 2, 21 November 2019.

be appointed by the ruling political party.[32] In that sense, as Šimić asserts, public schools in BiH are 'state-sponsored' which means that their promotion of a specific perception of the past is obligatory, and students have no choice but to attend these classes and be exposed to certain interpretations of facts and values.[33] In other words, children, as future peace- or war-makers are deemed to almost by default be exposed to nationalism in their schooling.[34] Schools across BiH teach at least three different histories, as there is no common curriculum across different cantons or entities and, as established in Chapter 4, there is no general consensus about the fundamental elements of the war. The fact that BiH never established a state-wide fact-finding commission or inquiry opens 'space for manipulation' about how history is taught.[35]

Due to the country's complex political structure explained in Chapter 3, there are currently twelve ministries of education (ten for each canton and two for each entity) as well as an education department in the Brčko District.[36] In both segregated and desegregated schools in Federation BiH, students are exposed to either Croatian or Bosniak versions of history. In schools designed for ethnic Croats in BiH, for instance, textbooks from the Republic of Croatia are used in the curricula, whereby BiH schools are treated as an extension of Croatian territory.[37] In public schools in Republika Srpska, pupils of all ethnicities are obliged to learn the 'Serbian' version of history. These relationships between the mainland and its perceived outposts in BiH are formal ones – in 2020, Republika Srpska and Serbia signed an Agreement on Cooperation in Education which established a synchronisation of curricula in the fields of history, geography, music, language, and literature.[38]

Therein, when it comes to learning about the wars of the 1990s, students are either exposed to different histories about the 1990s or they

[32] BN, 'I škole postale stranački plijen: Kako se biraju direktori?' (*BN*, 2 July 2021) www.rtvbn.com/4008627/i-skole-postale-stranacki-plijen-kako-se-biraju-direktori accessed 31 March 2023.

[33] Šimić, 'To Believe or Not to Believe', p. 156.

[34] Interview with Gordon Bacon, 3 October 2019.

[35] Šimić, 'To Believe or Not to Believe'.

[36] Rodoljub Jovanović and Dea Marić, 'Controversy in the Classroom: How History Teachers in the Western Balkans Approach Difficult Topics?' (2020) 52 Journal of Curriculum Studies 636.

[37] Šimić, 'To Believe or Not to Believe'.

[38] Erduan Katana, 'Dvije istorije u školi u Srebrenici' (*Radio Slobodna Evropa*, 13 October 2020) www.slobodnaevropa.org/a/bih-rs-srbija-nastavni-plan/30891299.html accessed 31 March 2023.

are not exposed to any history of this period at all, using books and materials from the former Yugoslavia. Research with history teachers across Western Balkans shows that teachers from BiH and Serbia in particular find talking about the 1990s to be the most challenging topic.[39] Current curricula do not leave much space for discussions about this period and generally provide teachers with little to no guidance about how to approach the topic. For these reasons, some teachers in BiH choose to end their history lessons in 1992, while others in Serbia skip the period between 1992 and 1995 and end their lessons in 1999 or 2000.[40]

When students do learn about the history of the 1990s in public schools, each of the three core history teachings promotes events and historical figures narrated to belong to Serbian, Croatian, or Bosniak histories in isolation from others. As is usual practice in history-making, common narratives of collective victimhood and/or heroism are promoted through these history textbooks and fed to three different audiences. History teaching is used to reinforce ethnic divisions and rebuild national identity and as such plays a key role in the maintenance of a certain post-conflict status quo.[41] As Jozelić claims, history education in BiH 'is predominantly constructed around instilling in young people a positive story about the national past, a loyalty to the state, a convincing and positive sense of identity and belonging and a social solidarity limited to their own group'.[42] Here we see competing attempts to secure the self through education as, '[b]y allowing such one-dimensional approaches and textbooks containing newly constructed histories, the state indirectly maintains an awareness of an ethnonational identity'.[43] As Šimić asserts, these history textbooks fail to develop awareness about different ethnic groups' 'common heritage' and instead promote a narrative in which each history has developed 'in a vacuum' and 'without a mutual relationship'.[44] Similarly to truth recovery processes discussed in Chapter 4, I observe how education has become a battleground for

[39] Jovanović and Marić, 'Controversy in the Classroom'.

[40] ibid.

[41] Jasna Jozelić, 'Teaching History with an Ethno-Nationalistic Approach: History Textbooks in the Education System of Bosnia and Herzegovina' in Gorana Ognjenović and Jasna Jozelić (eds.), *Nationhood and Politicization of History in School Textbooks* (Palgrave Macmillan 2020) p. 214.

[42] ibid, p. 215.

[43] ibid, p. 221.

[44] Šimić, 'To Believe or Not to Believe', p. 173.

identity formation, as demonstrated through identity's two core functions of sameness and difference which are activated through the narratives found in these history textbooks.[45] In Bosnian, Croatian, and Serbian history textbooks alike, the actors make sense of themselves, and what makes them the same or different in BiH, the Western Balkans, and the world in relation to the other actor or both actors. Formal education is used as a forum where these identity narratives are interpreted and, eventually secured in a way that the narrative identity, as Lerner suggests, constitutes the actors 'dynamically over time' giving them 'ideational continuity'.[46] In that sense, the educational system in BiH has not helped enforce pre-existing Bosniak, Bosnian Serb, and Bosnian Croat identities but aided the evolution of these *identities as difference* in young people for very political agendas. The 'difference' function has been used to sanitise one's past from what could be embarrassing, shameful, or difficult to face, and make sense of it in the present in a way that magnifies or even straightforwardly qualifies one's victimhood through negation of the victimhood of the other.

In an environment of multiple competing truth recovery and history-making projects, these victimhood-based identities are positioned as under continuous threat. That said, some common trends in history teaching about the war in BiH include categorisations of victims as 'our own' and war criminals as 'others', encouraging stereotypes of eternal victimhood, hegemony, and repression, and delegating blame and responsibility for the eruption of violence in war to 'the other side'.[47] Current history classes, asserted one practitioner, teach students about 'wrong' kinds of heroes who should, by all logic, be proclaimed war criminals.[48] By way of illustration, Bosnian Serb geography textbooks posit Republika Srpska as an independent state and Belgrade as the capital of all Serbs, while a Bosnian Croat geography textbook lists BiH as a centuries-old Croat state and positions Zagreb as the capital.[49]

[45] Adam B Lerner, *From the Ashes of History: Collective Trauma and the Making of International Politics* (Oxford University Press 2022).

[46] ibid, p. 74.

[47] Andrea Soldo and others, *Obrazovanje u BiH: Čemu (Ne) Učimo Djecu? Analiza sadržaja udžbenika nacionalne grupe predmeta u osnovnim školama* (Mas Media Sarajevo/Fond otvoreno društvo BiH 2017) www.promente.org/downloads/cemuucimodjecu.pdf accessed 31 March 2023.

[48] Interview with Saliha Đuderija, 17 December 2019.

[49] Anes Alic, 'Bosnia and Herzegovina: Teaching Intolerance' (*Open Society Foundations*, 2 June 2008) https://shorturl.at/dsPW0 accessed 31 March 2023.

Bosnian geography textbooks taught to Bosniak students position BiH as always under attack from the East and West and all Serbs as complicit in aggression and genocide on BiH.[50] Differences in the teachings of history reflect some of the ongoing public debates over different elements of the war, such as, for instance, the character of the war, which continues to be debated by different factions of the society and with that, the responsibility for the war and its atrocities. One academic said, 'it is a paradox that these children in Republika Srpska, and Serbia too, have such curricula, such an approach that what happened here was some sort of civil war, that neighbours got into a fight over some land'.[51]

Missing from these textbooks is a history education about BiH for Bosnian-Herzegovinians, and a history of coexistence, as most Bosnian Croat and Bosnian Serb students end up learning about Croatian and Serbian histories, acquiring Croatian and Serbian collective identities and feeling attachment to the two national flags, despite having lived their entire lives in BiH. As one professor of history stated in an interview for Radio Sarajevo, the history books in Republika Srpska 'do not allow children to know, understand and love the state of BiH and to build togetherness and the future with other peoples'.[52] Through these distorted interpretations and no alternative found in history education, young people are susceptible to new divisions, it is believed. One interviewee said,

> Unfortunately, today we see that children are being fed some sort of animosity towards people of different religions, divisions, and hatred … You saw the case when children who weren't even in anyone's thoughts in the 1990s let alone born then today favour certain criminals and chant different offensive songs, while not even knowing what these songs mean. Those children are 10, 12 years old. They dress and put on themselves different insignia that could not have come from children's minds. … In this way we are creating generations who will be a lot more extreme than those in the past who brought us to what happened.[53]

Other practitioners also identified the contents of history education in BiH as particularly divisive, dangerous, and actively contributing to the

[50] ibid.

[51] Interview with representative 1 of the Institute for research on crimes against humanity and international law, 7 November 2019.

[52] L.K., 'O udžbeniku istorije u RS-u: "Djeci ne daju da znaju, shvate i vole državu BiH"' (*Radio Sarajevo*, 18 September 2022) https://radiosarajevo.ba/metromahala/teme/historija/313288 accessed 31 March 2023.

[53] Interview with Selma Džihanović, 10 February 2020.

creation of new *mrzitelja*, new 'haters',[54] more extreme and radical than those who took part in the conflict in the 1990s.[55] One academic held

> nobody actively prepared me for war (in school). Nobody told me who were my enemies. Maybe this happened to some people but in the school I went to, for me the war came out of nowhere. . . . At this moment, we are actively preparing the children in our educational system for new conflicts, telling them who their enemies are and how to behave in this conflict.[56]

These animosities people talk about are sometimes visible inside as well as outside schools and affect children through formal as well as informal and non-formal schooling. One practitioner shared a personal story of what happened to their child in their hometown of Brčko, otherwise known for its special administrative status and ethnic diversity.

> We were standing at the square one day . . . my youngest son [three years old] was a very chatty and sociable child, joyful. Some kids were playing ball and he approached them. Those kids were older than him, maybe 10-12 years old, both boys and girls. They were playing with him, playing for a long time, especially the girls, they liked him. Then one kid asked him 'what's your name?' He said [Muslim name]. Suddenly, the group of boys and girls around him dispersed in a second and you could hear them whisper. Nobody around him, the child was left alone. Look, these were ten-year-old children we are talking about . . . who are [brainwashed] from birth, I think. All three [ethnicities] do that. Ten-year-old children whispering [about my son] 'he's one of them, don't play with him.'[57]

In this section, I have provided a brief overview of how formal education has been used to shape and securitise ethnic identities in post-war BiH and explained why such an educational system makes people doubt whether there are meaningful assurances of conflict non-recurrence in the country. These divisive and harmful processes in the education system have partly been facilitated by the international community intervening in BiH with the conclusion of the peace agreement. In the next two sections, I elaborate on more informal and non-formal forms of education about the war attempted and undertaken in the past two decades and discuss them in relation to the global project of transitional justice to claim that transitional justice institutions, and particularly the

[54] Interview with Goran Šimić, 12 December 2019.
[55] Interview with Selma Džihanović.
[56] Interview with Goran Šimić.
[57] Interview with Anonymous 2, 13 December 2019.

ICTY, have engaged in a widening of their roles to undertake educational capabilities in a struggle to maintain their own legitimacy and therefore survival in this specific context. In doing so, the new educators have limited and simplified education about the war in ways that directly contradict the prevention needs of the BiH society.

5.3 A Court as an Educator, Nay, Civilizer

In the absence of common core curricula and shared sources of history education in BiH, the ICTY played a key role as an educator through its Outreach office. Quantitatively speaking, the most widespread form of non-formal education about the war came from the ICTY's Outreach office. Rather than observing the ICTY's Outreach office as a benevolent way to produce common narratives of the war and disseminate them to BiH youth, in this section I am interested in why the ICTY would undertake such a role and the productive power behind it.

Soon after kickstarting its first trials, the Tribunal came to a realisation that the effects of its work were impeded by multiple manipulative and distorted narratives about it in the media and public speech. Amid growing criticism, the Tribunal was simultaneously concerned with its public image in the former Yugoslavia and the world public opinion of its legitimacy and effectiveness. In response, it took upon itself its seemingly righteous task to both write history and educate about it. In the 1998 Annual Report, it was stated, 'it is not enough simply to create a record. Its power lies in its dissemination, most crucially within the former Yugoslavia'.[58] For these reasons, the Tribunal felt it was necessary to establish even stronger contacts with the local population, to which information about the historical record in progress must be disseminated. Its response to this fear of losing legitimacy was to create an outreach office in 1998, the first of its kind.

In Tribunal's own words, the Outreach programme was created with the purpose of promoting the Tribunal's role 'as an agency of reconciliation' in the region.[59] It was through the efforts of the

[58] International Criminal Tribunal for the former Yugoslavia, 'Fifth Annual Report of the International Tribunal for the Prosecution of Persons Responsible for Serious Violations of International Humanitarian Law Committed in the Territory of the Former Yugoslavia since 1991' (10 August 1998) UN Doc. A/53/219, S/1998/737, para 296.

[59] International Criminal Tribunal for the former Yugoslavia, 'Ninth Annual Report of the International Tribunal for the Prosecution of Persons Responsible for Serious Violations

Outreach programme that both 'the legal and social impact of the Tribunal's work' would be strengthened.[60] Essentially, the Outreach office has functioned as a public relations agency that, as public relations agencies usually do, manages the reputation and moulds the legacy of the Tribunal.[61] The Outreach office's activities included translating the ICTY's official documents into the language of the former Yugoslavia and organising live audio and broadcasts of all public court sessions. Once the domestic courts began to adjudicate war crimes cases, the Outreach office was tasked with transferring the Tribunal's 'know-how' to the region.[62]

The Outreach office's other job was to convince local populations of the ICTY's social values which make it not only authoritative but also superior vis-à-vis other potential pools of authority in the transitional justice sphere, a problem discussed at length in Chapter 4. In 2003 and 2004, the Outreach office, by the virtue of its mandate, started organising conferences, workshops, symposiums, and community events across the former Yugoslavia, with a range of involved stakeholders, including victims' associations, non-governmental organisations, and legal professionals. These early events tended to provide insights into the operations and decision-making of the Tribunal at the stages of investigation, indictment, and prosecution, all with the aim of, in the ICTY's own words, enabling the local populations to better understand how the Tribunal serves justice, prevents revisionism, and fosters reconciliation.[63] In addition to organising outreach events, representatives of the Outreach office also appeared as speakers and participants in a range of other conferences and events organised by the likes of the OSCE, the

of International Humanitarian Law Committed in the Territory of the Former Yugoslavia since 1991' (4 September 2002) UN Doc. A/57/379, S/2002/985, para 265.

60 International Criminal Tribunal for the former Yugoslavia, 'Tenth Annual Report of the International Tribunal for the Prosecution of Persons Responsible for Serious Violations of International Humanitarian Law Committed in the Territory of the Former Yugoslavia since 1991' (20 August 2003) UN Doc. A/58/297, S/2003/829, para 286.

61 Christine Schwobel-Patel, *Marketing Global Justice: The Political Economy of International Criminal Law* (Cambridge University Press 2021).

62 International Residual Mechanism for Criminal Tribunals, *Read More on the Outreach Programme,* www.icty.org/en/content/read-more-outreach-programme accessed 6 December 2021.

63 International Criminal Tribunal for the former Yugoslavia, 'Eleventh Annual Report of the International Tribunal for the Prosecution of Persons Responsible for Serious Violations of International Humanitarian Law Committed in the Territory of the Former Yugoslavia since 1991' (16 August 2004) UN Doc. A/59/215, S/2004/627, para 320.

European Commission, and local NGOs. While some of these conferences concerned the judicial process and the legal values of the ICTY, others required the representatives of the Tribunal to weigh in on a range of values of transitional justice, primarily truth and reconciliation. Such events, among others, included the 'Establishing the Truth in the Aftermath of Conflict: Current Initiatives and Perspectives in the West Balkans' conference organised by three regional NGOs in May 2006; the 'The Truth about the Srebrenica Massacre'[64] conference organised in July 2006 by local victim groups in BiH; the International Conference on Establishing Truth after Armed Conflicts, organised by three regional NGOs in February 2007 in Zagreb, Croatia; the 'Mechanisms of Establishing the Truth' conference organised by a victims' association called Izvor in March 2007. Perhaps the most bizarre of the appearances was the Outreach representative's participation in the panel discussion organised at the popular Exit music festival in Serbia (then the Federal Republic of Yugoslavia) in 2002. The panel discussion was entitled 'What is the truth?' and was broadcast live on a local TV channel.[65]

Soon after the establishment and spread of these various outreach activities, the Tribunal could proudly report the improvements in its public image, measured by way of increased media enquiries and the enhanced support the Outreach programme offered to the regional media in their reporting of the activities of the Tribunal.[66] Some years later, the ICTY assessed its communication efforts with outside audiences and its public images by counting the page views of its website, established in 2008.[67] In addition to the website, the Outreach programme also engaged in documentary-making to, among others, mark the

[64] This was the official name of the conference at that time and should not be understood as minimisation of this crime legally qualified as genocide.

[65] International Criminal Tribunal for the former Yugoslavia, *2002*, www.icty.org/en/outreach/activities-archive/2002 accessed 31 March 2023.

[66] International Criminal Tribunal for the former Yugoslavia, 'Eleventh Annual Report'.

[67] In 2011, the ICTY reported that the website had 400,000 page views in May alone, setting the record for monthly views. See International Criminal Tribunal for the former Yugoslavia, 'Eighteenth Annual Report of the International Tribunal for the Prosecution of Persons Responsible for Serious Violations of International Humanitarian Law Committed in the Territory of the Former Yugoslavia since 1991' (31 July 2011) UN Doc. A/66/210, S/2011/473, para 83. In 2016, it was reported that the Tribunal's website reached more than 2.2 million page views. See International Criminal Tribunal for the former Yugoslavia, 'Twenty-Third Annual Report of the International Tribunal for the Prosecution of Persons Responsible for Serious Violations of International Humanitarian Law Committed in the Territory of the Former Yugoslavia since 1991' (1 August 2016) UN Doc. A/71/263, S/2016/670, para 73.

twentieth anniversary of the Srebrenica genocide. While the documentaries are focused on illuminating the public on the ICTY's key cases and contributions to international criminal law, they are claimed to also carry 'educational value' and therefore have been used in educational contexts around the world.[68] These documentaries were broadcast on numerous television stations in BiH and elsewhere and continue to be publicly accessible on the ICTY's website. The Outreach office therefore actively and consciously worked on constructing the image of the ICTY and its attached values to the former Yugoslav societies. In 2005, the annual report of the ICTY claimed that the Tribunal was being 'active in the reconciliation process by making the activities of the Tribunal accessible, transparent and relevant to the regions in the former Yugoslavia'.[69]

The peak of the Tribunal's outreach activities was reached when the Outreach office expanded its reach beyond educating 'the public' to in fact enter the public education arenas in BiH, Serbia, and Croatia. The 'Youth Outreach' programme started in 2011 and was most intensive between 2012 and 2015, with a decline of activities towards the closure of the ICTY until today. At least 10,000 students from all parts of BiH participated in presentations and discussions about the tribunal and its work.[70] The Youth Outreach workshops took place in schools and included materials such as facts and figures about the conflict stemming from the ICTY judgements, concrete ongoing and future cases, as well as any specifics of legal procedures at the ICTY. In the publicly available promotional materials of the Youth Outreach programme, interviewed students report better awareness of their past and hopes that educational programmes like these bring hope for a peaceful future.[71] It is further stated that 'through this project, the Outreach team set out to harness their [students'] ability to step away from the past and to view it more *objectively*'.[72]

[68] International Criminal Tribunal for the former Yugoslavia, *Documentaries*, www.icty.org/en/outreach/documentaries accessed 31 March 2023.

[69] International Criminal Tribunal for the former Yugoslavia, 'Twelfth Annual Report of the International Tribunal for the Prosecution of Persons Responsible for Serious Violations of International Humanitarian Law Committed in the Territory of the Former Yugoslavia since 1991' (17 August 2005) UN Doc. A/60/267, S/2005/532, para 4.

[70] United Nations, International Criminal Tribunal for the former Yugoslavia. *Outreach. 15 godina Outreach-a na MKSJ-u* (ICTY Outreach 2016); Interview with independent transitional justice expert, 5 December 2019.

[71] International Criminal Tribunal for the former Yugoslavia, *Youth Outreach*, www.icty.org/en/outreach/youth-outreach accessed 31 March 2023.

[72] ibid (my emphasis).

In a conversation with an independent expert previously involved in Youth Outreach programmes, it became obvious that the 'objective' presentation of facts involved difficult conversations about very personal matters.

> It is a fact that young people live in a deeply segregated society, that they simply don't have any contact with the youth from other communities ... Young people live all practical consequences of the events of the 1990s, to the point where at one Youth Outreach workshop we showed a photograph of a murder committed by Goran Jelisić in Brčko, where you can see dead civilians ... When the students were asked 'do you know where this is?' in the sense that these murders often took place in the town centre, close to the police station, to see if anyone would recognize these buildings, one girl said 'I recognize this place, that's my uncle [in the picture] who was killed.' In a school in Višegrad when we spoke about rape, one girl kept asking the question about false witnesses and people falsely testifying before the court. I tried to explain the mechanisms of disrespecting the court and that this is not in the interest of justice and of the Office of the Prosecutor, that they wish to have credible witnesses during the process ... Then I saw that we were wasting time discussing some topic where she was not receiving a satisfactory answer. At the end of the workshop, we stayed chatting for a short while and I asked her why she was so interested in false testimonies. She said 'my father was indicted for rape before the Court of BiH.' For her, it was unbelievable that her father, before her birth or ever could commit rape or participate in these events in any way. Therefore, young people are directly or indirectly affected by all these events, and you can see this every day.[73]

When it comes to the Youth Outreach programme, the Outreach office's evaluations show that 70 per cent of those students reported having learned something about the ICTY after only one workshop while 90 per cent of them left believing that those indicted for war crimes should face a trial no matter their social or ethnic status.[74] Eventually, the Youth Outreach programme also included teachers across the country. By way of example, in 2017 history teachers were invited to a three-day workshop called 'Learning history that is not yet history', where the Youth Outreach programme was presented and promoted.[75]

The ICTY has served as an educator in many other spaces around BiH. For instance, the Memorial Centre Srebrenica heavily relies on the ICTY judgements to educate about the truth about the genocide in Srebrenica,

[73] Interview with independent transitional justice expert.

[74] International Criminal Tribunal for the former Yugoslavia, *Outreach*.

[75] International Criminal Tribunal for the former Yugoslavia, *Youth Outreach*.

teaching for 'Never Again'. The Memorial Centre channels its educational aspirations towards thousands of pupils from middle schools and high schools in Federation BiH, who visit the Centre on organised school visits to learn about the genocide. In addition to being a space for informal education for pupils, the Centre is also visited by thousands of tourists and activists around the world. The space hosts numerous posters with photographs of perpetrators and the sentences issued by the ICTY and video projections of testimonies. When I visited the Memorial Centre in November 2019, I watched a short introductory film together with other visitors. The chronology of the events in Srebrenica in the film was reconstructed based on the ICTY findings. The ICTY was seen as inherently objective.

Contrary to the frequent treatment of the ICTY and domestic courts' judgements as universal and complete truths, these documents are inclusive of a specific, selective, and above-all constructed – and not 'found' – narrative of the past, a narrative that can be complemented or directly challenged by other existing and yet to be constructed narratives.[76] As evident in the case of the ICTY, the Tribunal consciously developed an education-oriented role in order to save its own legitimacy and therefore cannot possibly be treated as an objective, neutral actor with an all-encompassing history of the conflict in the making. As Barrie Sander argues, the historical record produced through these judgements is a result of contestation, a deliberation on who and what is selected (and who and what is not) and how they are judged; it is 'always the product of the situated choices' of the actors involved in the international criminal law processes.[77] As a result, Sander finds that international criminal tribunals tend to create hegemonic histories by constructing three particular types of historical narratives: apologetic, that are influenced by the international and domestic balance of power of states; spectacular, that highlight more immediate forms of physical violence as opposed to other types of violations; and narrowly contextualised historical narratives that omit reference to broader international and particularly economic networks and actors.[78]

[76] Sander, for instance, distinguishes between situational and case selectivity international criminal tribunals resort to, with the former concerning the mass atrocity situations that are prioritised over others and the latter concerning the individuals targeted for prosecutions within these situations. Barrie Sander, *Doing Justice to History: Confronting the Past in International Criminal Courts* (Oxford University Press 2021).

[77] ibid, p. 6.

[78] ibid.

Nevertheless, both the history-making and educational capabilities of the ICTY and, to a lesser extent, domestic courts were quickly claimed as the most authoritative by different international actors involved in the transitional justice processes in BiH. There are two key implications of this development. First, in promoting its own educational and history-making capabilities, the ICTY has utilised the old trope of civilisationalism, positioning local histories in BiH as faulty, failing to fully acknowledge the links between history and identity, whereby 'uncivilised' histories are interpreted as 'uncivilised' peoples by different political communities. Already in 1994, while the war in BiH was still ongoing, the ICTY was presented as a 'civilised' approach to justice, and an 'alternative to . . . desire for revenge' that was somehow seen as characteristic of 'the region'.[79] It was stated that '[t]he history of the region clearly shows that clinging to feelings of "collective responsibility" easily degenerates into resentment, hatred and frustration and inevitably leads to further violence and new crimes'.[80] From the start, the Tribunal adopted a rather imperial rhetoric and outlook towards the region, positioning itself as a necessary condition for peace without which the region would succumb to seemingly 'ancient' and inescapable interethnic hatred. Through its Outreach program, the Tribunal built an image of itself as a source and educator of history, maybe not a complete history, but a historical record that was promoted as a condition for other core values such as prevention of further conflict. This branding move has promoted a relationship of dependency of the local populations on the ICTY and the domestic courts whereby people in BiH were persistently told that their past histories were essentially wrong as they led to violence and that for this reason, these people needed the Tribunal as a neutral and perhaps only legitimate arbiter of 'civilised' history. To illustrate, in its final annual report of 2017, the Tribunal asserted that '[n]ational and communal identities founded on false histories are inherently sources of regional tension and distrust'.[81] For this reason, the Tribunal took the

[79] International Criminal Tribunal for the former Yugoslavia, 'Annual Report of the International Tribunal for the Prosecution of Persons Responsible for Serious Violations of International Humanitarian Law Committed in the Territory of the Former Yugoslavia since 1991' (29 August 1994) UN Doc. A/49/342 S/1994/1007, paras 15–16.

[80] ibid, para 16.

[81] International Criminal Tribunal for the former Yugoslavia, 'Twenty-Fourth and Final Annual Report of the International Tribunal for the Prosecution of Persons Responsible for Serious Violations of International Humanitarian Law Committed in the Territory of

task of facilitating a 'shared agreement on the recent past' without which, it was said, a peaceful future could not be secured.[82] As discussed in Chapter 4, this results in further resistance to the ICTY and other transitional justice efforts imposed or proposed by the international community. Importantly, the ICTY Outreach office has dealt with the education about 'the correct' history in impersonal, technical ways that aim to draw broader lessons for peace and reconciliation based on the legal procedure. Missing from these efforts was a consideration of how this history teaching can complement or be reconciled with, even if only in part, with the histories taught in formal education as well as lived experiences, in ways that would not propose that the only way forward to sustainable peace is through rejection of 'national and communal identities' and instead raise awareness of identities as fluid and capable of transforming.

Second, the organically proposed transitional justice developments that seek to ameliorate some of the harms of segregated, ethnonationalist education in BiH can be limited in scope and application through the international transitional justice actors' linking of these practices to the legacies of the ICTY. I elaborate on the second point in more detail in Section 5.4.

5.4 'As Established'

As an area of intervention, education, together with memorialisation, was largely bypassed in the grand scheme of the transitional justice project. Yet, that they are perceived as important in the prevention of further conflict had been detected in the relatively early stages of transitional justice policymaking in BiH. Observe, for instance, *the Draft Transitional Justice Strategy 2012–2016* for BiH which was initiated by the UNDP and BiH Council of Ministers and devised by local experts in cooperation between the BiH Ministry of Justice and the Ministry of Human Rights and Refugees. The strategy was set out to create 'an acceptable platform for effective and realistic mechanisms and activities which would correct the injustices and heal the traumas created by the armed conflicts 1992–1995, return public trust in institutions and prevent repetition of

the Former Yugoslavia since 1991' (1 August 2017) UN Doc. A/72/266, S/2017/662, para 51.

[82] ibid.

human rights violations and war crimes'.[83] The work done towards compiling a draft transitional justice strategy included establishing an expert working group with representatives from different governmental and entity-level agencies and civil society organisations, and numerous consultations with the public across the country, particularly victims' and veterans' associations.

The strategy was evidently influenced by the transitional justice blueprint. It outlined the four basic pillars of transitional justice as criminal justice, truth recovery, and fact-finding; reparations and memorials; and institutional reforms. Furthermore, numerous foreign consultants with previous experiences working on transitional justice in other contexts were asked to advise the working group. The expert group also went on an organised trip to Germany to learn about German experiences of transition post-1989. One of the interviewed members of the working group stated:

> People from the International Center for Transitional Justice were there too, people from all over. However, I cannot say that they were particularly helpful because in fact their understanding of the problems in BiH was insufficient for them to be able to offer high-quality solutions. It was based on working in some other countries because when you come from Chile and say 'you know, I think you need a forum here, not a fact-finding commission' ... But the BiH context simply isn't like that.[84]

Unsurprisingly then, the strategy also suggested new context-specific interpretations of and needs for non-recurrence that arose out of a broad consensus about transitional justice priorities among the experts and in consultation with hundreds of members of the public. A crucial element of the overall rationale for building a comprehensive transitional justice strategy was to step away from a model of transitional justice predominantly oriented towards criminal justice and its institutions. In shaping the aims of the transitional justice strategy, the working group identified that while criminal trials are believed to be the single most influential mechanism on individuals and societies in transition, the problems of transitional justice go beyond prosecutions and call for non-judicial activities. The strategy argued that both judicial and non-judicial mechanisms in an 'integrated, complementary and holistic performance' can achieve the

83 Ministarstvo ljudskih prava i izbjeglica i Ministarstvo pravde Bosne i Herzegovina, 'Strategija tranzicijske pravde u Bosni i Hercegovini 2012–2016 – radna verzija' https://shorturl.at/bwxz4 p. 6.

84 Interview with Šimić.

necessary capacity for ensuring a successful process of dealing with the legacies of the past by the state and society and can lead to justice.[85]

More specifically, one of the key strategic goals of the transitional justice strategy was to build and preserve collective memories by building memorials and nurturing a dialogue about the past with the goal of preventing repetition of atrocities.[86] In particular, the strategy recommended establishing 'sites of conscience' in BiH, which would develop pedagogical and dialogical functions of memorials with the goal of preventing repetition of 'traumatic past' and building and protecting democratic values, a culture of remembrance and human rights.[87] The sites of conscience would be borne out of a process of consultation with the public and in line with relevant legal frameworks. Sites of conscience are therefore not only touristic sites but also venues of dialogue about the legacies of the past war as well as all ongoing social processes that are influenced, shaped, or triggered by these legacies. The sites of conscience, the strategy suggested, would be sites where a 'world heritage' is created and kept alive with the goal of non-recurrence of atrocities in BiH and beyond. The proposal for sites of conscience reflects a hope that more transethnic spaces can be nurtured in BiH, a hope sparked by student protests in Jajce.

To help fulfil this objective, the strategy also recommended that standards and criteria for building memorials and conducting commemorative activities are established and that a dialogue about the past is nurtured through adequate memorialisation practices, all with the purpose of building a culture of remembrance. These recommended actions were all buttressed by research into public opinion and numerous consultations with the public. For instance, the working group conducted surveys that showed that over 75 per cent of surveyed citizens of BiH thought that there should be an FBiH-wide legislation regulating memorialisation, and a vast majority (with varying degrees across ethnic groups) believed that it was necessary to start a nationwide dialogue about the past.[88] This dialogue would, among other things, include informing and educating people about the need to build sites of conscience in BiH, a process led by the government as well as civil society

[85] Ministarstvo ljudskih prava i izbjeglica i Ministarstvo pravde Bosne i Herzegovina, 'Strategija tranzicijske pravde'.
[86] ibid.
[87] ibid.
[88] ibid.

organisations who should benefit from a transparent allocation of government funding to keep the dialogue alive. In addition to enhancing dialogue and regulating memorialisation, the strategy also suggested that the government authorities should consider building a special memorial commemorating all victims of the war (regardless of their ethnicity) in the capital city as well as in local communities where memorials have tended to honour the victims of majority ethnicity in that municipality and completely neglect the minorities. This, the working group asserted, would help recognise the pain and suffering of victims' family members and contribute to overcoming divisions in BiH society.

The strategy's interpretation of the practices and processes that are necessary for non-recurrence were buttressed by international legal frameworks in the sense that the drafters referred to different UN agencies and guidelines to stress the importance of a specific issue; for example, where the UN Working Group on Enforced Disappearances also called for legislation regulating memorialisation in BiH. Yet, in shaping their ideas and plan of action, the drafters were primarily led by lived experiences and political realities and imaginings in their country at that specific moment in time. For the interviewed drafters, the strategy therefore felt personal but universal, a framework for practice that can be used as an inspiration for societies transitioning from conflict across the world.[89]

In the eyes of those who participated in the drafting process, compiling the draft strategy was a genuinely complex, tense, and long-term process. Despite the working group producing a coherent document with concrete objectives and a plan of action, the strategy was never formally adopted by the BiH Parliament or the Council of Ministers. All respondents who worked on the strategy identified that despite the differences, the working group was initially working well until representatives of the Republika Srpska entity retreated towards the very end of the process. A couple of interviewees suggested that the key problem was that the main funder, the UNDP, was in charge of negotiating the implementation of the strategy with political stakeholders and eventually lost interest in the strategy too quickly after it took longer than expected to achieve desirable results. 'There was no pressure from the international community because they exclusively defined this as a "project" and I still don't know why that was', the chair of the expert working group stated in our

[89] Interview with Šimić.

interview.[90] The funders then abandoned the entire project altogether at a time when domestic institutions needed an extra 'push' from the international community to proceed with the initiative. The overwhelming impression is that the funders treated the strategy as just another project that can be dropped if not performing satisfactorily and not as perhaps one of the most important processes in the post-conflict lives of people of BiH. The chair of the expert group further asserted,

> One of the key reasons, in my view, that our transitional justice strategy did not succeed was due to our request for changes in the educational sector and that all children of BiH hear all three or four 'truths' and decide for themselves . . . We did not need to bring something that perhaps is so nationally sensitive, but we could have at least start talking about what is war and different types of crimes without putting a 'label' on anyone.[91]

Even though the strategy was eventually dropped as a project, it still comes up in conversations about transitional justice both in BiH and abroad. For example, the European Commission reports about BiH tend to urge the country to establish a comprehensive country-wide transitional justice policy.[92] Some of the ideas about prevention of further conflict found in the Strategy have been revived in international transitional justice policy circles. In a recent, very detailed report on BiH, the UN Special Rapporteur on the promotion of truth, justice, reparation, and guarantees of non-repetition recognised 'education, culture and the media' as 'guarantees of non-recurrence' in a section where he observed the dangers of schoolchildren being taught different narratives about the conflict.[93] Memorialisation, too, was discussed as a new, separate pillar of transitional justice, as BiH was scolded for the scarcity of efforts to commemorate 'all violations committed during the conflict and commemorating all victims', something that the transitional justice strategy working group had discussed at length.[94]

Yet, in the recommendations to state actors about how to act on these identified guarantees of non-recurrence needs, a pull back to the core components of the transitional justice structure is noted. Namely for both

[90] Interview with Đuderija.
[91] ibid.
[92] European Commission, 'Bosnia and Herzegovina 2022 Report' (12 October 2022) SWD (2022) 336.
[93] Human Rights Council, 'Visit to Bosnia and Herzegovina Report of the Special Rapporteur on the Promotion of Truth, Justice, Reparation and Guarantees of Non-recurrence*' (8 July 2022) A/HRC/51/34/Add.2.
[94] ibid, para 67.

memorialisation and education, it is recommended that the state adopt 'comprehensive legislation and policies on memorialization processes, which entail plural and accurate accounts of past violations' and 'policies in the fields of education, culture and the media to provide society with plural and accurate accounts of past violations' '*as established by international and national courts*'.[95] Public officials, such as teachers, the judiciary, and security personnel, are to be trained on human rights and historical memory, which includes 'an examination of comprehensive and accurate accounts of the violations committed and the responsibilities of State and entity- or district-level institutions, *as established by domestic and international courts*'.[96]

These practices by international transitional justice entrepreneurs are referent to the work of the ICTY and domestic courts adjudicating atrocity crimes, as sources from which the standard of truth to be memorialised and educated is derived. The practice of linking should be seen as one of maintaining the structure and transitional justice as a global project. Through these examples, we see confirmation of the idea that ICTY and domestic courts can write and teach history, an idea that, as explained in Section 5.3, has served a specific purpose of boosting the legitimacy of the ICTY and local populations' dependency on it. It is not by any means an international legal standard that 'accurate accounts', or truth recovery for that matter, cannot go beyond (and not against) what is established by judicial institutions. This linking practice confirms and maintains the structure of transitional justice itself. As Giddens asserts, 'the most important aspects of structure are rules and resources recursively involved in institutions'.[97] Furthermore, institutions and all the norms and ideas enshrined in them are among the more enduring elements of social life and they give structures form through time and space.[98] For transitional justice, this means that as a global project, it can only exist securely not only through the legal frameworks and norms that underpin it but also through and as long as the institutions which enforce those norms exist. In particular, in today's BiH, where almost thirty years have passed since the end of the war, the global project of transitional justice might struggle for relevance. The ICTY officially completed its

[95] ibid, paras 12 and 113 (my emphasis).
[96] ibid, para 120.
[97] Anthony Giddens, *The Constitution of Society: Outline of the Theory of Structuration* (Polity Press 1984) p. 24.
[98] ibid.

mandate in 2017, and its successor, the International Residual Mechanism for Criminal Tribunals, was dealing with its final cases at the time of writing this book. Domestic courts adjudicating international crimes are working at an increasingly slower rate, as witnesses and defendants age, die, and overall grow reluctant to participate in the legal process. As legal institutions, courts give the structure of transitional justice legitimation, in the context of BiH as well as globally. Therefore, that international transitional justice entrepreneurs such as the UN Special Rapporteur find it important to protect the reputation and contributions of the ICTY and domestic courts should, among others, be read as an attempt to keep the global project of transitional justice itself relevant and legitimate.

What this practice of structure maintenance does for concrete non-recurrence needs in BiH is that it tries to avoid the messiness of truth recovery, education, and memorialisation in post-conflict societies and solve the issue of clashing ethnonationalist histories with an 'objective', externally sourced history. There are thousands of stories that criminal justice institutions cannot capture that, if heard, could significantly shape our understandings and practices of both memory and education. Linking education and memory to established judicial facts is by default a violent, exclusionary process where some knowledge is treated as authoritative or foundational at the expense of others. Beyond this, because these institutions are ad hoc and have finite mandates, they have, by and large, already 'found' the 'plural and accurate accounts of past violations' that the Special Rapporteur talked about. Notwithstanding potential different interpretations of court archives, the process of extraction of said accounts is completed as the International Residual Mechanism for Criminal Tribunal finalises its last cases. This suggests that the element of truth that needs to be integrated into education and memorialisation is fixed; finite. This is very much in contrast to the transitional justice expert group's proposal to practice prevention as a 'dialogue', a process of building conscience and memory, open to all, necessary for all, and kept 'alive' in years to come through open negotiations.

5.5 Conclusion

My intent in this chapter has been first and foremost to show how the current education system in BiH founded on ethnic divisions produces numerous anxieties about the future of peace in this country. With concrete examples from Bosniak, Bosnian Serb, and Bosnian Croat textbooks and curricula, I have illustrated how each political community aims to shape, securitise, and secure a certain collective identity through the teachings of history. I did not aspire to claim that the global project of transitional justice alone is responsible for ethnic segregation in education, but it certainly helped it, primarily through the OSCE's 'Two Schools Under One Roof' policy. In this policy, we can see both the short-sightedness of international actors who did not plan for the long-term ramifications of ethnic segregation in schools and a continuous, deep misunderstanding of ethnic identities and ontological security needs of groups in critical situations.

The second aim of this chapter has been to critically discuss the ongoing engagements and aspirations in the sphere of education by different international transitional justice actors. Much of this discussion has been centred on explaining how and why the ICTY undertook a role as an educator and showing how aspiring, desegregated education and memorialisation efforts in BiH tend to be linked back to the work of the ICTY by international transitional justice entrepreneurs. The rationale of limiting education about the war to those truths established by the ICTY and domestic courts is of course one of protecting the legacies of these institutions and the global project of transitional justice itself. The point of my critique is never to deny, trivialise, or minimise ICTY and domestic courts' judgements. The point is to remember that they are after all judgements, which come with their own violent knowledge production processes and tend to be presented as fixed truths, whereas in fact, the prevention needs and priorities in BiH suggest that learning and remembering the past has to be a shared, organic, contentious, and ongoing process. In efforts to keep international criminal justice and with it the whole project of transitional justice relevant in BiH, the actors I have discussed in this chapter are approaching prevention of conflict recurrence, but also history and identity in sterile, pretend-objective, and myopic ways. In that sense, in this chapter I have hoped to show that the global project has its own survival needs and existential worries and that addressing these can clash with or straightforwardly be epistemologically violent towards the needs of the BiH society.

6

'My Landlord, a War Criminal!'

Glorification, Denial, and Troubled Relationships with One's Past Self

6.1 Enver

In September 2019, *Toplane*, a public electrical company in the Sarajevo canton, appointed a new director. The man, called Enver Zornić, was recommended for the position by both the local government and the Social Democratic Party (SDP) of Bosnia and Herzegovina (BiH), of which he was a member. I had never met Mr Zornić, but we had a mutual acquaintance. In December 2019, I met this mutual acquaintance in their office for an interview. In discussing conflict (non-)repetition in BiH, the interviewee felt important that they shared the shocking story of their former landlord, whom they became friends with upon moving from a town in northern Bosnia, to Sarajevo.

> My landlord was Enver, and I was very good friends with him. He was some sort of commander in the war, but I met him [because] he had a firm. I ordered some furniture, and his firm got the job via a tender, so he delivered this furniture to me . . . I [then] lived in his flat [in Sarajevo] for 4–5 years and had good relations with Enver. Then, he was named the director of Toplane because he is in the SDP and . . . Op! Suddenly it was all over the news that Enver Zornić, my friend, was convicted for committing war crimes. War crimes![1]

Zornić's crimes had been committed and prosecuted during wartime, shortly before the International Criminal Tribunal for the former Yugoslavia (ICTY) was established and long before domestic courts were restructured and subsequently received jurisdiction to prosecute such matters. In 1993, the Sarajevo Regional Military Court found Zornić, who was deputy commander in charge of the security of the 6th

[1] Interview with Anonymous 2, 13 December 2019.

Mountain Brigade in the Army of BiH, and several other members of the Army responsible for the murders of three civilians, Jagoda Janković, Sreten Ninković, and Josip Gogalo. The three victims were each held captive by Zornić's unit, promised safe release after having been questioned but were instead taken to an abandoned house and shot in the head. The media reported that the three bodies were then burned on site and that Zornić was aware of the crimes his subordinates committed and is furthermore believed to have ordered them and provided the petrol to set the victims' bodies on fire.[2] He was subsequently found guilty on three counts of murder by way of command responsibility and destruction of evidence by the Sarajevo Regional Military Court. The Court sentenced him to ten years and three months in prison. This meant that Zornić spent the rest of the war in prison, serving a total of three years of his sentence. Released seven years early, Zornić had been pardoned three times by the Presidency of BiH.

Why would a convicted war(time) criminal be pardoned by the Presidency and, years later, recommended for a highly regarded public office by local government officials? After a local newspaper uncovered the story of Zornić's involvement in the war, debates were had about whether he was indeed a convicted *war* criminal or, simply, a criminal. Because Zornić had been found guilty of murder and not war crimes, this technicality was used to diminish his responsibility and justify his position of prominence in the BiH public life, despite the fact that his crimes were committed in the context of war and that the victims of his crimes were captured, defenceless civilians. In one of the articles trying to settle the debate about Zornić's future in BiH public life, Muhidin Kapo, the head of the jury in Zornić's 1993 trial, is quoted saying that legal qualification was 'appropriate' and given sentences 'fair'. 'People do things in war that they wouldn't even think of doing during peacetime. As far as I know that case was reviewed by the Hague [ICTY] and was rated as properly undertaken', Mr Kapo was quoted saying.[3] Others held that cases like Zornić's were many. During wartime, people like Zornić were prosecuted within their own ethnic groups on allegations of

[2] Aleksandar Brezar and Admir Muslimovic, 'Murder or War Crime? Why Bosnia Had a Dilemma' (*BIRN*, 16 October 2019) https://shorturl.at/qxLQZ accessed 5 April 2023; Selma Boračić-Mršo, 'Slučaj ubistava iz' 93: Da li će director Toplana Sarajevo podnijeti ostavku?' (*Radio Slobodna Evropa*, 25 September 2019) www.slobodnaevropa.org/a/bih-ratni-zlocini-enver-Zornić/30183304.html accessed 5 April 2023.

[3] Brezar and Muslimovic, 'Murder or War Crimes?'.

committing crimes against civilians of other ethnic groups, like Zornić's victims, which is possibly why their crimes were devalued in qualification and the issued sentences were generally milder. Not 'officially' having any war criminals among the ranks of the Army of the Republic of Bosnia and Herzegovina (ARBiH) was deemed important because any declaration that certain members of ARBiH were also engaging in systematic abuse of civilians and violations of international humanitarian law would, it was feared, damage BiH's independence claim with the international community. In other words, uncovering war crimes of the party who were clearly the primary victim of the war, in the sense of causalities and legality, would have seemingly tainted the purity of this victimhood upon which, as discussed, the contemporary Bosniak identity is built. The victimhood identity of this community is by and large recognised in international society, offering an avenue for pursuing the security of the self.

This is how the BiH public eventually ended up with the likes of Enver Zornić who, after serving less than a third of his already devalued sentence, continued to prosper, conduct business, rent flats in Sarajevo, engage in politics, and rise through the ranks for twenty-four years until the same public, and some of his newly acquired friends, to their horror, learned about his troublesome past. In the concrete case of Zornić, the 'proper' thing – in alignment with the political community's current identity – was not to forgive and forget but, once forced to remember, undertake performative punishing. Following the news of his criminality, Zornić was dismissed as Director of Toplane and kicked out of his political party. While Zornić did lose positions of power as a punishment for his crimes, he nevertheless was allowed to continue to work for the same public company in another role suitable for his qualifications.[4]

Zornić, a convicted war(time) criminal, was therefore not ostracised from public life, and he, at the time of writing this book, has not come forward to confess and apologise to the victims' families. His minimal 'punishment' is a rarity in post-war BiH, and Zornić was rather unlucky to lose a rather profitable job on the account of his role in the killing of three civilians thirty years ago. Many other convicted and acquitted war and wartime criminals not only walk freely, like Zornić does, but continue to actively shape intellectual, political, educational, economic, health, and social life in BiH. Other notable examples include Fikret

[4] Er. M. 'Smijenjeni director Enver Zornić ipak ostaje raditi u Toplanama' (*Klix*, 21 October 2019) https://shorturl.at/twxIM accessed 5 April 2023.

Abdić, the mayor of Velika Kladuša, who assumed the post after completing his sentence for committing war crimes in Bosanska Krajina between 1993 and 1995, and Blagoje Simić, who was named director of a local health centre after serving his fifteen-year-long sentence for war crimes.[5]

Troublesome relationships with past regimes have been part and parcel of global political life. Not recognising perpetrators among one's own ranks, downplaying one's group's atrocities, and providing pardons and immunities to war criminals might remind one of life before the neoliberal world order, a life that burgeoning structures of international human rights and international criminal justice promised to put a halt to. While amnesties in some shape or form continue to be part of domestic politics worldwide, the United Nations have been very explicit in forbidding amnesties for atrocity crimes, namely genocide, crimes against humanity, and war crimes.[6] One of the core mechanisms of doing so has been the international criminal tribunal, the first of which was the ICTY. What we have witnessed in the past thirty years globally is calls for evermore accountability and an undoubtful dominance of the anti-impunity norm in the repertoire of human rights and humanitarian norms available to the global project of transitional justice.

So, what then happened in BiH? What accountability for the BiH society? In this chapter, I identify glorification of convicted and suspected war criminals and denial, minimisation, or trivialisation of their violent actions (hereinafter 'atrocity crimes denial') as widespread, systematic, and one of the key sources of the anxieties relating to conflict recurrence in BiH. Domestic political elites are not innocent in this ordeal, as the creation of heroes and martyrs out of those suspected or convicted for war crimes and promoting their individual prosecutions as collective persecutions are practices that serve very carefully crafted nationalist agendas and help the likes of Milorad Dodik stay in power. In many ways, the roots of this orchestration of national myths predate transitional justice in BiH and the war itself.

My intent in this chapter, however, is to analytically link these practices to the transitional justice project and discuss how international

[5] Eventually Simić was demoted to deputy director. See Nejra Džaferagić, 'Život nakon odsluženja kazne za ratni zločin: Između suočavanja s prošlošću i načelničkih fotelja' (*BIRN*, 20 April 2021) https://shorturl.at/abioX/ accessed 21 April 2021.

[6] Office of the United Nations High Commissioner for Human Rights, *Rule-of-Law Tools for Post-conflict States: Amnesties* (United Nations 2009).

normative commitments after the war have shaped them. First, I propose that the past practices of legal and institutional reform such as vetting lacked transparency and were generally conducted in an ineffective way, prioritising quick and inexpensive fixes for the sake of painting a picture that the international community was doing something meaningful. The outcome was a legal structure that allowed war criminals to flourish and to be glorified. The responsibility for it all fell on the back of ethnonationalist politicians, and the identified culture of denialism was labelled as a 'civilisational issue' by the same international community to reinstate its relevance by trying to fix this 'uncivilised' practice yet again. Second and relatedly, I show these denialist practices, by no means uniquely Balkan phenomena, served to re-position the former Yugoslav states as outliers to Europe and perpetuate their stigmatisation in the international society, as actors begin to think of themselves as being perceived as 'deviant', pariahs, or outliers. This positioning has served the ethnonationalist elites well by allowing them to turn their aggravated stigma into a badge of honour. Instead of a civilisational issue, glorification of war criminals and atrocity crimes denial are phenomena more usefully understood, I propose, as ontological security-seeking behaviours in situations of shame partly helped by the actors of the global transitional justice project.

This chapter proceeds in four sections. Section 6.2 discusses the extent and shape of atrocity crimes denial and glorification of war criminals in BiH, as well as in neighbouring countries, demonstrating how these threaten any existing security assurances. In Section 6.3, I reframe the identified problem by suggesting that it is an inseparable product of the global transitional justice project and particularly the past practices of vetting and criminal prosecutions which were lacking transparency and were overall ineffective. I then show how the international community involved in transitional justice processes in BiH has relieved itself from responsibility for the consequences of such vetting and instead began to refer to the widespread atrocity crimes denial as a civilisational issue. I use a common comparison between Germany as a leader in good 'dealing with the past' and BiH to explore denial and glorification as forms of stigma management and discuss them in the context of different actors' forging of (troubled) relationships with their past selves in times of rupture. In Section 6.4, I talk about more recent legal developments imposed by the High Representative to fix these 'uncivilised' issues and explain why these amendments triggered behaviour that made assurances of non-recurrence even more questionable. Finally, I provide a brief conclusion in Section 6.5, proposing some more fruitful ways to think about how atrocity crimes denial and glorification of war criminals can be diminished.

6.2 Everyone Is Concerned

The phenomena I am discussing in this chapter take several forms. There are people like Enver Zornić whom the public knows committed war crimes but were never adequately prosecuted and convicted for such, although they might have been prosecuted for a lesser crime. They deny their war crimes and have court records to support them. Then, there are people like Fikret Abdić, who were convicted of war crimes, served their sentences, and now continue to sit in positions of political power. Even some of those convicted for their involvement in the Srebrenica genocide have already served their sentences and have returned to their normal lives in BiH and Serbia.[7] The issue is then one of seemingly rewarding convicted war criminals for successfully serving their sentences, even when there is no sense of remorse, no apology, or anything that would suggest to the survivors and victims' families that justice, in a less legal understanding, has been served. Then, there are of course people who were never prosecuted or were prosecuted but were never convicted. Criminal justice processes regarding atrocity crimes in BiH are still ongoing but operating at an ever-slower rate, and it is possible that only a minority of those yet to be prosecuted before will have their day in court before it all ends. Others, like Croatian generals Ante Gotovina and Mladen Markač, or Naser Orić of the ARBiH, have been acquitted which in the legal sense means that it could not be proven beyond reasonable doubt that they were responsible for a specific violation, but does not mean that this specific act did not happen or was not illegal, nor does it necessarily mean that the acquitted person had not committed any crimes whatsoever during the war (although it might).

Yet, that it is too little too late to reflect on the impacts of these phenomena on victims' personal safety and security is undoubted. Unprosecuted, early-released, acquitted perpetrators and those who already served their sentences, in many cases, continue to live in the

[7] Although three of the high-profile perpetrators in this category have had their identities changed and continue to live abroad. See Admir Muslimović, 'Osuđeni za Srebrenicu: Žrtve ogorčene novim životom zločinaca' (*Detektor*, 7 July 2017) https://shorturl.at/arGPU accessed 3 April 2023.

same environment in which they committed war crimes. 'Here [in BiH], the situation is such that our heroes are the other side's war criminals, and we live in an environment where people who committed these crimes, they live here, in our surroundings. We bump into them, and then we prosecute them ... they are here and so are the victims', two prosecutors in the Brčko district told me.[8] The Mothers of Srebrenica also reported 'constantly seeing war criminals around Srebrenica', and keeping a list of 'around 400 such people who in any way participated in genocide and who now work for the police and public institutions'.[9] The two prosecutors explained that in such an environment, in ongoing criminal cases, alleged perpetrators frequently influence victims and witnesses through intimidation. Survivors of wartime sexual violence have been particularly discouraged from pursuing criminal cases because of short sentences being issued for such violations. 'What's the point, they think ... when the perpetrator will be sentenced to one-year imprisonment, they will pay and continue to see the victim [around]'.[10] That suspected and convicted war criminals live in our neighbourhoods is thus logically a core cause of insecurity among victims and survivors.

These are individual cases. They are foremostly threats to the personal safety of those who directly faced them and their actions in wartime or otherwise fear for their well-being living in a community with known murderers and rapists. I often walked around Sarajevo – or Belgrade for that matter – thinking if I would walk past a war criminal. However, most people in BiH, Serbia, and Croatia do not go about their days thinking about these things or worry about all the released or acquitted war criminals they share living space with. Notwithstanding how gruesome and disrespectful these individual cases might be for individual victims, survivors, and their families, it could be argued that a few acquitted and early-released war criminals walking around BiH towns and villages can be considered an inevitable by-product of the war. In other words, after a conflict on such a mass scale, no society could hide all the people involved in perpetrating atrocities away from public life. Yet, beyond these still very problematic individual cases, glorification of war criminals and atrocity crimes denial have been collective, strategic,

[8] Interviews with Prosecutor 1 and Prosecutor 2, the Prosecutor's Office of the Brčko District, 13 November 2019.

[9] Muslimović, 'Osuđeni za Srebrenicu'.

[10] Interviews with the Prosecutor's Office of the Brčko District.

and planned occurrences sponsored and promoted by political elites across the spectrum. The fact that the state and its different institutions not only have convicted or suspected war criminals among their ranks but in fact actively protect, promote, and glorify such individuals is a key trigger of the anxiety relating to conflict recurrence. The manifestations of such a phenomenon can be found across not only BiH but also Serbia and Croatia.

Convicted war criminals have been openly glorified in public discourse and public spaces. The most visible way in which this has been done is through naming streets and public squares after war criminals and framing their involvement in the war as 'heroic' or 'martyr-like'. To illustrate, one of the three presidents of BiH at that time, Serb representative Milorad Dodik, was the person who officially opened a student accommodation hall named 'Radovan Karadžić' after the former President of Republika Srpska convicted for genocide and war crimes by the ICTY.[11] The student hall was funded by Republika Srpska and given a name after the man who, in Dodik's words, 'set the foundation of the entity'.[12] If ever passing through the village of Bozanovići, one might encounter the 'General Mladić Street', also convicted for genocide by the ICTY, while in Posušje, one might find themselves in the Janko Bobetko Street, commemorating a Croatian general indicted by the ICTY but died before extradition. In the city of Bihać, on BiH's north-eastern border with Croatia, a street carries the name of Rasim Delić, likewise convicted by the ICTY.[13] In public speech among the political elites in both Republika Srpska and Serbia, Ratko Mladić is frequently hailed as a Serbian hero without whom 'Serb sacrifice' and 'suffering' in the war would have been even greater.[14] One of the most public-facing war criminals in Serbia, Vojislav Šešelj, spent eleven years in custody in the Hague in a long case about his involvement in inciting war crimes using political speeches. He had been released temporarily in 2014 to undertake cancer treatment, after which he refused to return to the Hague and

[11] See TrebinjeLive, 'PALE-Dodik otvorio studentski dom "dr Radovan Karadžić"' (*TrebinjeLive*, 20 March 2016) https://shorturl.at/avwBK accessed 28 January 2020.

[12] RTS, 'Dodik otvorio Studentski dom "Radovan Karadžić"' (*RTS*, 20 March 2016) https://shorturl.at/hiEJR accessed 5 April 2023.

[13] Nejra Džaferović, 'Ulice i trgovi u BiH nose imena ratnih zločinaca' (*BIRN*, 19 May 2020) https://shorturl.at/dwyI0 accessed 29 November 2020.

[14] Snežana Mitrović, 'Reakcije iz RS: Ratko Mladić je bio i ostao ratni heroj' (*N1 BiH*, 9 June 2021) https://shorturl.at/iuBN8 accessed 5 April 2023.

Serbia refused to extradite him, only to formally be acquitted of war crimes in 2016.[15] He, however, was eventually convicted of crimes against humanity in a partial overturn of the decision by the International Residual Mechanism for Criminal Tribunals in 2018.[16] Having already served his ten-year sentence through the time he spent in detention, Šešelj continues to enjoy a prosperous political career in Serbia, having even served as an MP, mocking the ICTY in public, and publishing multiple books each year which include titles such as *I won again* (2014), *There is no end to the Hague Tribunal's madness* (2017), *The Hague has been missing me again* (2018), and *There was no genocide in Srebrenica* (2018; in three volumes).[17]

In 2019, when Slobodan Praljak was found guilty of war crimes by the ICTY and subsequently drank poison, taking his own life in the courtroom, the then President of Croatia, Kolinda Grabar Kitarović, posted an 'in memoriam' photo commemorating the war criminal on her Facebook account.[18] Branimir Glavaš, a former Croatian general who had been convicted of torturing and murdering Serbian civilians in Croatia's town of Osijek in 2010, was released after less than five years of his sentence in Mostar, BiH. Upon his return to Croatia in early 2015, where he would be subject to a new trial before the Supreme Court, Glavaš was greeted by a warm 'welcome home' event on Freedom Square in Osijek with notable Croatian singers performing to an audience of 1,500 people.[19] By October 2016, Glavaš had been appointed a Member of the Croatian Parliament. It is important to stress that high levels of glorification of war criminals and atrocity crimes denial come from outside BiH, first and foremost Serbia and secondarily Croatia, and occasionally Montenegro. Therefore, the source of anxiety about potential conflict repetition here spreads transnationally, making meaningful assurances of non-recurrence dependent on outside actors.

[15] Denis Dzidic, 'Serbian Nationalist Leader Seselj Convicted of Wartime Crimes' (*BIRN*, 11 April 2018) https://shorturl.at/dqyN2 accessed 3 April 2023.

[16] International Residual Mechanism for Criminal Tribunals, *ŠEŠELJ, Vojislav (MICT-16-99)*, www.irmct.org/en/cases/mict-16-99 accessed 3 April 2023.

[17] Srpska Radikalna Stranka, *Sabrana dela prof. dr Vojislava Šešelja*, https://shorturl.at/diQR1 accessed 3 April 2023.

[18] N1info, 'Kolinda Grabar-Kitarović komentirala objavu fotografije Slobodana Praljka' (*N1*, 3 December 2019) https://shorturl.at/txFJO accessed 28 January 2020.

[19] Sven Milekic, 'Glavas Returns to Warm Welcome in Croatia' (*BIRN*, 2 February 2015) https://balkaninsight.com/2015/02/02/branimir-glavas-returns-to-croatia/ accessed 3 April 2023.

This widespread, systematic revisionism and atrocity crimes denial have made quite a few people I interviewed doubtful of the transitional justice processes and the security assurances their proponents promised. One member of the civil society in Bijeljina said that these phenomena suggest that despite the myriad measures of institutional reform implemented in post-war BiH, people 'still cannot be 100 per cent sure some "things" will not happen', alluding to potential resurgences of armed hostilities and atrocities.[20] Another local interviewee working for an international organisation in BiH suggested that 'the whole narrative of denial and glorification relativises the peacebuilding process and puts . . . "Never Again" under a huge question mark'.[21] Seeing people directly responsible for certain atrocity crimes in decision-making positions causes ordinary people to feel insecure in their daily lives, a practitioner explained.[22]

Even people working within the existing institutions of the transitional justice project, such as criminal justice institutions, felt discouraged about the meaning and utility of their work in a climate largely defined by denial. A prosecutor from East Sarajevo observed that the weakening of victims' interests to participate in criminal justice processes was partly a consequence of the widespread denial of the judicial truth determined by the ICTY and domestic courts.[23] Their colleagues from Brčko also stressed how political elites build their campaigns on denial of crimes and glorification of people who should unequivocally be labelled as perpetrators.[24] '[T]his affects both these current and any future perpetrators', the prosecutors from Brčko concluded.[25] As explained in Chapter 5, the ICTY itself is well-known to have justified its Outreach program, the first of its kind for an international tribunal, in part as a reaction to a brewing culture of denial that had negatively impacted its work.[26] When in 2019, I met with a transitional justice expert formerly involved in the Outreach activities, they perceived the revisionism and denial to be even further aggravated despite the actions of the ICTY

[20] Interview with representative 1 of the Helsinki Committee for Human Rights RS, 12 November 2019.

[21] Interview with representative 1 of the OSCE, 21 November 2019.

[22] Interview with Saliha Đuderija, 17 December 2019.

[23] Interview with Prosecutor from the Prosecutor's Office of East Sarajevo, 29 November 2019.

[24] Interviews with the Prosecutor's Office of the Brčko District.

[25] ibid.

[26] Interview with independent transitional justice expert, 5 December 2019.

Outreach.[27] The key promised role of international and domestic criminal tribunals in transitional justice, that of general deterrence, is feared to be failing, seemingly *despite* all efforts.

Needless to say, everyone is concerned about these developments. In the past few years, different entities comprising the international community, such as the Council for Europe, the European Union, the UN General Assembly, and individual states such as Germany and the UK, expressed concern about the widespread glorification of war criminals and atrocity crimes denial in BiH.[28] In a recent report on BiH, the UN Special Rapporteur for truth, justice reparations, and guarantees of non-repetition stated that he 'is alarmed at the concerning instances of denial of atrocity crimes, the concomitant rejection or relativisation of war crimes rulings of the [ICTY] . . . and the glorification, in various forms, of convicted war criminals'.[29] Who is to blame? Ethnonationalist politicians who deny, trivialise, minimise, and glorify atrocity crimes and their criminals for political gains. What is to be done? The political elites and public figures are urged to 'stop engaging in irresponsible behaviour that sows division and undermines peace'.[30] What is needed is more accountability, more obedience, and more careful observance of the anti-impunity norm and the guidance and recommendations put forward by the said members of the international community.

Yet, I would argue that this kind of 'concerned' thinking does not get the BiH society anywhere other than to drag it even more deeply into the insecurities produced by such overt denialism. There are two key aspects of the social world missing from these expressed concerns and seemingly given no agency in creating and solving the problem at stake – the project of transitional justice itself and the people of BiH. I deal with the former in the following section and with the latter in Chapter 7. My intent here is to reframe the problem that keeps non-recurrence on shaky grounds and suggest that the widespread, systematic glorification of war criminals and

[27] ibid.

[28] AlJazeera, 'Ne prestaje glorifikacija ratnih zločina i zločinaca u regiji' (*AlJazeera*, 14 January 2019) https://shorturl.at/cdxM1 accessed 5 April 2023; InfoRadar, 'EU: Poricanje genocida, revizionizam i glorifikacija ratnih zločinaca u suprotnosti s temeljnim evropskim vrednostima' (*InfoRadar*, 8 June 2021) https://shorturl.at/ovwJ9 accessed 5 April 2023.

[29] Human Rights Council, 'Visit to Bosnia and Herzegovina Report of the Special Rapporteur on the Promotion of Truth, Justice, Reparation and Guarantees of Non-recurrence*' (8 July 2022) A/HRC/51/34/Add.2, para 84.

[30] ibid, para 88.

atrocity crimes denial are not at best an accidental by-product or, at worst, completely detached from the transitional justice project in BiH. They do not happen at such a systematic level *despite* the transitional justice structure in BiH but, at least partly, *because of it*. How exactly did the project of transitional justice directly aid such overt denial?

6.3 'The Politicians Are ... Rubbish!'

Previously, I identified an obsession with linking the principle of non-recurrence to the state, its laws and institutions, in both IHRL and international transitional justice policy. I showed that equating guarantees of non-recurrence with measures of institutional reform is commonplace in transitional justice practice and scholarship and that the two concepts are sometimes even being used interchangeably. At the same time, in Chapter 3, I also suggested that institutional reform has been one of the most developed areas of transitional justice-related interventions in post-war BiH. Courts, police, and armed forces have all been vetted, restructured, and transformed with the promise of 'Never Again'. Cleansed state institutions, the premise is, can no longer hurt their own subjects.

Years later, the BiH state continues to hurt its citizens through fragmentation, stagnation, economic depravity, and memory politics. Regarding vetting more specifically, most interlocutors held that the past vetting processes conducted in BiH, as explained in Chapter 3, were insufficient, suffering from a lack of transparency and stringency. The end result is that, despite seemingly widespread vetting across sectors, we still see known war criminals assume positions of power in these same sectors. On the account of transparency, the process of recertification in the police was particularly singled out as problematic. The criteria for non-recertification were not transparent to the public, and the non-recertified police officers had no means of challenging the decisions as they were not granted an appeals procedure. 'It could be the case that someone was not recertified as a police officer because he lacked education; it was found out that he was a baker, so he could no longer work as a police officer. But at the same time, it could be the case that he was not recertified because he participated in the Srebrenica genocide', a practitioner asserted.[31] This information was never shared with the BiH public

[31] Interview with representative 1 of the Helsinki Committee for Human Rights RS.

who continue to live with the adverse outcomes of such recertification processes. Furthermore, even after the reform was conducted, there was suspicion among the public that certain officers who actively took part in enabling or perpetrating atrocities in the war were left in positions of power. Overall, a legal expert asserted, this ruined the public trust in the renewed institutions.[32] In judicial circles, one municipal judge adjudicating war crimes shared their belief that the specific criteria for the vetting of judges and prosecutors, conducted by the High Judicial and Prosecutorial Council, were insufficiently transparent and therefore, potentially biased.[33] The judge further held that the lack of transparency resulted in numerous ongoing disciplinary processes against judges and even occasional controversial appointments of individuals with criminal records. Those stories eventually found their way into the media, the judge explained to me, and citizens' trust in state institutions further deteriorated.

Moreover, despite the seemingly comprehensive reform of state structures, both glorification of war criminals and atrocity denial had technically been legal until 2021. The individual cases of convicted war criminals assuming political offices are without a doubt legal. The BiH constitution allows convicted war criminals who have served their sentences to re-enter public life.[34] BiH criminal laws allow for short sentences (an average of 4.77 years and as short as one year) and loose consideration of mitigating circumstances such as 'marital status' for perpetrators of rape and sexual violence, a violation that affected the lives of between 12,000 and 50,000 women during the war.[35] The Criminal Codes of BiH (Article 42(a)) and Federation BiH (Article 43(a)) allow for sentences of up to twelve months to be 'exchanged' with a financial penalty if the

[32] Interview with member of the RECOM Coalition Working Group, 14 November 2019.

[33] Interview with judge of the Municipal Court of East Sarajevo, 3 December 2019.

[34] Article 9(1) of the Constitution of Bosnia and Herzegovina states: 'No person who is serving a sentence imposed by the International Tribunal for the Former Yugoslavia, and no person who is under indictment by the Tribunal and who has failed to comply with an order to appeal before the Tribunal, may stand as a candidate or hold any appointive, elective, or other public office in the territory of Bosnia and Herzegovina'. See Annex 4 of the General Framework Agreement for Peace in Bosnia and Herzegovina (Dayton Peace Agreement), Dayton, OH, initiated 21 November 1995, signed in Paris 14 December 1995, UN Doc. A/50/79C, S/1995/999.

[35] Kyle Delbyck, *Kažnjavanje ratnog seksualnog nasilja. Smijernice za suzbijanje nedosljednosti u odmjeravanju kazni* (TRIAL International 2018) https://shorturl.at/bepwB accessed 5 April 2023.

perpetrator requests it, which means that many perpetrators convicted of wartime rape and sexual violence have walked back into their communities having served minimal or no time in prison.[36]

The other, more systematic and direct acts of glorifying war criminals and denying court judgements are immoral, but up until 2021, they were not necessarily illegal. At the time of my field research, there was no legislation at the central level that criminalised denial, trivialisation, and minimisation of atrocity crimes, and such matters were handled either on the entity level or not at all. Such legislation was absent from the package of measures passed or nudged by the High Representative in the first years after the conflict. A draft law that would make denial, minimisation, justification, or approval of Holocaust, genocide, and crimes against humanity had been unsuccessfully circulating in the BiH Parliament since 2011.[37] While the media reporting on these instances of glorification and denial spiked in 2019 and 2020, there was little hope for the realisation of the desired legal improvement. Eventually, the draft law was voted against again in April 2021.[38]

This is not to say that institutional reform is not valuable for assurance of conflict non-recurrence but to highlight the importance of understanding that the existing institutional reform in BiH was done poorly and sloppily by focusing on wrong priorities such as speed, measuring effectiveness through metrics, and reducing costs. A more comprehensive reform, specifically vetting, would be more transparent, stringent, categorical, and overarching within and across sectors. Why was such a reform not conducted at a time when all the attention and many resources were directed towards restructuring BiH institutions and rewriting its laws? The interviewed members of the international community who led some of these reformative projects held that the goals of such projects do not always match the actual mandates given to the bodies conducting the reform. For instance, a former Commissioner of the UN International Police Task Force in BiH stated that, although he was under the impression that the goal of the IPTF was to 'open accountable methods of professional policing and rebuilding their

[36] ibid.

[37] Parlamentarna skupština Bosne i Hercegovine, *Prijedlog zakona o zabrani negiranja, minimiziranja, opravdavanja ili odobravanja holokausta, zločina genocida i zločina protiv čovječnosti*, www.parlament.ba/law/LawDetails?lawId=733 accessed 11 June 2021.

[38] Nejra Džaferagić, 'BiH pod pritiskom da usvoji zakon o poricanju genocida u Srebrenici' (*BIRN*, 16 April 2021) https://shorturl.at/klZ68 accessed 24 May 2021.

relationships with the citizens', the practice proved not to be the case.[39] He further claimed,

> The major constraint was the notion of IPTF as a monitoring, advising, and training force *without any authority* to introduce or impose institution- and capacity-building initiatives. It was obvious that many police officers desperately needed to re-connect with their European counterparts but were constrained from doing so by their political masters fearful of progressive external influences. I arranged regular meetings . . . but the imperative for both sides was establishing territorial control for the future.[40]

As a result, the former Commissioner added, it was 'nigh on impossible to enforce recognisable international standards of impartial police conduct on local police behaviour' and no political commanders were vetted for political ends.[41] As a result, institutional reforms in BiH were presented as necessary, relatively quick, and relatively inexpensive 'fixes', leaving an impression that the international community, embodied in the UN and its agencies, cared and was doing 'something' to prevent mass human rights and humanitarian law abuses from being committed ever again.

The failures and omissions of these processes of institutional reform are often presented through the frames of 'civilisation'. One of the interviewees from the civil society sector usefully illustrated the situation.

> There was no common approach to what we wanted to do [regarding institutional reform] . . . You [the engineers of institutional reform in BiH] opened Pandora's box which you could not close. And then you retreat to your countries [with all the documentation about vetting processes] and said 'yes, those Balkan people are savages, look at what they are doing, they really are savages and should not be helped.'[42]

In an obvious way, in today's BiH, the fact that the international community cared and did 'something' is largely interpreted as an assurance of non-recurrence in the law, relieving the same community from responsibility for the woes and pains experienced by BiH citizens precisely as a consequence of such a quick and messy reform. The blame and therefore responsibility are redirected ethnonationalist politicians, or 'rubbish, full

39 Written correspondence with Richard Monk, former Chief of the UN International Police Task Force in Bosnia and Herzegovina, 25 November 2019.
40 ibid (my emphasis).
41 ibid.
42 Interview with representative 1 of the Helsinki Committee for Human Rights RS.

rubbish' as the High Representative Schmidt referred to them in 2022.[43] The problems of glorification of war crimes and atrocity crimes denial are constructed as a 'civilisational issue'. And while the European Parliament found it important, regarding the 2021 European Commission report on BiH, to reiterate that 'the denial of genocide, celebrating war crimes and war criminals . . . are contrary to European values and aspirations',[44] it is also important to stress that the initial vetting processes were not harmonised with international law and standards. As I explained above, in many ways, the legal structure in post-war BiH allowed war criminals to assume positions of power and be celebrated in public spaces.

This very process is one of stigmatisation; what makes the modern world hang together,[45] what constitutes international society;[46] and what is needed to sustain transitional justice as a project that some collective actors simply need and, when it does not work out, did not try hard enough to fulfil. Stigma, as explained previously, is an attribute that classifies an actor as different, deviant, and less desirable than other actors in a collective. Stigmatisation occurs when that actor sees themselves as different, deviant, and failing to reach a standard of civilisation in the eyes of others, understanding that their attributes make them undesirable, judged, and somehow special in a negative way.[47] As a process of classification of acceptable and unacceptable behaviours, it is a key to the idea of civilisation, creating distinctions between us (the 'normal') and them (the 'deviant').[48] Stigmatising one who seemingly does not comply with the international normative order sustains the order itself by reinforcing the notion of 'normality' untainted by the challengers, failures, and 'rubbish' politicians.[49] It therefore keeps alive

43 N1 Info, 'Schmidt ljutito: Ja brinem o ovoj državi! Ovo je grad u kojem su ljudi izgubili živote. . .' (18 August 2022) www.youtube.com/watch?v=LWsU-UZa138 accessed 30 September 2022.

44 European Parliament, 'Resolution on the 2021 Commission report on Bosnia and Herzegovina' (6 July 2022) (2021/2245(INI)).

45 Ayşe Zarakol, 'What Made the Modern World Hang Together: Socialisation or Stigmatisation?' (2014) 6 International Theory 311.

46 Rebecca Adler-Nissen, 'Stigma Management in International Relations: Transgressive Identities, Norms, and Order in International Society' (2014) 68 International Organization 143.

47 Zarakol, 'What Made the Modern World Hang Together'.

48 Adler-Nissen, 'Stigma Management'.

49 ibid.

both the notion of certain standards that bring the 'normal' together and the hierarchical relations in such an order.

Stigmatisation impacts collective behaviours, identities, and narratives.[50] People have internalised this sentiment of deviance. Several of my interlocutors held that atrocity denial was what separated BiH from 'the civilised' world. One interlocutor observed that 'we still deny some things that we should strongly judge, and not deny, we make ludicrous something that is a universal definition of evil'.[51] Another said, 'unlike in most civilized countries, we do not have a law that prohibits genocide and war crimes denial'.[52] The key to progress, they asserted, would be to become a part of a community where genocide and war crimes denial is prohibited and sanctioned. 'Why don't our emigres do this [denial] in France, the UK . . . but they respect the laws of the country they are in, the laws of the EU, and they are hard-working, respected members of their communities?'[53]

It may be superfluous yet necessary to state that historical revisionism and atrocity crimes denial are not by any means unique to the Balkan states, as revisionist states have lived and died in international relations for as long as there have been international relations. There is no European standard against denial of all atrocity crimes or all genocides for this matter. There is instead a standard of recognition first and foremost the Holocaust and then other atrocity crimes adjudicated by the handful of international criminal tribunals established so far. Framing revisionism and denial in BiH as 'a civilisational issue' is therefore intellectually unhelpful because it re-positions the Western Balkans as an outlier on the European continent, deliberately not looking for traces of such revisionism among the 'civilised' nations of the continent, for instance, former imperial powers such as Britain which to date have not fully and systematically acknowledged the scale and brutality of the empire's atrocities. Furthermore, it is a dangerous frame because it, in fact, helps those same 'rubbish' politicians advance their agendas. In repositioning the Western Balkans as an uncivilised area, this practice perpetuates old tropes of the 'wild' and 'untamed' Balkans. Like in the past, now again, this contradiction with the Balkans helps (Western) Europe build and confirm its standards, its positive image, and the

50 Zarakol, 'What Made the Modern World Hang Together'.

51 ibid.

52 Interview with independent transitional justice expert.

53 ibid.

necessity of its further projects.[54] However, these tropes are conveniently used by political elites as a trigger to not only undertake revisionist behaviour but also present it as a fight against anti-imperialist powers, a positive development. Without trying to take away agency from anyone engaging in such genocide denialism, when one employs the binary of the civilised versus uncivilised, 'rubbish', scum of the Earth versus progressive and enlightened people, then one can expect the Othered to utilise the same binary in their reaction. And what the person traditionally labelled as 'uncivilised' sees on the other side of the binary is not the 'civilised enlightener', but the oppressive imperialist denying the person their right to exist – or at least an opportunity to abuse such views. From a scholarly point of view, these tensions in framing are pretty 'textbook' and unsolvable in their current form because they trigger one another and allow the narratives of 'civilisation' and 'imperialism' to be co-opted.

On that note, the question of agency deserves further elaboration. As stigmatised collective actors make sense of self in the world, they deal with their stigma in different ways. Adler-Nissen calls this stigma management strategies.[55] She differentiates between stigma recognition, that is, identifying with and internalising the value judgement of the 'normal'; counter-stigmatisation, that is, turning one's stigma into an emblem of pride; and stigma rejection, that is, accepting the classification of deviance but insisting on being no different than others in international society.[56]

One interlocutor posited,

> Why aren't court judgments recognized? . . . I was watching Angela [Merkel] the other day. She goes to Auschwitz and says, pay attention please, 'these crimes, the Holocaust, which Germany committed in World War II are an inseparable part of German identity.' And over here, [they are saying] 'it wasn't us' . . . This is where we are different from the civilized world.[57]

This quote illustrates a common perception found elsewhere in the world that Germany is a good example of how to 'deal with the past'. Ever since Willy Brandt's act of apology for the Holocaust in 1970, and more intensively so post-unification, the memory of the Holocaust has proliferated in Germany with numerous monuments, memorials, educational

[54] Maria Todorova, *Imagining the Balkans* (Oxford University Press 1997).
[55] Adler-Nissen, 'Stigma Management'.
[56] ibid.
[57] Interview with Goran Šimić, 12 December 2019.

programmes, and symbolic acts of acknowledging the responsibility of the German state and German people in the Holocaust. To put this in the language of non-recurrence, the German state appears to have been cleansed of its rotten apples and rotten ideology to the point where it can find a sense of ontological security in facing the crimes of Nazi Germany for what they were. This is even though many former Nazi officials continued to have prosperous public positions in the society after the war, some even assuming posts very similar to what they had before or during the war.[58] Germany's stigma management strategy, therefore, has been one of stigma recognition.[59]

In the BiH space, we see multiple competing stigmas and multiple evolving stigma management strategies, some of which question the stigma and others turn it into a badge of honour.[60] None can be interpreted as stigma recognition. Yet, the 'wishing we were Germany' sentiment is not that helpful to combat the widespread atrocity crimes denial and glorification of war criminals. There are two core problems with Germany being set as the standard of 'good' dealings with the past others ought to achieve. First, there are many differences between Germany and BiH, most importantly in the nature and execution of the wars and in the structures of the two respective societies. When observing why different groups in BiH might reject or even be proud of the stigma they endured for committing heinous crimes in the 1990s, it can be claimed that, unlike Germany, in BiH organic discussions about the war are yet to be encouraged in the mainstream and, unlike Germany, the primary victims of the war in BiH cannot be treated as some sort of historical abstraction.[61]

Second, the governing of the past through international or hybrid criminal tribunals discussed here has primarily been imposed on non-Western countries, with the exception of Germany. It is therefore unsurprising that it is precisely Germany, as an exceptional case of a Western European state subject to an international criminal tribunal after World War II, that is being used here as the example of 'good' dealing with the past to continue to shame those unable to reach the set standard of civilisation. Therefore, perhaps the most important difference between

[58] Clint Smith, 'Monuments to the Unthinkable' (*The Atlantic*, 14 November 2022) https://shorturl.at/devT7 accessed 3 April 2023.

[59] Adler-Nissen, 'Stigma Management'.

[60] ibid.

[61] ibid; Smith, 'Monuments to the Unthinkable'.

the two countries is that, unlike Germany, BiH has always been on the margins of Europe and the West.

What we see when we unpack the binary of the civilised versus uncivilised is a much more complex tale of the causes and fuels of and responsibility for glorification and denial. While glorification and atrocity crimes denial can certainly be caused by endogenous factors such as the capture of political power and populist politics, they are also a result of extraneous factors, including the international normative order that imposes the new 'rules of the game' onto the state.[62] The rules of the game into which BiH, as well as its neighbours Serbia and Croatia, were (re-)admitted into international society in the late 1990s and early 2000s were significantly different from what most societies transitioning from conflict and mass human rights abuse had known before. As a result of the human rights and transitional justice developments in the 1980s and early 1990s, the international normative order carried quite a few new and emerging norms into these states. At the forefront was the anti-impunity norm which, as discussed in Chapter 4, had had its internal structure altered so that courts could undertake additional social values such as truth recovery and reconciliation and has generally been positioned as superior over other norms, and particularly other desirable behaviours otherwise constituting these norms.

For BiH, Croatia, and Serbia, committing atrocity crimes so grave that a special international criminal tribunal is established to adjudicate them triggers a sense of shame as the actions that were committed within the borders of these states and by their armed forces are put on display for the whole world to see. These pressures can trigger ontological insecurity in states because they involve a process of separation and status loss which can also be perceived as discrimination, an unjustly different treatment in comparison with other states in similar situations.[63] The international criminal tribunals in Rwanda and the former Yugoslavia were significantly different from the Nuremberg tribunal because of their emphasis on civilian sufferings and because they were not imposed by the 'victors' of an international armed conflict but by the international community as a changed, 'evolved' way of dealing with the mess resulting from state failure to take care of one's own population. As explained

[62] See generally, Alexander E Wendt, 'The Agent-Structure Problem in International Relations Theory' (1987) 41 International Organisation 335 and Alexander E Wendt, *Social Theory of International Politics* (Cambridge University Press 1999).

[63] Adler-Nissen, 'Stigma Management'.

previously, the ICTY and other imposed transitional justice processes by their nature have served to disrupt some of the core national myths in the (re-)making, posing problems for political elites to maintain a coherent biographical narrative. Yet, much of the institutional reform had been cosmetic, and practising ethnonationalism on steroids proved to be prolific, leading to votes as well as personal wealth. As court judgements were issued, suspects were acquitted, and some of the first convicted criminals had served their sentences, maintaining that close connection with the past self without much discussion about who that past self was became a prevalent way to handle the rupture, at least in narrative. That said, to add to the list of reasons of what makes BiH different from Germany, unlike in Germany, there has been no *temporal othering* among any of the groups discussed here and their former selves, no 'sudden and radical' ruptures with the past for the purpose of 'Never Again' that served to securitise one's own past.[64] Quite the opposite, glorification of war criminals and denial of atrocity crimes can be understood as strategies that help make sense – and even be proud – of one's former self in a climate where much of the world is telling you to feel shame about one's own past.

These past selves, particularly in BiH, are still seen as being on trial in different shapes and forms, and the country is still in the international community's spotlight for its numerous failings, which are very rarely discussed as shared failings of the international community and a myriad of actors who came (and stayed) to 'fix' BiH. Instead, what we see is stigmatisation and a popular belief that BiH was offered a chance but failed to join the club of the 'civilised', maintaining the relevance of the international community and its projects. Some of those who stayed, such as the High Representative, have attempted to tackle the issues of glorification of war criminals and atrocity crimes denial, which most evidently hamper any non-recurrence assurances in the long run, by imposing further legal amendments. In the next and final section, I discuss why such amendments might in fact end up harming BiH's road to 'Never Again'.

6.4 One Last Thing before You Go

At the time of my fieldwork in 2019 and 2020, the way to tackle such pervasive glorification and denial was through the civilisational tool of

[64] Bahar Rumelili, 'Breaking with Europe's Pasts: Memory, Reconciliation, and Ontological (In)Security' (2018) 27 European Security 280, p. 290.

law. Passing a legislation which would prohibit atrocity crimes denial was perceived as a matter of urgency; perhaps it was not a magical tool for solving all the woes but nevertheless a necessary foundation. When asked about what is needed to ensure non-recurrence in BiH, one activist said 'passing a law prohibiting genocide denial and glorification of fascist organisations is urgent. Urgent! So that we no longer witness the marching of the order of chetniks in Višegrad, the commemoration of Draža [Mihailović] in Bileća, . . . naming a school after an Ustaša in Sarajevo'.[65]

Hence why in 2021, after many concerned groups turned to the Office of the High Representative to enforce legislation criminalising genocide denial, the resulting legislation reflected the superiority of courts as the sole appropriate institutions for truth-making, sparking one of the most serious political crises in BiH. The legislation was imposed at the very end of Valentin Inzko's term as High Representative after much concern about the increasing instances of genocide denial and glorification of war criminals in public spaces. This legal amendment was preceded by repeated appeals from different citizen groups. Certain international non-governmental organisations, most prominently TRIAL International, also took an interest in advocating for legislative changes. When I interviewed one of their representatives in 2019, they announced an initiative to create and publish a policy paper on atrocity crimes denial which, they said, came out of a realisation that focusing narrowly on atrocity crimes prosecutions, which the organisation used to do, was insufficient to see core justice improvements in society.[66] Their goal was to eliminate atrocity crimes denial from public discourse. Before the mentioned legal amendments were adopted, the programme coordinator gave a speech about transitional justice in BiH before the UN Security Council.[67] In this speech, atrocity crimes denial was in focus, as it was stated that, as war criminals are glorified in textbooks, celebrated in demonstrations and political rallies, and some even appointed to official government functions, 'the authorities . . . seem in no rush to put an end to the historical denial'.[68] The reference to non-recurrence was worded as a warning. In the words of the speaker: 'Three generations

[65] Interview with representative of the Youth Initiative for Human Rights BiH, 11 December 2019.

[66] Interview with representative of TRIAL International, 22 November 2019.

[67] Trial International, *Trial International before the UN Security Council*, https://shorturl.at/yBJN0 accessed 13 May 2024.

[68] ibid.

have now tasted the poison of hatred. Very little is done to prevent the same fate from happening to the next generation'.[69] Their report was published later in the year with a clear focus on recommending possible models of regulating atrocity crimes denial in BiH by means of law.[70] The paper suggested that the banning of denial by law was extremely important in order to 'finally acknowledge the truth about the war in our country, punish war criminals, individual perpetrators – rather than to let an entire ethnic group carry a stigma of crime – and also to make sure that such crimes would never be repeated'.[71]

Throughout 2019 and 2020, Inzko repeatedly urged the authorities to amend the Criminal Code to this end, promising to enforce the legislation himself through his legislative powers. The High Representative's threats caused small but nevertheless important changes. The most notable was the removal of the previously mentioned 'Radovan Karadžić' plaque on a student dormitory in Pale, Republika Srpska.[72] After it had been officially placed on the dormitory in 2016, the plaque was critiqued by concerned citizens, particularly after Karadžić was convicted of genocide by the ICTY in 2019. This led the High Representative to threaten to forbid Dodik, who inaugurated the plaque, from travelling to the EU member states if he did not order the plaque to be removed. The threats ultimately triggered a removal of the plaque in December 2020.[73] Notwithstanding this success, at the time of my fieldwork, many of my interlocutors doubted that the High Representative would follow through with his promises, seeing how he had not used his Bonn powers to impose decisions since 2014. Yet, as a result of a combination of these pressures and perhaps a worry about his own legacy, seeing that his mandate was ending with barely any use of the powers, Inzko responded. He surprised the BiH public when on 23 July 2021 he issued a decision enacting the Law on Amendment to the Criminal Code of BiH which, among others, criminalised public

[69] ibid.

[70] Lejla Gačanica and Caroline Finkeldey, *Calling War Atrocities by Their Right Name. Regulating a Ban on Denial, Trivialisation, Justification or Condonation of Genocide, the Holocaust, Crimes against Humanity or War Crimes* (forumZFD – TRIAL International 2019) https://shorturl.at/mrTUW accessed 5 April 2023.

[71] ibid.

[72] Lamija Grebo and Vladimir Kovačević, 'Uklonjena tabla sa imenom Radovana Karadžića' (*BIRN*, 10 December 2020) https://shorturl.at/bcsDK accessed 8 June 2021.

[73] ibid.

condonement, denial, gross trivialisation, or attempts at justification of genocide, crimes against humanity, or war crimes.[74]

I identify two core issues with this piece of legislation being put forward as a 'solution' to glorification of war criminals and atrocity crimes denial. The first issue is the actions and reactions this legislative amendment invited since Inzko's action. Notably, there is the problem of enforcement. In the first year since the law was enacted, there were forty applications pending before the Office of the Prosecutor in BiH, without a single filed indictment.[75] This is unsurprising considering the Office of the Prosecutor had repeatedly been critiqued for not bringing forward many indictments that would reflect the personnel and resources it has at its disposal.[76] The Office of the High Representative of the United Nations in Bosnia and Herzegovina's response to the issues of glorification and denial was therefore one that exhibits, once again, incredible trust in the BiH state, a trust, as vast empirical evidence on the (lack of) work done by the federal institutions shows, that is not well-deserved. Thus, the legal amendment, while an important step in aligning BiH laws and 'values' with those of the European Union, was in the immediate period after its enactment of little importance for everyday lives and security and its importance remains symbolic. Then, there is the issue of political deadlock triggered by Inzko's move. The immediate reaction from Republika Srpska manifested in an agreement by major RS political parties' representatives to boycott the federal institutions of BiH, namely the Parliament, the Council of Ministers, and the Presidency.[77] Just a week after the legislative amendments were enacted, the Republika Srpska Assembly formally rejected the legislation, calling it a 'revision' of history aimed at 'insulting' Serbian people who were 'the true victims of genocide in World War II' and 'diminishing' their 'victimhood'.[78]

[74] For more information about the implemented amendments, see Office of the High Representative, *HR's Decision on Enacting the Law on Amendment to the Criminal Code of Bosnia and Herzegovina*, https://shorturl.at/KRX39 accessed 9 August 2021.

[75] Milorad Milojević, 'U prvoj godini zabrane 40 prijava za negiranje genocida u Srebrenici' (*Radio Slobodna Evropa*, 28 June 2022) https://shorturl.at/nqFLW accessed 5 April 2023.

[76] Emina Dizdarević, 'Tužilaštvo BiH u 2021. podiglo manje optužnica za korupciju nego godinu dana ranije' (*BIRN*, 29 December 2021) https://shorturl.at/jFLX9 accessed 5 April 2023.

[77] Gojko Veselinović and Meliha Kešmer, 'Stranke iz RS-a bojkotuju institucije BiH zbog zabrane negiranja genocida' (*Radio Slobodna Evropa*, 26 July 2021) https://shorturl.at/hN349 accessed 5 April 2023.

[78] Dragan Maksimović, 'Republika Srpska odbacila Inzkov zakon' (*DW*, 31 July 2021) https://shorturl.at/nrJN1 accessed 5 April 2023.

It was then agreed, by passing a new law, that the legal amendments would not be implemented by the Republika Srpska institutions.[79] Republika Srpska Assembly further retaliated by passing a law aimed to prohibit any public acts suggesting that Republika Srpska is an 'aggressor' or 'genocidal entity' and punish them by imprisonment.[80]

The second issue is one of the sources of knowledge that can and cannot be legally denied, trivialised, and minimised, and thus an issue of power and agency. The enforced amendment, as expected, made a crucial, and perhaps necessary mistake. This legislative amendment restricts the conceptualisation of the said crimes as per the judgements of a handful of tribunals: the Nuremberg Tribunal, the ICTY, the ICC, and the courts of BiH. As such, this act of prohibition of atrocity crimes denial therefore does not restrict glorification of individuals who committed violent acts in WWII or later conflicts but were never prosecuted or otherwise acquitted. It does not stop people like Enver Zornić from being glorified – not that he has been – because he was only convicted of ordinary crimes (in wartime) or prevent the continuing celebration of controversial individuals such as Dragoljub Draža Mihailović who was the commander of the royalist Chetnik forces in World War II. After the war, Mihailović was captured, tried, and convicted of high treason and war crimes by the Supreme Court of the Federal People's Republic of Yugoslavia and was subsequently executed. Nevertheless, Mihailović was rehabilitated by a Belgrade court in 2015, which proclaimed the 1946 conviction as 'void'.[81] Statues of Mihailović today can be found in both Republika Srpska and Serbia. Mihailović is but one example of an individual who is outside the scope of Inzko's legal ways of combatting denial, yet who continues to be glorified through street art and memorials, including in Republika Srpska, while also being very clearly associated, by different communities, with Serb nationalism and violence. Importantly, the legal amendment neglects the lived experiences and pockets of truth-recovery that take place outside these named institutions

[79] Gojko Veselinović, Maja Žuvela, and Meliha Kešmer, 'Skupština RS-a proglasila zabranu negiranja genocida "neprimjenjivom"' (*Radio Slobodna Evropa*, 30 July 2021) https://shorturl.at/nsEGK accessed 5 April 2023.

[80] Elvira Jukić-Mujkić, 'Zabranjeno negiranje, ali daleko od priznanja genocida' (*Osservatorio balcani e caucaso transeuropa*, 6 August 2021) https://shorturl.at/oAN58 accessed 5 April 2023.

[81] Sven Milekic and Marija Ristic, 'Serbia Rehabilitates WWII Chetnik Leader Mihailovic' (*BIRN*, 14 May 2015) https://balkaninsight.com/2015/05/14/serbia-rehabilitates-wwii-chetnik-leader-mihailovic accessed 30 May 2024.

of criminal justice all over BiH, which serve to directly challenge this blatant glorification and atrocity crimes denial. To these, and other practices of and for 'Never Again' with, despite and, possibly, against the global project of transitional justice I turn to in Chapter 7.

6.5 Conclusion

In this chapter, I have presented systematic, state-supported, widespread practices of atrocity crimes denial and glorification of war criminals as sources of anxiety around potential conflict recurrence and have sought to explain them as phenomena in relation to the global transitional justice project. I have complicated the assertion that atrocity crimes denial places BiH and other former Yugoslav states among the 'uncivilised' and argued that such phenomena are intrinsically linked to the institutionalised forms of transitional justice, primarily vetting and criminal prosecutions which largely created the enabling conditions for such behaviours.

I have used frequent comparisons between Germany and BiH and expressed a longing for BiH to be as good at 'dealing with the past' as Germany to propose that atrocity crimes denial and glorification of war criminals can be analysed through a lens of stigma management strategies that multiple groups resort to in attempts to find and sustain ontological security. In the case of Zornić and many other suspected or convicted war criminals found in the Army of BiH, the violence of the past self has been suppressed or even entirely erased to elevate the claims of victimhood. In the case of Bosnian Serb and Serbian political elites, as well as Bosnian Croat and Croatian political elites, there has not been a clear separation from the violent past self, but rather an active campaign of reframing that violence as an achievement; a necessity.

For BiH in particular, what needed to be encouraged in the early years of transition was breaking up with its wartime self which, it was not, seeing that BiH in the very Dayton Peace Agreement itself is a meeting point for securities of multiple beings, each entity developing and securing its own biographical narrative, as discussed in Chapters 4 and 5. The three core 'constituent peoples' in BiH exist, legally speaking, only in relation to the war, and only as parties that were once in the war, and now they live together in an overly complex political system as a consequence of it. This makes any temporal othering from the former, wartime self challenging, if not impossible. If BiH, Serbia, and Croatia have ever had an opportunity to break up with their past selves, the regimes and individuals who comprised them, that moment has now passed. It is therefore unsurprising that some 'fresh' faces on the political scene of Republika Srpska, for example, such as Draško Stanivuković or Jelena Trivić, while opponents to the long-lasting ethnonationalist leader Milorad Dodik, ended up performing their Serbhood in similar ways, for example, taking pictures with far-right chetnik groups[82] or denying that what happened in Srebrenica was a genocide.[83] Denying some actions perceived as injustices and elevating other actions perceived as heroic, for many people, is part and parcel of what it means to be a Serb in BiH. It is outside the scope of this book to think through all possible ways forward, but what is clear is that atrocity crimes denial and glorification of war criminals can be reduced but not eliminated through blanket prohibition and imposition of laws. This is just a perpetuation of all sorts of outside interference that ethnonationalist elites such as Dodik use to sustain their politics. Instead, these practices need to be thought about in relation to truth recovery, education, and memorialisation, and not in a vacuum, as they depend on there not being a state-wide fact-finding process, or a public dialogue about the past, and they depend on there being segregated ethnicity-based education. In Chapter 7, I discuss how different actors engage in myriad practices for non-recurrence and challenge this post-conflict status quo by prioritising intersections over isolations.

[82] Dragan Bursać, 'Kome smeta (po)četnik Draško Stanivuković?' (*Radio Sarajevo*, 10 February 2020) https://shorturl.at/qAGJL 4 April 2023.

[83] A. B., 'Ona je budućnost RS-a/Jelena Trivić: Tužite me koliko hoćete, u Srebrenici nije bilo genocida' (*Oslobođenje*, 23 July 2021) https://shorturl.at/lBJTV 4 April 2023.

7

Agency amid Anxiety

7.1 Personal

> The war has made us all unhappy and destroyed us altogether. I have decided, after everything, to fight and to try my best to make sure the war never happens again. To live in hatred with the other is horrific. To live in peace and love with another who is different is the most valuable thing in the world.
>
> Hikmeta Rizvanović (exhibition '*Lično*')

> If we let the past pass under the bridge, we have built a future for ourselves and everyone around us. Let peace be our future. Everything passes; only the future remains.
>
> Goran Dragojević (exhibition '*Lično*')

Lično. Personal. This was the name of a photography exhibition that portrayed about a dozen survivors of war. The exhibition was created in 2017 by Bosnia and Herzegovina (BiH) artist Velija Hasanbegović and supported by the Catholic Relief Services within their US Aid-funded project Pro-Future. I attended one of the iterations of the exhibition in Sarajevo in 2019. I remember feeling overwhelmed by emotions as some of the survivors gave their speeches to the audience. Some of it was sadness for those who perished, for what the war had done to our societies, but some of it was hope and gratitude. As one of the survivors proudly pointed to his granddaughter in the audience, I remember feeling, distinctly, like what I was witnessing was also a celebration of life. The survivors were victims of wars but heroes of peace, it was said, and 'peace does not have an alternative'.[1] While the portraits, shot in black and white, and testimonies were a window to the painful past, each

[1] Fokus.ba, 'Otvorena izložba "Lično": U ratu nema pobjednika' (*Fokus.ba*, 2017) www.fokus.ba/kultura/otvorena-izlozba-licno-u-ratu-nema-pobjednika/673146/ accessed 9 August 2023.

message attached to them, as the two exemplified above, was a message for the future, a message of love, peace, and unity. The language of and desire for meaningful 'Never Again' were demonstrated in every corner of the exhibition.

The exhibition, with its portraits, messages, and speakers, travelled around the country, including formal spaces of governance such as the BiH Parliament as well as religious sites. There were, I was told, different versions of the narrative section for different audiences. When I met them in their office, spokespeople of the Pro-Future project explained to me that I heard the short version at the exhibition, 'but they [the speakers] also have 20-minute versions of their stories, when they talk to young people. One of their messages is, "War is not a Hollywood movie. At the end of it, you don't kiss a girl and leave the scene. There is no happy ending for anyone."'[2] The idea was, the spokespeople explained, to unequivocally show that there are no winners in war – everyone loses.[3]

I wondered then if these individuals' enthusiasm and hope for the future despite (or perhaps because of) devastating pasts can also be observed at collective levels, if and how post-conflict societies can establish 'personal' connections with the past in a way that reaffirms their ownership of it; or even, 'get personal' with the past. Could the transitional justice project ever support these attitudes and connections to the past as a personal matter, something that concerns and involves everyone? Up until this point, my book has complicated that possibility as it pointed to new and aggravated anxieties, insecurities, and grievances in the light of the transitional justice project. Preceding chapters focused on the transitional justice project as a structure which, with its core tenets of how to deal with the past, its institutions, norm clusters, and civilisational missions, shapes common perceptions of recurrence and non-recurrence in and for BiH. Through stories, illustrations, and examples from the past three decades of transitional justice in BiH, I have sought to show how the project can make post-conflict societies more anxious about the future and durability of peace. Yet, the interactions between the structure and agency, between the project and the people, are not a one-way street. Instead, people across different strata of our global and local societies interact with the transitional justice project in ways that sustain it,

[2] Interviews with representative 1 and representative 2 of the PRO-FUTURE Project, Catholic Relief Services, 18 November 2019.

[3] ibid.

challenge it, or even change it.[4] Taking a step back from the structure, I discuss here how the ways in which societies both deal with the past and ensure 'Never Again' can exist and indeed flourish outside and beyond the constraints of the global project. In this chapter, I want to shift the reader's attention to the people and collectives like those I refer to above who may or may not experience everyday anxiety about renewed war but contribute to its prevention day in and day out. This chapter is about stories, illustrations, and examples of nurturing connections in a divisive and deeply anxious environment. Based on these stories, I conceptualise non-recurrence beyond governance as not only resistance but also co-existence, binding, and healing; as work; as homework you take home; a self-assignment.[5]

A lot of what I will discuss in this chapter has to do with elements and characteristics not awarded high value within the transitional justice project, such as *interpersonal, transethnic, reflective,* and *dialogical.* The decision to include this chapter in the book was inspired by the burgeoning scholarship on imaging the world otherwise,[6] feminist scholarship on joy, love, and hope in and after the war,[7] and by my personal experiences of healing together with people in post-Yugoslav spaces. Like many scholars have argued before me, 'dealing' with the past in post-conflict settings extends way beyond the global project of transitional justice.[8] However, this chapter's goal is not to provide an overview of different

[4] Anthony Giddens, *The Constitution of Society: Outline of the Theory of Structuration* (Polity Press 1984) p. 14.

[5] Sarah Ahmed, *Living a Feminist Life* (Duke University Press 2017) p. 7.

[6] Laura A Meek and Julia Alejandra Morales Fontanilla, 'Otherwise' (2022) 3 Feminist Anthropology 274; Cynthia E Cohen, 'Reimagining Transitional Justice' (2020) 14 International Journal of Transitional Justice 1; Jonas Rusche, 'Imagining Peace Outside of Liberal Statebuilding: Anarchist Theory as Pathway to Emancipatory Peacefacilitation' (2022) 47 Alternatives 18; Elena B Stavrevska, 'On Feminist Anger and Imagining Peace Otherwise' (*LSE Blog*, 10 November 2021) https://blogs.lse.ac.uk/wps/2021/11/10/on-feminist-anger-and-imagining-peace-otherwise/ accessed 1 August 2023.

[7] Roxani Krystalli and Philipp Schulz, 'Taking Love and Care Seriously: An Emergent Research Agenda for Remaking Worlds in the Wake of Violence' (2022) 24 International Studies Review 1.

[8] Daniela Lai, 'Transitional Justice and Its Discontents: Socioeconomic Justice in Bosnia and Herzegovina and the Limits of International Intervention' (2016) 10 Journal of Intervention and Statebuilding 361; Kieran McEvoy, 'Beyond Legalism: Towards a Thicker Understanding of Transitional Justice' (2007) 34 Journal of Law and Society 411; Oliver P Richmond and Audra Mitchell, 'Peacebuilding and Critical Forms of Agency: From Resistance to Subsistence' (2011) 36 Alternatives: Global, Local, Political 326.

forms of 'local' agency or exercises of transitional justice. It is instead, starting from a point of interconnectivity of global(s) and local(s), to explore some of the ways in which more meaningful forms of 'Never Again' are promoted in connection – or disconnection for that matter – with the global project.

Most examples explored in this chapter stem from the work of non-governmental actors such as civil society organisations, but the reader should note that these actors ought not to be romanticised. Many of these practices are in fact projects funded by different, typically foreign funding bodies. As such, they have their own limitations and are not immune to criticism. It is outside the scope of this book to discuss in depth the selection and design biases of these specific non-governmental actors. There is always the question of 'what is the point?' of these initiatives if the problems are as structural and grave as I identified them in previous chapters. But this question to me gives away a sense of haste, a perception that only the quickly visible changes count. Yet we are here talking about some of the most painstaking and complex processes humankind could phantom; to expect things to be done with haste would be to set oneself up for giving up. As one of the people supporting *Lično* and other similar projects said, 'this is all being written into some peace history of BiH . . . When you run metrics or you read the news, you look around, it is hard to see any impact. But this doesn't discourage us because we are aware that this is a long process'.[9]

Section 7.2 provides an overview of key ontological security work on the positive potential of being anxious or living in anxious times and what facing one's anxiety might bring. In Section 7.3, I illustrate how both the limits and merits of judicial truth recovery can be accommodated, providing multiple examples that different practitioners in BiH have identified as their ways of ensuring 'Never Again'. Section 7.4 is about selected practices for 'Never Again' that completely reorient the focus away from state-obsessed formal transitional justice processes to the human and personal levels. What they illustrate are attempts to foster trust among people and in people, and, in doing so, they act not necessarily against but certainly despite the transitional justice project.[10]

[9] Interviews with representatives of the PRO-FUTURE Project.

[10] Evans uses a similar classification to distinguish between scholarly interventions which are 'in' transitional justice (i.e., seeking to improve transitional justice as a field), 'beyond' transitional justice (i.e., parallel frames that may complement or even reject transitional justice) and 'against' transitional justice (i.e., alternatives to the existing framework). See

Section 7.5 summarises, briefly, what these described practices have in common and how they might expand scholarly understandings of what non-recurrence is and what it entails. Finally, in Section 7.6, in place of a conclusion, I open the possibility that the global transitional justice project cannot be reimagined but must instead be abolished. This is essentially a thought exercise in which I offer musings and invite further reflections on what humanity might gain by accepting that the past may be ungovernable.

7.2 Anxiety as a Possibility for Change

Previously in this book, I discussed anxiety about renewed conflict as something that could be either paralysing and detrimental to action or open new possibilities for social and political change, focusing, however, primarily on the negative effects of anxiety. Much of Chapter 2 was built on Giddens' work on ontological (in)security or more contemporary work inspired by him. Missing from Giddens' account of anxiety is its positive potential and an exploration of what happens when one embraces rather than attempts to fight one's own anxiety. Scholars of ontological security have shown that anxiety can open possibilities for critical reflection, creativity, innovation, and, ultimately, social and political change during and after critical situations.[11] Anxiety can activate a wilful agency that confronts and accepts mortality, unpredictability, and fortune and can turn out to be emancipatory and self-actualising.[12] Embracing what Gustafsson and Kirckel-Choi call 'normal' (as opposed to neurotic) anxiety[13] and dwelling on ambivalence is said to expand

Matthew Evans, 'In, Against, and Beyond Transitional Justice' in Matthew Evans (ed.), *Beyond Transitional Justice Transformative Justice and the State of the Field (or Non-field)* (Routledge 2022) pp. 3–10.

11 Maria Mälksoo, 'The Transitional Justice and Foreign Policy Nexus: The Inefficient Causation of State Ontological Security-Seeking' (2019) 21 International Studies Review 373; Catarina Kinnvall and Jennifer Mitzen, 'Anxiety, Fear, and Ontological Security in World Politics: Thinking with and beyond Giddens' (2020) 12 International Theory 240; Bahar Rumelili, *Conflict Resolution and Ontological Security: Peace Anxieties* (Routledge 2015).

12 Bahar Rumelili, '[Our] Age of Anxiety: Existentialism and the Current State of International Relations' (2021) 24 Journal of International Relations and Development 1020.

13 Karl Gustafsson and Nina C Krickel-Choi, 'Returning to the Roots of Ontological Security: Insights from the Existentialist Anxiety Literature' (2020) 26 European Journal of International Relations 875, p. 877.

political space as political actors generate and select alternative possibilities.[14]

In the context of transitional justice, Mälksoo, for instance, argues that anxiety caused by critical situations such as transitions can 'open up space for breaking the habitual conflict patterns and the intersubjective negotiation and reformulation of identities'.[15] What is desired for more reflexive and less divisive transitional justice, therefore, is the 'ability for introspection, adaptability and aptitude to cope with change' while dealing with the past and the role one's self had in such a past.[16] Rumelili sees the positive value of anxiety in that it can facilitate the renegotiation of identities and promote conciliatory ways of being. For instance, she explains how anxiety can unsettle systems of meaning and inspire anxious actors to 'make a leap of faith into trust' and alternative identifications and interests which are not conflictual or antagonistic.[17] Thus, speaking of anxieties linked to conflict resolution, Rumelili holds that anxiety can be 'both a necessary condition and an undermining force' for peace processes, as it both 'generates a longing for a return to conflict' and 'provides the actors with the necessary realm of individual freedom and choice to enact change'.[18] Gustafsson on the other hand links anxiety to creativity, that is, having possibilities to create both oneself and one's daily activities.[19] Building on May, Gustafsson proposes that creativity as 'the process of bringing something new into being' can be both constructive and destructive.[20]

This literature proposes that anxiety helps understand and bridge the gaps between expectations and reality and, ultimately, make sense of the world. Unlike in neurotic anxiety investigated by Giddens, in normal anxiety, the gap between expectation and reality can be bridged as expectations are used to creatively transform reality.[21] In other words, anxiety can reveal the limitations and pitfalls of

[14] Kinnvall and Mitzen, 'Anxiety, Fear and Ontological Security', p. 247.
[15] Mälksoo, 'The Transitional Justice and Foreign Policy Nexus', p. 385.
[16] ibid.
[17] Rumelili, '[Our] Age of Anxiety', p. 1033.
[18] Rumelili, *Conflict Resolution and Ontological Security*, p. 13.
[19] Karl Gustafsson, 'Why Is Anxiety's Positive Potential so Rarely Realised? Creativity and Change in International Politics' (2021) 24 Journal of International Relations and Development 1044, p. 1046.
[20] May cited in ibid.
[21] Gustafsson and Krickel-Choi, 'Returning to the Roots of Ontological Security', p. 889.

existing orders and inspire a need to address them.[22] The positive potential of anxiety, therefore, lies in bridging the gaps between expectations and reality that cause friction in our relationships with others and in our own identities.

Bridging these gaps requires facing anxiety rather than seeking to destroy it. Gustafsson, for instance, argues that the positive potential of anxiety is hardly ever realised because creative ideas can often appear threatening, whereas familiar ideas are easier to accept.[23] Translating this into the area of transitional justice practice, it can be envisaged that the practitioners working on new, creative ways to ensure 'Never Again' alongside or beyond the transitional justice project may find it challenging to have their ideas appreciated and accepted into the mainstream. As Gustafsson claims, 'getting used to the new' is a process whereby the new is not static but instead 'gradually adapted to bridge the cleavage between expectation and reality'.[24] Indeed, almost all practices I explore in this chapter are contested by certain audiences. Yet perhaps contestation is a part of the point if a debate, or even better a dialogue, emerges out of it. How do political communities who are so often told to fear another war act for a more meaningful 'Never Again'? What sort of practices do actors prioritise as beneficial to non-recurrence and adding to the successes of transitional justice or even undoing some of the harms it has caused? The following examples provide useful illustrations in response to these questions.

7.3 With (and beyond) Transitional Justice

In previous chapters, I have both critiqued the International Criminal Tribunal for the former Yugoslavia (ICTY) and domestic courts for their inability and inaptness to produce full historical accounts of the war and raised a concern about many attempts to revise the truth recovered by the ICTY that are in fact instances of historical revisionism and denialism harmful for any meaningful assurances of 'Never Again'. In this section, I propose that the way forward out of this deadlock may be through truth recovery which is appreciative of the fact-finding capabilities of the ICTY and domestic courts yet at the same time critical of their claimed values

[22] Bahar Rumelili, 'Introduction to the Special Issue Anxiety and Change in International Relations' (2022) 19 International Relations 1.

[23] Gustafsson, 'Why Is Anxiety's Positive Potential so Rarely Realised?', p. 1045.

[24] ibid, p. 1047.

of objectivity, neutrality, civilisation, and completeness. To illustrate what I mean by this, I provide a couple of examples of ongoing truth recovery practices that embrace the inherent multisiteness and contestedness of truth and channel them into spaces of memory and connectivity with the past. The practices do so in ways that complement judicial truths and do not challenge them on what is there, that is, the judgements, and the qualifications, but on what is *not there*, the people, the places, and the stories.

The ICTY archive and domestic court archives have served as a key legitimating foundation for various actors working on truth recovery and fact-finding for 'Never Again' in BiH and the wider region.[25] For many of these actors, the ICTY archive is always the starting point rather than the final outcome of truth recovery processes. Actors build upon contexts and issues already dealt with by international and domestic courts while referring to court records to stress the severity, pervasiveness, complexity and/or roots of the conflict, and protection against any accusations of revisionism.[26] Yet, the same actors embrace the idea that there are truths that courts have not yet told and probably never will be due to the temporal, procedural, and content limitations of judicial proceedings.

For example, the largest network of investigative journalists in former Yugoslavia, the Balkan Investigative Reporting Network (BIRN) has a transitional justice stream whereby they investigate and monitor a whole range of transitional justice events and developments. Their task is, in their view, finding and communicating facts, which contributes to the values of transitional justice such as non-recurrence. Through their reporting, republished by numerous media outlets across post-Yugoslav space, the collective seeks to fight against the loss of information over time and allowing 'propaganda to become the truth'.[27] The struggle is ultimately one against the current political climate of revisionism and denialism. For them, the ICTY archive is the biggest hub of 'established facts'.[28] When asked about dealing with the widespread historical revisionism and denialism, BIRN's programme coordinator explained, 'what we are really trying to do is stick to court-established facts. We stick to

[25] Maja Davidović, 'Reconciling Complexities of Time in Criminal Justice and Transitional Justice' (2021) 21 International Criminal Law Review 935.

[26] ibid.

[27] Interview with representative of the Balkan Investigative Research Network, 19 February 2020.

[28] ibid.

court-established facts, and court materials are things we refer to. The editorial control is rather strict when it comes to this question, and I think that is a very good thing'.[29]

To that end, in their documentation database, BIRN ensures that all entries are linked to either direct court judgements or other databases where judgements are available and translated. Occasionally, these are complemented by non-judicial sources such as private documentation initiatives by victims' families. 'However', the interlocutor added, 'sometimes it is simply necessary to find ways to report about matters that were never adjudicated before, where nobody was proclaimed criminally responsible'.[30] In that case, the reportage would not focus on individual criminal responsibility but rather invite interpretations from the audience by presenting evidence from numerous sources and victims' and survivors' testimonies.

This pattern of adhering to the ICTY archive to the extent possible but acknowledging that there are significant gaps in both truth and memory that need to be filled is very common among civil society actors working on transitional justice issues in BiH. Take, for instance, the Research and Documentation Centre (RDC), a BiH-based NGO whose largest fact-finding initiative called the *Bosnian Atlas of War Crimes* sought to document *all* human losses and atrocity crimes committed on the territory of BiH between 1992 and 1995. In the organisation's own words, the Atlas was borne out of the decade-long research conducted by the RDC and made available to the wider public 'to help historical remembrance based on available and trustworthy facts, change the social climate in which argumentative social dialogue is absent, and the climate of . . . politicisation of the recent past dominates' all seen as potentially leading to new conflicts.[31]

In the *Atlas*, court judgements are incorporated where applicable and the *Atlas* remains faithful to court qualification of wrongful acts. For example, the only atrocity classified as 'genocide' on the *Atlas* map is the one in Srebrenica, as per the ICTY's jurisprudence. Yet, the events and violations included in the *Atlas* expand beyond those adjudicated by the ICTY and domestic courts to document the destruction of religious

[29] ibid.
[30] ibid.
[31] Research and Documentation Center, *Bosnian War Crimes Atlas 92–95*, http://mnemos.ba/en/home/index accessed 27 April 2021.

objects and hospitals, as well as forced displacement, among many others.

The *Atlas* is therefore respectful of ICTY's legacy but fully aware of the limitations of such institutions. In our interview, the director of the RDC referred to the 'stereotypes built around the ICTY', suggesting it would reconcile and write history.[32] 'That is not its job', he explained. 'A court is an instrument of criminal responsibility'.[33] The *Atlas*, which uses Google Earth for visual presentation of the findings, is a well-known and used tool by the researchers of the BiH conflict. In addition, many survivors, and victims' families contribute to it by providing information, photographs of personal possessions of the victims, and so on, making the *Atlas* a platform that more closely reflects the lived experiences of violence and justice than criminal justice institutions can do in isolation. As a result, the *Atlas* has over 4,500 informative 'dots', that is, markings on the map of BiH containing information about the violation committed and lives lost. In the first month since it went live, it was visited by 16,000 people.[34]

Sometimes, truth recovery is done in more experiential ways where sites of atrocities are visited and numerous competing stories of the war are heard, and then judged together against any existing court judgements on the case or the area. Many of these practices have more direct educational components and take place within informal educational programmes such as training, summer schools, and fellowships. Offering only a limited scope for participation, these activities are designed at the intersection of education, memorialisation, art, and archives and aim to provide an immersive, comprehensive 'dealing with the past' experience to those who take part. Accepting court records as a source of knowledge about the conflict, these programmes by civil society organisations utilise court records as educational materials. Nevertheless, the education does not consist of only presenting court-established facts but also of further expanding on the criminal justice foundations. To do so, these actors tend to use more experiential tools to trigger empathetic feelings and emotional connections between those educated and those they need to be educated about.

32 Interview with representative of the Research and Documentation Center, 21 January 2020.

33 ibid.

34 ibid.

In the case of a group of activists from the Centre for Non-Violent Action (CNA) who mark the unmarked sites of atrocity across BiH, their markings are usually, but not always, buttressed by court rulings establishing that a war crime took place on that site, which gives legitimacy to their cause. The activists mark the unmarked sites of atrocities across the country physically by placing a commemorative plaque on-site with some basic information about what happened. 'Our foundation, something that is necessary and that we pay much attention to is that our information about the sites come from court judgements, which means that we spend a lot of time reading these judgements and extracting information out of them', their representative told me.[35] 'At the same time', they continued, 'we incorporate lived experience, information about certain atrocities being committed when, for example, somebody who participated in the war knows about certain locations, places'.[36] Almost all commemorated sites are buttressed by court judgements and when a court ruling is missing, the activists rely on, among others, personal memories of survivors or war veterans to gather information about what happened at a particular site before placing a commemorative plaque on location. The educational afterlives of such memorialisation are digital. The organisation uses photographs of the physical memorialisation and boosts them via platforms such as Facebook directly into local communities where the said atrocity happened. For the CNA, the photographs, followed by information about the atrocity, provide a means to challenge dominant discourses in the community which typically suppress and silence minority experiences.

For the Youth Initiative for Human Rights in BiH, this kind of practice creates spaces for competing stories of conflict to be heard directly from actors who played different roles in the same conflict areas.[37] 'Of course, court judgments are a part of our work, and we base all our work on facts . . . We simply hate working *ex-cathedra*', their programme coordinator said.[38] The participants of their summer school project, 'School of Distinct Memories', are exposed to different conflict actors who narrate their own interpretations of the conflict and then led into a discussion about these competing narratives. 'To create a connection between

[35] Interview with representative of the Center for Non-violent Action, 4 February 2020.
[36] ibid.
[37] Interview with representative of the Youth Initiative for Human Rights BiH, 11 December 2019.
[38] ibid.

participants and the topic we are dealing with, we typically visit the sites of atrocity. Lecturers are typically either journalists or researchers or victims' family members, survivors. For some, I wonder how come they are not in prison'.[39] Here, the coordinator was referring to a former commander of the HVO who volunteered as a lecturer in the School of Distinct Memories. The goal of the school, the coordinator said, was not to bring in lecturers who will talk about 'roses flourishing in war', that is, whitewash the war by focusing on heroism. There is no assumption that any of these lecturers' stories should be taken at their face value. Instead, the coordinator explained

> The whole approach to the school is that we are not creating a dialogue between lecturers and participants. We are not interested in that. Lecturers are there to voice their narrative, the narrative of their region, community, and what they think is true. Then it is up to the participants and us coordinators to have a dialogue based on our reflections and debates about what we just heard from these lecturers. The goal is for them [the participants] to question, research whatever they are interested in without creating a conflict.[40]

These narratives are then judged against each other and against any existing judgements on the case or the area by the participants to create a consensus among them about what happened. 'For example, this one lecturer in Herzegovina has a story about how Heliodrom[41] was a hotel. But then we also talk to a Heliodrom camp survivor later in the same day. That is the goal, to expose narratives'.[42]

These practices take place within spaces and discourses of contestation. When the *Atlas* was published, many rejected it as an authoritative source of information. The Centre's director reported that resistance came primarily from his own ethnic group [Bosniak] for coming up with a lower number of victims than was originally estimated in public discourse immediately after the conflict.[43] When it comes to marking

39 ibid.

40 ibid.

41 Heliodrom was a detention camp located south of Mostar where non-Croat prisoners were tortured, assaulted, and starved. The camp was run by members of the wartime Croat entity Herceg-Bosna, along with the HVO, some of whom, like Jadranko Prlić, were convicted by the ICTY for being part of a joint criminal enterprise set to ethnically cleanse certain areas of BiH through, among others, a network of detention camps which included Heliodrom.

42 Interview with Youth Initiative for Human Rights BiH.

43 Interview with Research and Documentation Center.

unmarked sites of atrocity, CNA reported that most plaques they place are removed on the same day, sometimes within the first thirty minutes. When I asked why this could be the case, their programme coordinator asserted 'simply because a vow of silence is nurtured in certain communities. It is here as a person, as a phenomenon in everyone. So, they remove [the plaques] . . . to forget, to not talk about it, to not threaten what is theirs . . . the "ethnic purity."'[44] Despite the pervasive challenges, the CNA's persistence and presence on the field have gained them politicians' support in certain communities and led to the permanent marking of a couple of sites of atrocity and organisation of inter-ethnic commemorative events, making small fractures in this vow of silence.

7.4 Despite Transitional Justice

In working towards a more meaningful 'Never Again' for BiH, certain actors acknowledge the possibility that the transitional justice project does more harm than good. What we get as a result of the existing bias towards the state as both the problem and the solution in transitional justice, one civil society activist posited, is a state of 'permanent truce'.[45] 'What is needed', they suggested, is to reconnect on the human level.[46] What if, instead of seeking to establish our trust towards the state, we sought to re-establish trust among people first and foremost?[47]

Here, specifically prominent interventions work on the culture of public speech. These activities which have to do with encouraging personal reckoning with past crimes and dialogue in public speech do not go against the transitional justice project but equally neither do they go with it. The transitional justice project is there, often kept separate from the truly 'hard' work that needs to be done to secure a future where sustainable peace is more likely. Here 'Never Again' becomes a primarily personal process, a personal journey through changing people's consciousness, outside or alongside schools, truth commissions, and fact-finding inquiries. 'Societal consciousness is most important. And such consciousness is divided in BiH', an MPI representative suggested.[48]

[44] Interview with the Center for Non-violent Action.
[45] ibid.
[46] ibid.
[47] ibid.
[48] Interview with representative of the Missing Persons Institute, 17 December 2019.

'Conflict is not over in our heads', a practitioner told me.[49] They further explained:

> We can always argue about things we disagree on in a cultured, nice way. But what is currently present in our culture of [public] speech . . . Look at our internet portals. It is horrible. People are scared when they read such comments. It doesn't matter if it is a Serb, Croat or Bosniak, there is so much hatred and animosity. We are now in a situation where we are trying to finish the war in our heads. A small number of people managed to do that; they overcame. A significant number of people, unfortunately, still have a problem with it.[50]

Diminishing historical revisionism and atrocity crimes denial to the point where they are no longer a major source of conflict repetition anxiety is an endeavour broader than the scope of the institutionalised form of transitional justice. It is holistic, inclusive of dissemination of the truth about the war, education, provision of mental health services, and listening to the 'other' and 'othered' in public speech. After all, it would require integrating the 'person' and 'personal' into dealing with the past, a form of 'dealing' often invisible in the global project of transitional justice beyond a few established perpetrators and established victims. To quote the same practitioner,

> [I]t is important to include our parliaments, our public lives, our televisions, our education [in the process of transitional justice]. We simply have to speak out, publicly and openly, testify about our problems, our troubles, about what we love and do not love, what we accept and do not accept . . . and the listener should not see that as a personal attack.[51]

'We can't make any progress [regarding guarantees of non-recurrence]', a participant from the ICMP added, 'as long as government officials here [in BiH] and the entire region do not come out and say "look, people, revealing the locations of mass graves anonymously, not publicly, is not a betrayal of your people. It is totally fine."'[52] What is missing to promote a more meaningful 'Never Again', it was held, is a political culture where there is the explicit willingness of the leading parties across the region to face their demons, accept the established facts, and reframe such actions from 'embarrassments' and 'betrayals' to heroic, responsible acts. The

49 Interview with Saliha Đuderija, 17 December 2019.
50 ibid.
51 ibid.
52 Interview with representative of the International Commission on Missing Persons, 6 December 2019.

process, my interlocutors told me, is an organic one, from the bottom-up and within. 'No pressure would yield results. It would be best to organically develop consciousness by having people sit down, realise what is a good option and implement their own initiative. Pressures from some Higher Representatives, Americans, Russians, the English, Germans … No'.[53]

Nurturing such a culture of public speech and willingness to engage more meaningfully and holistically with the processes of dealing with the past could be a prerequisite to diminish other sources of insecurities mentioned in earlier chapters, particularly as many of them are linked to trying to secure a collective 'victim' identity or the fear of the main perception of their collective identity being that of 'deviance'. To get to the point of establishing a nationwide truth recovery programme, educational reform, and eliminating strategic atrocity crimes denial, political elites need to create adequate political conditions for such action. It is to remember and mourn all victims of war together, building community and not reminding people of what sets them apart. It is to proactively create 'a society without divisions', a society where all diversities would be respected and messages of togetherness would transfer to the youth.[54] It is to enforce the democratic foundation of the society that respects the rule of law, equality, human rights, and freedoms.[55] Such activities may not contribute to the creation of an authoritative source of the truth, but they facilitate 'sentimental education' where similarities among people may begin to outweigh their differences.[56]

Examples of this form of activism are perhaps more plentiful than one realises. 'Positive stories do not make it to the front pages', one participant complained.[57] 'It is the negative news that sells, and positive stories are easily lost in the crowd'.[58] At the Catholic Relief Services Pro-Future project section, mentioned in the context of the exhibition *Lično*, activists have devised a 'Platform for Peace', a mechanism which obliges the signatory parties – over seventy-five local municipalities, parliaments, and universities – to a set of peacebuilding values and actions and establishes a collective, multi-ethnic, multi-entity vision, a *transethnic*

53 Interview with the Missing Persons Institute.
54 ibid.
55 Interview with the Research and Documentation Center.
56 See Payam Akhavan, *Reducing Genocide to Law: Definition, Meaning, and the Ultimate Crime* (Cambridge University Press 2012) p. 173.
57 Interviews with representatives of the PRO-FUTURE Project.
58 ibid.

space. To name a few manifestations of such action, municipality leaders from different ethnic groups/majority-ethnicity towns have organised joint commemorations for victims of all three ethnic groups, war veterans from all three key armies have shared with the BiH youth their insights into the dangers and pain of war, and religious communities have undertaken interfaith exchanges.[59] The project, above all, seeks to enhance an inclusive culture of public speech, where different ethnicities, collective memories, and circumstances are not obstacles to finding a collective vision for the future of BiH. 'The project starts with the assumption that other narratives should be heard. And that we should not necessarily be prevented from having a conversation with those different from us because of individual or collective historical and political narratives', the two activists held.[60] The action plan of the Platform for Peace also envisaged offering interfaith and interethnic support to the individuals and communities affected by hate speech or physical violence. The representatives of the project stated

> What we are doing is building empathy in people because if you go cold on what happened … These are alive, open wounds but if you go coldheartedly towards them with media content, or whatever sources … It is truly important that people hear out something different, something that can open their eyes. With this you wake up empathy and understanding, decreasing this war-mongering energy although … is there really some research that shows how many people are truly war 'ready'? In our collaboration with young people, students, young politicians … we are building a new political culture … by offering them a political academy about values … forgotten values. Empathy, humanity, care for the other and the different.[61]

Through such a process- and value-oriented practice, the activists seek not to measure but to *create*, unlike the architects of the institutional reforms did in the early transitional years. 'It is crucial that whatever we put our energy and knowledge into, we *create resilience*. This is perhaps closest to the term you are using, non-recurrence', the activists told me.[62] Another activist from the CNA spoke of the *creation of trust* among individuals and communities to prevent conflict repetition. Their organisation works with war veterans, as people with lived experience of

[59] ibid.
[60] ibid.
[61] ibid.
[62] ibid.

fighting. 'Nobody knows better than them what it means to fight in a war and when a person like that chooses non-recurrence, and furthermore works on prevention of conflict repetition, then this is the right path to follow', the activist told me.[63] Veterans, often as many as thirty or forty of them, from formerly belligerent parties within BiH but also from Serbia, visit commemorations and public events together with the CNA. This creates 'a different picture', the activist posited, 'one of trust'.[64]

These processes are also deeply contested. Observing neighbouring Serbia, for instance, intense contestation over how key actors of the war are framed can be detected. Serbian civil society has for a long time been well-organised and outspoken against the atrocities committed by the Serbian government, both current and preceding ones, and Belgrade continues to host some of the region's key transitional-justice-oriented civil society organisations such as the Humanitarian Law Centre, Women in Black, and the Youth Initiative for Human Rights. As of lately, out of necessity, the efforts of many of these activists have been directed towards identifying and removing commemorations of Ratko Mladić in public spaces around the country. Ratko Mladić, who, to remind the reader, was a general of the Republika Srpska Army during the war and the commander in charge of 'delivering' the Srebrenica genocide, has over the years been shaped and integrated into Serbian collective memory as a heroic figure, his sacrifice only buttressed by the recent ICTY genocide conviction. One can hardly walk around Belgrade without noticing at least one mural or graffiti dedicated to Mladić, and many other cities and towns in Serbia are no exception.

Such a way of commemorating and celebrating a convicted genocidaire culminated in civil tensions in Belgrade in late 2021. A large mural of Ratko Mladić with the inscription 'General, we thank your mother' was painted on the wall of a residential building. On the International Day of Fighting Fascism, activists attempted to remove the mural, but their gathering was prohibited by the police. This resulted in activists' attempts to destroy the mural with paint and eggs during which several activists were arrested, and the police continued to protect the mural. Such events led to further protests at the location, with people protesting activists' arrest and state protection of the mural. Tensions arose between

[63] Interview with the Center for Non-violent Action.
[64] ibid.

the activists and small groups of counter-protestors defending the wall. Video footage of the clashes between the two factions of the public, as reported by Radio Free Europe, shows protestors shouting, 'The wall will fall!', as the counter-protestors shouted, 'There was no genocide!'[65] The issue being negotiated in these communities' different individual and collective memories is therefore not only the involvement of Ratko Mladić in the Srebrenica genocide or the war overall but also the overall qualification of the atrocities committed in Srebrenica. As such, the clashes manifest both genocide denial and its challengers at work.

While the right-wing counter-protestors organised their own gatherings of support for Mladić and furthermore guarded the mural almost every day, the local authorities eventually agreed to remove the mural. Yet, hundreds of similar images of and messages to Ratko Mladić exist around the country. In Belgrade, activists organised to report known murals and graffiti to the city authorities, demanding that they are removed but received no response. This is why the Youth Initiative for Human Rights also turned to 'the human level' in September 2022. Named 'Da istina više ne kasni' or 'Lest truth is late again', the Initiative's campaign to map the murals and graffiti dedicated to Ratko Mladić across Serbia asked citizens to submit photos and locations of the commemorations. The campaign is aimed at demonstrating the true scale of glorification of war criminals and atrocities in Serbia to the public as well as local authorities in charge of public spaces. More than 300 murals and graffiti dedicated to Ratko Mladić have been identified so far, most of them located in Belgrade.[66] In the organisation's own words, the campaign is

> a response to the institutions' refusal to do their job and is a part of the fight for the truth which is directed towards making our country respectful. The campaign is inspired by the fight for a future without armed conflict, which will only be possible by facing war legacies and having a conversation about established facts, as well as deconstructing nationalistic and chauvinistic narratives which celebrate war criminals.[67]

[65] Nevena Bogdanovic, Predrag Urosevic, and Andy Heil, 'Graffiti War: Battle in the Streets over Ratko Mladic Mural' (*Radio Free Europe*, 10 November 2021) www.rferl.org/a/serbia-mladic-mural-protests/31555357.html accessed 7 December 2021.

[66] Beta, 'YIHR Demands Removal of Mladic Murals across Serbia' (*N1Info*, 13 March 2023) https://shorturl.at/cdryz accessed 9 August 2023.

[67] YIHR Serbia, 'Kampanja mapiranja murala i grafita: "Da istina više ne kasni"' (*YIHR*, n.d.) www.yihr.rs/bhs/kampanja-mapiranja-murala-i-grafita-da-istina-vise-ne-kasni/ accessed 9 August 2023.

The campaign, like other projects and practices described in this section, seeks to put people in conversation about dealing with the past, both nationally and regionally. They are reactive to the visible consequences of the global project of transitional justice such as the ontological insecurities the court convictions have boosted for both states and ethnic communities. These activists' practices challenge the common, legal form of guarantees of non-recurrence by suggesting that the state and their institutions continue to be sources of insecurity despite their reforms. They go beyond and despite (but not against) the institutionalised forms of transitional justice by emphasising values previously neglected by the global project or otherwise assigned to norms and institutions which cannot organically 'produce' such values, such as international criminal tribunals. Finally, to play their role in ensuring non-recurrence of conflict, the actors focus on the *creation* of skills, networks, and a sense of ownership that can foster people's sense of security in their everyday lives and collective senses of self by making them a part – and not mere recipients – of the process.

7.5 Non-recurrence as Work

These identified practices for 'Never Again' with and despite transitional justice show us that, for people in a post-conflict society, ensuring 'Never Again' means getting comfortable with the utterly uncomfortable matters and committing to the seemingly never-ending *work* of listening and questioning. It means being open to considering how past violence has shaped one's own present and even asking some fundamental questions about the self – both individual and collective. Even though individuals are required to put in the work, these stories of meaningful work towards 'Never Again' are first and foremost stories about community, interdependence, boundness, and emotions. Because divisions in the BiH society are sustained by both the formal peace process and communal silences in the everyday, conversing about the past comes out as a common thread across the different practices highlighted by practitioners as meaningful. What the practices I described in previous sections do is encourage dialogue about competing narratives and prioritise discussions over debates. There is an acknowledgement of the plurality of narratives, and, using multiple sources, some of these actors seek to invite multiple interpretations from the audience. The goal is to reach some sort of convergence of narratives, but not through imposition of an authoritative source of such a narrative nor through acceptance of historical revisionism. Instead, the convergence is continuously created and negotiated the more people question and unpack the dominant narrative(s).

Practices centred on communal, dialogical, and personal 'dealings' with the past do not measure quantifiable outcomes to assess whether the society is any closer to 'Never Again'. Instead, they seek to create; their desired outcome is creation. This includes the creation of skills such as critical thinking, the creation of emotional connections and empathy with the other and othered, creation of shared experiences in transethnic spaces, and the creation of trust in one another to take care of the shared future. It is not an erasure of differences nor pretending that ethnicity-based identities are not as strong as ever in BiH. It is instead about coming to the full realisation that both the past and the future are shared across ethnic groups and that the real enemy of peace lies elsewhere.

Ultimately, what these practices do is integrate the human, personal, and emotional back into the processes of dealing with the past. The transitional justice project is in many ways centred on the individual but in a rather depersonalised manner. I am here describing actions beyond the victim versus perpetrator binary, beyond their roles in the judicial process, and beyond being identified as threats to sustainable peace. This form of integration provides an acknowledgement that reckoning is individual as well as collective and that at both levels it is shared. When we focus on what is going well in BiH in addition to everything that has gone poorly, we see ways of understanding the future and peace that the transitional justice project, as it was practised in BiH, could not have accommodated. This outlook uncovers that despite lots of animosities and divisions, there is still lots of love, care, and community in these processes of dealing with the past.[68]

Looking at what sort of practices people find meaningful for 'Never Again' demonstrates that the scope of the imperative to prevent renewed conflict is much broader than the scope of the project of transitional justice. These practices of 'Never Again' put forward a different mode of being to that of neoliberal legalism. Unlike in human rights law and much of transitional justice, non-recurrence is detached from the state and its institutions as practitioners pay no faithful allegiance for the state to be transformed and enact necessary changes. But perhaps more importantly, non-recurrence is here constructed as a form of *work*, rather than an actionable goal; an open-ended, fluid process whose completion

[68] Krystalli and Schulz, 'Taking Love and Care Seriously'.

date is unknown and which relies on other people joining the workforce. It is not a stress- or contestation-free or necessarily peaceful form of labour, but it is the work itself that counts and eases some of the anxieties which suggest, hopefully falsely, that the future can only be as grim as or worse than the past. Dealing with the past as everyone's personal matter, as various examples in this chapter show, is a way for individuals and communities to reclaim ownership over their own pasts and remake their world.

7.6 In Place of a Conclusion: Against Transitional Justice?

This chapter was an exercise in observing creative practices aimed at ensuring a long-lasting 'Never Again' in BiH in the everyday. Practices and practitioners discussed in this chapter are, in most cases, openly critical of the transitional justice project, but at the same time acknowledge its merits or utilise, to their own advantage, its tools. It was not my intent to propose how the project could be reformed to better align with the ideas and needs of 'Never Again', yet this chapter, in particular, might suggest that I am, after all, a reformist. This is a debate I am happy to entertain in the concluding chapter. Here, instead of a conclusion, I wish to undertake another thought exercise much closer to what I believe about the transitional justice project on most days. It is possible, and maybe even probable, that the global transitional justice project cannot be reformed for it must be abolished. It is possible, and maybe even probable, that the transitional justice project is, with its characteristics and embeddedness in deeper structures, violent, discriminatory, and harmful to the prevention of renewed conflicts. That, because it has its survival needs, shown here in this book to be harmful to 'Never Again', the project should no longer exist. One scenario is that the international community does away with the imperative of 'dealing' with the past through a set of norms, laws, and institutions today known as belonging to some sort of 'transitional justice' package. In a way, it would mean to accept that different political communities' pasts cannot be governed.

There are vibrant conversations about the possibility of rejecting the global project of transitional justice as a form of governance over our pasts in post- and decolonial transitional justice scholarship. Already in 2012, Vielle put forward a provocation for transitional justice scholars, asking if transitional justice is, in fact, a colonising field on the basis of the overt tendencies of its legalistic paradigm to silence other ways of knowing.[69] Moyo, for instance, challenges the perceived necessity and inevitability of transitional justice mechanisms for post-colonial states to be able to establish credibility and legitimacy.[70] She notes the civilising impulses of transitional justice as well as international law, which underpins it, and calls for decolonisation of these fields.[71] In a similar vein, Park argues that transitional justice as a project is incapable of confronting settler colonialism due to its liberal teleology and suggests that only a radicalised transitional justice which, among others, abandons such teleology and challenges the legitimacy of the settler state could aid decolonisation.[72] Sesay's work goes further, inviting us to consider whether the transitional justice project which aims to maintain a certain normative and social order may in fact be fully irreconcilable with the needs and urgencies of decolonisation as a process which would require dismantling existing systems of doing and knowing.[73] Somewhat similar to the examples in this chapter, others yet have proposed that the power is not only in the hands of the structure, showing how the so-called subjects of the global project of transitional justice have unpacked and contextualised the proposed model to reclaim the processes of dealing with the past as their own, as a form of resistance.[74]

How can this proposal be supported? Duthie proposes that even if we assume that transitional justice is developed 'with the best of intentions', which I do not, it is a deeply contested and political process that inevitably triggers 'unexpected outcomes'.[75] He further argues that this is because of 'frictions' between global transitional justice mechanisms and local realities, whether that is problems of translation of universal standards or interactions between global and local understandings of certain values or

[69] Stephanie Vielle, 'Transitional Justice: A Colonizing Field?' (2012) 4 Amsterdam Law Forum 58.

[70] Khanyisela Moyo, *Postcolonial Transitional Justice: Zimbabwe and Beyond* (Routledge 2020).

[71] ibid.

[72] Augustine SJ Park, 'Settler Colonialism, Decolonization and Radicalizing Transitional Justice' (2020) 14 International Journal of Transitional Justice 260.

[73] Mohamed Sesay, 'Decolonization of Postcolonial Africa: A Structural Justice Project More Radical Than Transitional Justice' (2022) 16 International Journal of Transitional Justice 254.

[74] Noha Aboueldahab, 'Transitional Justice as Repression and Resistance: Practices in the Arab World' (2023) 21 Journal of International Criminal Justice 701.

[75] Roger Duthie, 'Afterword: The Consequences of Transitional Justice in Particular Contexts' in Alexander Laban Hinton (ed.), *Transitional Justice: Global Mechanisms and Local Realities after Genocide and Mass Violence* (Rutgers University Press 2010) p. 249.

categories of dealing with the past.[76] In particular, Duthie provides examples of spaces where the project's truth recovery mission interacts with numerous conflict narratives. The claim that transitional justice produces contestation and friction can be used both in defence of the project and against it. That the project triggers people to debate and challenge certain narratives of the past can be part and parcel of the process of creating a consensus or creating history, for that matter. Debating, after all, is better than silence or oppression of narratives. But the problems of the transitional justice project are much broader than that there is multiplicity and complexity of truths about the past. In the context of truth recovery, as this book has shown, the problem lies in both creating and sustaining authoritative sources of truth. In both of these processes, the transitional justice project harms those who are supposed to benefit from it.

In defence of the transitional justice project, despite 'unintended consequences', Duthie puts forward two claims. First, such consequences should be expected, and they can to some extent be mitigated; second, our expectations of transitional justice 'should be modest and realistic' to start with.[77] It is with claims such as these that the myth of benevolence of the transitional justice project persists. 'If the project means well, then it must be good' is a shallow argument and largely what prevents us from imagining a future without, say, international criminal tribunals as a form of governance. When faults are detected, which have been numerous times with the ICTY and the International Criminal Tribunal for Rwanda, we – the global society of the civilised – should inspire to make sure that the future tribunals are better is the logic of such myth of benevolence. Yet we must not dare propose that perhaps tribunals are ill-suited for justice-seeking efforts in whatever new context the tribunal model has travelled to, because that would mean that we are against justice. It is the conflation of positive values most people aspire to in post-conflict settings (justice, truth, and non-recurrence) with the mechanisms of transitional justice (tribunals, commissions, and institutional reform) that is both the biggest success of the transitional justice project and one of its most devastating, and I would argue intended consequences.

To effectively imagine a future without the project of transitional justice, it would be useful to look into ways of dealing with the past that defy the contours of the project. Zinaida Miller, for instance, proposes

[76] ibid, p. 250.
[77] ibid, pp. 252–3.

that 'the institutionalisation and naturalisation of transitional justice work have helped to produce a dominant conception of the relationship between time and justice', a process she calls temporal governance.[78] It is possible to resist the linear trajectory of temporal governance whereby we move from the past to the present to the future linearly and whereby the transitional justice moment represents 'a rupture' between the past and the present.[79] Miller explores this possibility, through numerous examples of dealing with colonial pasts, to *undo*, and not merely *rethink*, colonial temporalities.[80] For instance, Miller points to the direction of movements such as Black Lives Matter which focuses on continuities between the past and present and direct links between slavery and present injustice and inequality, challenging the central idea of transitional justice that atrocities one is dealing with belong in the past.[81]

Movements like these shift the focus away from the truth of the past to the truths of the past *and* the present, from individual perpetrators to multigenerational responsibility, and from repairing the wrong to that which cannot be repaired. They deal with the past against the very key premises of the transitional justice project, sometimes without awareness or care for the project itself, and sometimes with a conviction that the transitional justice project sits, rather comfortably, 'on a spectrum of colonial bureaucratic violence'.[82] To defy the contours of the transitional justice project would therefore mean not to forget or silence the past, but rather to reclaim it 'in a critical, counter-linear way'.[83] Similarly to many of the practices I was describing earlier in the chapter, escaping the contours of the transitional justice project very much ends up being about reclaiming one's ownership of their own past, both individual and collective. It is with these thoughts in mind that I now proceed to the concluding chapter of this book where I further entertain the idea of reform, or perhaps rather, a rebirth of transitional justice as a guiding light of the ungovernable dealings with the past. Where are we at the moment and what does the future hold for prevention of conflict repetition and transitional justice, together or apart?

[78] Zinaida Miller, 'Temporal Governance: The Times of Transitional Justice' (2021) 21 International Criminal Law Review 848, p. 850.
[79] Davidović, 'Reconciling Complexities of Time'.
[80] Miller, 'Temporal Governance', p. 872.
[81] ibid, p. 873.
[82] Jaymelee J Kim, 'Perspectives from the Ground' (2018) 4 Conflict and Society 116, p. 116.
[83] Rose Parfitt cited in Miller, 'Temporal Governance', p. 872.

8

Conclusion

The Never-Ending Promise

Bosnia and Herzegovina (BiH) is but one post-conflict country affected by some of the elements of the global transitional justice project since the 1990s. As I am writing the conclusion to this book in late 2023, Russia's war against Ukraine is still raging with no indications of when or how it may end. Yet, since the very early stages of Russia's full invasion of Ukraine, the Western international community has been committed to establishing a special jurisdiction tribunal of some kind, hybrid more likely than international, to compensate for the International Criminal Court's gaps in jurisdiction with respect to Russia.[1] New truth commissions have been launched in places such as Norway and Sweden;[2] the United Nations Secretary-General has published a new guidance note on transitional justice.[3] The transitional justice project is here to stay.

What kind of transitional justice is the Western international community exporting to more and more areas across the world? In this book, I have focused on three concrete characteristics of the transitional justice project that, when at work, can produce and perpetuate anxieties around renewed conflict and move post-conflict societies further away from meaningful assurances of non-recurrence. I have proposed that transitional justice should be considered as an institution-based, normatively hierarchical, and civilisational project. The three characteristics can of

1 See, for instance, European Commission, *Statement by President von der Leyen on the Establishment of the International Centre for the Prosecution of Crimes of Aggression against Ukraine*, https://ec.europa.eu/commission/presscorner/detail/en/statement_23_1363 accessed 28 November 2023.

2 Astrid Nonbo Andersen, Astri Dankertsen, and Otso Kortekangas, 'Will Norway's Truth and Reconciliation Process Bring Change?'(*Justice Info*, 29 August 2023) www.justiceinfo.net/en/120849-norway-truth-reconciliation-process-change.html accessed 28 November 2023; David Mac Dougall, 'Sweden Ordered to Apologise to Tornedalian Minority Community for Historical Abuses' (*Euronews*, 16 November 2023) https://shorturl.at/ORW27 accessed 28 November 2023.

3 United Nations Secretary-General, *Guidance Note of the Secretary General on Transitional Justice: A Strategic Tool for People, Prevention and Peace* (United Nations 2023).

course manifest together in a single practice, as this book is shown. In the case of BiH, the International Criminal Tribunal for the former Yugoslavia has been the primary institution ensuring the longevity of the transitional justice project, and a primary operator of the anti-impunity norm, positioned as superior to other norms found in the transitional justice family of norms. Simultaneously, as seen, for instance in the area of education, the International Criminal Tribunal for the former Yugoslavia has been positioned as a not merely objective but rather civilisational tool of history teaching, the *correct* way to create and disseminate history of the former Yugoslavia's wars to the former Yugoslav population, seemingly devoid of the perceived fallacies of local histories. This is an example of how these core characteristics of the transitional justice project operate in practice. Instead of summarising other examples any further, I would like to discuss what these characteristics mean for new and future transitional justice projects and the everyday practices of 'Never Again'.

First, as a structure that orders behaviours, separating those desirable from the less desirable ones, transitional justice needs institutions to survive. Out of the three characteristics I focused my analysis on, this one is the least controversial and possibly the least problematic. Institutions can be defenders of human rights as well as oppressors of those same rights. What this means in the context of non-recurrence, however, is that institutions of transitional justice, primarily courts but also truth commissions and other ad hoc mechanisms and task forces established to oversee different forms of reform of domestic institutions, make sense of their existence, mandates, and resources in relation to the goal of ensuring that mass violations of human rights are not repeated. That these institutions alone cannot provide meaningful assurances of non-recurrence is a moot point after everything the chapters on BiH have shown. They can, however, be an important, or even necessary start, securing what we have come to know as negative peace, a sheer absence of violence, which some scholars may also understand to mean guarantees of non-recurrence. The problems start to arise with the passage of time, as both the transitional justice project and other non-institutional forms of 'dealing with the past' develop. A transitional justice project that is not compatible with the imperative to ensuring 'Never Again' does not listen to any ongoing, organically grown dealings with the past happening alongside and despite it and adjust. Instead, it monopolises 'dealing with the past' as a practice in defence of its legitimacy and, ultimately, legacy. This is something, I hope, both scholars and practitioners of transitional justice for the present and the future will be able to recognise.

Second, my claim that transitional justice is a normatively hierarchical project is based on a single case study, and for this, it may be challenged. In relation to this claim in particular, BiH appears as a rather atypical case, considering that most states recipients of the transitional justice project are not subject to a UNSC-established international criminal tribunal. Hence the argument may hold in contexts where there are international or hybrid tribunals, which are increasing in numbers, but not others. Still, looking at other cases of transitional justice over time, it becomes clear that normative hierarchies creep in elsewhere, even in contexts where the adopted model of transitional justice is not centred on criminal justice and instead is more comprehensive or even void of criminal justice. In a 2023 article, Jinú Carvajalino and I show how the same normative hierarchy has been replicated in Colombia, a state often praised for doing transitional justice in a different, much more holistic way.[4] In Colombia, the government has made sustained efforts to break away from a model focused on criminal accountability, a decision visible in the comprehensive 2016 peace agreement between the government and FARC-EP. The 2016 peace accord established a judicial institution known as the Special Jurisdiction for Peace, as well as non-judicial institutions such as the Truth, Coexistence and Non-Repetition Commission. However, despite being in early stages, this process shows that a range of internal and external actors such as the ICC Office of the Prosecutor and different INGOs bring criminal accountability to the centre stage of transitional justice discussions in this country, not only giving this value some sort of priority over other values but also perceiving the Special Jurisdiction for Peace as a mechanism suitable for fulfilling this and a range of other values such as truth recovery and, ultimately, non-recurrence.[5]

This argument does not extend only to those models of transitional justice where there is a criminal tribunal established especially to deal with past violence. In South Africa, whose transitional justice model was led by a TRC instead of criminal trials, a normative hierarchy also emerged, marginalising certain values and behaviours constitutive to the transitional justice project over others. For instance, Renner writes

[4] Jinú Carvajalino and Maja Davidović, 'Escaping or Reinforcing Hierarchies? Norm Relations in Transitional Justice' (2023) 25 International Studies Review 1.

[5] ibid, pp. 15–16.

how the early calls for punitive criminal justice in the transitional South Africa were framed as 'bad' for representing values of revenge and thus contrary to the reconciliation discourse the TRC was promoting.[6] On the other hand, the South African TRC, as the primary operator of transitional justice in this country, was put forward as inherently 'good' and necessary to achieve not only truth recovery but also justice.

What this means for new and future transitional justice contexts and the promise of 'Never Again' is that a holistic, multi-pillar transitional justice, which international policymakers promise and promote, is incredibly difficult, if not impossible to undertake. With that, the ideas promoted by the likes of the UN Special Rapporteur for transitional justice of guarantees of non-recurrence as a 'function' cutting across all pillars of transitional justice, something that all tools of transitional justice ought to contribute to, are unattainable. These normative hierarchies I speak of are sustained by domestic and international influences. Domestically, populist politicians might advocate for more criminal accountability, harsher prison sentences, and other similar measures that ought to symbolise control over deviance. Internationally, the UN, the ICC, and other governmental and non-governmental organisations might, like they did in South Africa, question the legitimacy of transitional justice models that are not criminal justice 'heavy' for not aligning with international legal standards, or for not being 'tested before an international human rights body'.[7]

Lastly, my proposal that transitional justice is an inherently civilisational project should be the one, I hope, to invite most further research, as any discussions about the project's reform would depend on whether civilisational projects can ever not be civilisational and therefore ever not be violent. Both its institutions and normative hierarchies are markers of how civilisational the project is, demonstrating also its adaptability across contexts, histories, and hopes for the future.[8] The transitional justice project is not civilisational simply for suggesting that problematic pasts should be dealt with, or even in its proposal that some pasts are more problematic than others. Instead, the civilisational coat of the transitional

[6] Judith Renner, *Discourse, Normative Change and the Quest for Reconciliation in Global Politics* (Manchester University Press 2017).

[7] Office of the United Nations High Commissioner for Human Rights, *Rule-of-Law Tools for Post-conflict States: Amnesties* (United Nations 2009) p. 33.

[8] Ntina Tzouvala, *Capitalism as Civilisation: A History of International Law* (Cambridge University Press 2020).

justice project, this book demonstrates, is visible in the language of its multiple servants directed towards the subjects of transitional justice, all suggesting that there are correct, inherently good ways and those bad, barbaric even, ways of dealing with these problematic pasts. This binary needs to be sustained for the sake of the international order,[9] and its structures. Importantly, when those 'good ways' turn out to be good, the servants of transitional justice are there to take the credit for it, but, crucially, when they lead to the 'bad ways' of dealing with the past, there is no sense of responsibility by those same servants.

'Civilisation' here offers a frame for understanding both the successes and failures of transitional justice. Its successes are, of course, signs of progress, nearly always linear, from a bad place to a good place, for a problematic past to a peaceful future.[10] Yet the omissions of transitional justice, those presents that remain violent or futures that turn into unpredictable, uncertain presents, are often, I have argued in this book, internalised by the subjects of transitional justice as problems of the collective 'uncivilised' self. A lot of guilt and worry comes out of this perception that one's democratic leaders are doing something so deeply uncivilised, after already embarrassing their people and 'staining' their collective identities by waging wars and genocides and not being able, so it seemed, to take care of justice. This belief is not a banal problem. It is a classification that deepens the divides of our world between 'civilised' and 'uncivilised'; 'normal' and 'deviant'; 'moral beacons' and 'barbarians'. What this classification so skilfully hides is that behind the veil of 'civilised' lie numerous problematic behaviours, including denials of genocides, or people and harms previously erased and ignored. Therefore, atrocity crimes denial in BiH, Croatia, and Serbia are seriously problematic, but they are not unique, native, or inherent to this region and its people. If the project of transitional justice was able to communicate this, it may in fact lose its sense of self and its sense of purpose, as it currently has no to very little place in established democracies that once had empires, such as the United Kingdom which otherwise continue to engage in denial, trivialisation, or minimisation of their imperial

9 Rebecca Adler-Nissen, 'Stigma Management in International Relations: Transgressive Identities, Norms, and Order in International Society' (2014) 68 International Organization 143.

10 Zinaida Miller, 'Temporal Governance: The Times of Transitional Justice' (2021) 21 International Criminal Law Review 848.

atrocities.[11] This shows, at least in BiH, that as much as transitional justice can empower the victims about their individual cases, it can collectively shame groups or entire societies into thinking that they are incapable of taking care of their pasts, when in fact much of their ownership was taken away by the very same project. What this means for 'Never Again' is that meaningful assurances of non-recurrence cannot exist in societies or regions classified on the basis of collective shame and internalised sense of lack of worth to be admitted into the club of those who do things the correct way.

Establishing the core characteristics of transitional justice has served to put in conversation the global imperative of dealing with problematic pasts with the global imperative of preventing repetition of mass atrocities. The idea of preventing renewed hostilities and atrocities in places scarred by them is a powerful one. Packaged and presented in the famous 'Never Again' promise, this idea has arguably been one of the most powerful ideas in the human rights-led post-World War II era. It signals collective commitment to not only peace and international law but also human rights, recognising that there are horrors humans are capable of to which no human should be subjected. It also signals that mass atrocities are likely to be repeated, sooner or later, if no work is done to prevent them. This symbolism was only fortified by the post-World War II world which has grown ever more interconnected and interdependent, and where wars do not need to be international to be of global concern or of global impact.

In the period between the end of World War II and today, 'Never Again' transformed from a mere promise to an actionable goal, something that can be achieved, or as close as possible to it, with certain tools. This is where the transitional justice project has come into play, as a rather standardised, easily exportable project with numerous commonly used tools in its repertoire. In the transitional justice laboratories in the late 1980s and 1990s, there were no questions about whether the actionable goal and the proposed tools were at all compatible. Likewise, there were other potential tools that the transitional justice project could have added to its repertoire in those early days, such as, for instance, education reforms, as initially proposed by the Chilean TRC this book discussed in Chapter 1, or, for instance, people's unofficial and revolutionary tribunals

[11] Caroline Elkins, *Legacy of Violence* (Penguin 2023); Tom Lawson, *The Last Man: A British Genocide in Tasmania* (Bloomsbury 2015).

Zunino talks about in his prehistory of transitional justice.[12] For reasons now obvious, the transitional justice project ended up looking the way it looks today, deeply rooted in neoliberalism and legalism. We know that the pillars of transitional justice, and more notably their crown mechanisms, are not accidental but are products of very concrete historical circumstances of the 1990s when 'an autonomous discourse of transitional justice' developed based on paradigmatic contexts such as Argentina, South Africa, and the Eastern European transitions.[13] The rest, where 'the state was not the protagonist', such as education or people's tribunals, remained outside of transitional justice as a project because they did not quite fit with its characteristics.[14]

Among transitional justice reformists, scholarly debates will continue to be had about 'what works', and which tool is better or more effective in achieving which goal, including prevention of conflict repetition. My hope is that these conversations will show more appreciation for the idea that nothing might work and consideration of how and why the transitional justice interventions can perpetuate some of the grievances and animosities that led people to believe that another conflict is not only possible, but probable. How different institutions and tools of transitional justice can monopolise truth recovery processes, promote civilisational tropes, deepen ethnic segregation, discourage dialogue, and ignore non-institutionalised justice claims have all been discussed in this book, illustrating with clear examples from practice what the consequences are and how they are linked with people's anxieties around potential renewed conflict. This book has defined a path, through its adoption of an ontological security lens, for exploring this idea further in contexts similar to as well as uniquely distinct from BiH.

Now, onto prevention of conflict non-recurrence more concretely. What can BiH, as an early experiment in the transitional justice laboratory, teach scholars, practitioners, and policymakers about prevention of renewed conflict both during and after transitional justice interventions, and possibly, even without? To start with, lived experiences in BiH show us that the realities of 'Never Again' after a conflict are much broader than the realities of the transitional justice project. Of course they intersect and of course the transitional justice project continues to shape

[12] Marcos Zunino, *Justice Framed: A Genealogy of Transitional Justice* (Cambridge University Press 2019).

[13] ibid, p. 229.

[14] ibid, p. 235.

the perceptions and practices of non-recurrence, as the book has established. Yet, when we look at the very ideas of how 'Never Again' can be achieved, as discussed in Chapter 7 of the book, we see that at their core are mobilisation of people and resources far stronger, wider, and deeper than any political project, including transitional justice.

After all, these lived experiences of non-recurrence demonstrate that it is a process, not a project, whose expiration date my interlocutors and I never really discussed. It does not exist, or at least it is not perceivable in our lifetimes. When people spoke to me about 'Never Again', it was always with an outlook stretching beyond the lives of own physical lives. Of course, at times it is about very concrete, urgently needed changes in the law or policy, as is, for instance, in the case of criminalising genocide denial. However, many times it is also about the future generations, our children and their children, about some distant future of which we won't be a part but on which we will have a defining impact. Instead of being solely in your institutions or in your newspapers, 'Never Again' is everywhere – in your homes, schools, work, friendships, and romantic relationships. This is what it is meant by *non-recurrence as work* all members of society are expected to undertake at some level, at some point, in some form. Chapter 7 has alluded to the myriad of ways in which this is currently occurring in Bosnia and Herzegovina, and other ways in which different actors actively dreaming of non-recurrence aspire for it to feel present, whether that's through creating transethnic spaces, spending time in transethnic spaces, questioning those taken-for-granted truths, remaining curious and asking uncomfortable or seemingly unwanted questions, or simply growing love and understanding for those othered. This is how peace might in fact win over war. These processes of working towards 'Never Again', even when the end of the process is unimaginable or simply a faint vision of the world after us, will look different in different contexts. What will be at the core of these processes, at least in my assessment, is the practices of non-recurrence are not merely about changing the status quo ante, the state of being which led to the war and to the atrocities, as per international law and transitional justice. It is in fact, the case of BiH has shown, about the status quo post-post-conflict peacebuilding, state building, and transitional justice. It is about identifying how these processes have changed society for the better and for the worse, and facing the anxieties they may have worsened or altogether produced anew.

How, if at all, can the transitional justice project support, instead of obstructing, these practices of 'Never Again'? As explained before, these specific understandings of 'Never Again' in and for BiH did not develop in isolation from the transitional justice project but in response to it. The two global imperatives are therefore still very much linked, and as evidenced here, some of the fruits of transitional justice labour such as court archives are crucial for many civil society organisations' organising for a more meaningful and durable peace, serving as a factual as well as legitimating foundation.

Yet, going further to imagine what the project of transitional justice could be, there is a burning need for the project to be interested in how political communities are created and sustained because that is where ontological security is often found. This is a double-edged sword. Browning, for instance, proposes that one of the key processes by which individuals cope with anxieties and reclaim their sense of ontological security is through vicariously identifying with broader communities, meaning 'living through others' experiences and achievements'.[15] Identification with communities can therefore mean identifying with a national or ethnic group, like often has been the case in BiH, whereby the collective self becomes vulnerable to anxieties about the future of the collective's being, fostering new anxieties. But communities are not static and can be created from scratch in response to violence and harm and offer a space to process the anxieties stemming from belonging to other, more secure and rigid communities. Because they tend to be personal, the practices of non-recurrence described in Chapter 7 put people in a position where they face their anxieties – anxiety about whether there will be another war, anxiety about knowing about the past war and how horrendous its atrocities were, and anxiety about making the war feel 'real' by getting to know the people behind numbers and photographs. Oneself is in touch with the past, the present, and the future and all the contexts in which various selves are embedded in. A transitional justice not interested in these internal – as well as external – dynamics shaping ontological (in)securities of its presumed beneficiaries will always remain a civilisational transitional justice that seeks to impose ideas and behaviours rather than contribute to the beneficiaries' making sense of ideas and behaviours in post-conflict spaces.

To be a guiding light rather than the governor of collective efforts towards non-recurrence, the transitional justice project would need to maximise on its existing good sides and scale down on the violence.

[15] Christopher S Browning, '"Je suis en terrasse": Political Violence, Civilizational Politics and the Everyday Courage to Be' (2017) 39 Political Psychology 243, p. 251.

To do so, it needs to become interested in how it can support the work of non-recurrence and not treat it as a goal only itself can fulfil. Many scholars have interrogated community-based dealings with the past processes across the world that happen alongside and beyond the transitional justice project and have deeply transformative potentials.[16] I am here referring to the global project's potential, or rather, role. The job of the transitional justice project, if it were to be more compatible with the imperative 'Never Again', is to not actively hamper the creation of such communities during and after transition. This means acknowledging that its institutions, such as criminal tribunals, play only a small part in the society-wide long-term reckoning with the past; that the records produced by its institutions are by no means the only authoritative sources of truth nor are they definite; that it facilitates initiatives and inspires dealing with the past, but it surely cannot govern it. Perhaps the most difficult task would be for the transitional justice project to abandon its civilising mission, understanding that it is only a humble servant of the people who need to make sense of their own past for it to *become* past. As a package of measures, an ideal transitional justice project would serve the people, rather than discipline them. Enhancing these principles will be an essential task for scholars, policymakers, and anyone who thinks that the transitional justice project must remain a part and parcel of communities' dealings with violent pasts.

Lastly, while the future of the transitional justice project may be debated, the need for meaningful assurances of non-recurrence of mass atrocities remains more pertinent than ever, as the language of 'Never Again' reverberates across the world. As the world watched yet another war against Palestine, bloodier than most before, unfolding since early October 2023, 'Never Again' became a question, not merely a statement or a promise. Never Again for whom? What Never Again? Where is Never Again? People mobilising around the world to protest Israel's indiscriminate bombings and killings of Gazan civilians expressed doubts that 'Never Again' applied only to certain contexts and only to certain

[16] See, for instance, Clare D Dwyer, 'Expanding DDR: The Transformative Role of Former Prisoners in Community-Based Reintegration in Northern Ireland' (2012) 6 International Journal of Transitional Justice 274; Nadia Jmal and Virginie Ladisch, 'A Voices-Centered Approach to Transitional Justice: Youth-led Activism and Artistic Initiatives Open Spaces for Broad Community Engagement' (2022) 16 International Journal of Transitional Justice 118; Claudia Bernardi, 'The Disappeared Are Appearing: Murals that Recover Communal Memory' (2020) 14 International Journal of Transitional Justice 193.

kinds of victims.[17] It became obvious that one person's or one group's idea of 'Never Again' could be another person's or another group's living hell.

The lack of faith in meaningful assurances that mass atrocities will not be repeated and any efforts to prevent and stop them once they start is reflected in this book, which does not proclaim but instead asks if non-recurrence is meaningful, if Never Again is truly never. In the words of BiH author Lana Bastašić, upon her reflection on Israel's atrocities in Gaza, 'But *never again* is a feeble phrase. The world forgets, just like it has forgotten Bosnia. The *nevers* have been worn out and abandoned; the *again* keeps coming back in bigger numbers and darker stories'.[18] This book has hoped to show that, even if the world might have forgotten about BiH, BiH still has a lot to teach us about peace. There are no easy solutions, no straightforward way towards a meaningful 'Never Again'. There should not be. No courts, truth commissions, or reparation schemes can single-handedly bring meaning to 'Never Again' for an entire society wounded by inter-group killings, torture, and, eventually, a genocide. Everyone must participate in some capacity in what comes after these atrocities, whether that is some form of justice, closure, reconciliation, or trust; participate by listening, learning, empathising, staying curious, creating transethnic spaces, and starting discussions. The future of transitional justice, and particularly the international criminal justice components of it, if they wish to stay legitimate, is not to censor and control out of anxiety but to facilitate this participation for 'Never Again'. The point, after all, is that we must continue to 'deal' with our collective pasts, filled with violence, harm, and injustice, but some of those processes must remain ungovernable.

[17] There have been many debates about the meaning of Never Again since 7 October 2023, and the slogan has been mobilised by different actors to express solidarity with Israel as well as with Palestine. See, for instance, Philip Oltermann, 'Israel-Hamas War Opens Up German Debate over Meaning of "Never Again"' (*The Guardian*, 22 November 2023) www.theguardian.com/world/2023/nov/22/israel-hamas-war-opens-up-german-debate-over-meaning-of-never-again accessed 28 November 2023.

[18] Lana Bastašić, 'I Grew Up in Bosnia, Amid Fear and Hatred of Muslims. Now I See Germany's Mistakes over Gaza' (*The Guardian*, 23 October 2023) https://shorturl.at/ftDJZ accessed 28 November 2023.

Appendix

Table A.1 *List of all researched institutions, organisations, and mechanisms of transitional justice*

	Name	Data collection	Interview date and place
1	**Srebrenica Commission**	Desk research and interview	3 October 2019, Durham, UK
2	**International Commission on Missing Persons**	Desk research, interview, and field notes	3 November 2019, Durham, UK 6 December 2019, Sarajevo, BiH
3	**Nansen Dialogue Centre**	Desk research and interview	4 November 2019, Sarajevo, BiH
4	**Post-Conflict Research Center**	Desk research, interview, and field notes	6 November 2019, Sarajevo, BiH
5	**Institute for Research on Crimes against Humanity and International Law**	Desk research, interview, and field notes	7 November 2019, Sarajevo, BiH 15 November 2019, Sarajevo BiH
6	**Foundation Truth, Justice and Reconciliation**	Desk research and interview	11 November 2019, Sarajevo, BiH
7	**Helsinki Committee for Human Rights RS**	Desk research, interview, and field notes	12 November 2019, Bijeljina, BiH
8	**Transitional Justice Strategy Working Group**	Desk research and interview	12 November 2019, Bijeljina, BiH 13 December 2019, Sarajevo, BiH

Table A.1 (*cont.*)

	Name	Data collection	Interview date and place
			12 December 2019, Sarajevo BiH 17 December 2019, Sarajevo, BiH 17 December 2019, Sarajevo, BiH
9	**Basic Court of the Brčko District**	Desk research and interview	13 November 2019, Brčko, BiH
10	**Prosecutor's Office of the Brčko District**	Desk research and interview	13 November 2019, Brčko, BiH
11	**RECOM Coalition's Working Group**	Desk research and interview	14 November 2019, Sarajevo, BiH
12	**PRO-FUTURE**	Desk research and interview	18 November 2019, Sarajevo, BiH
13	**OSCE**	Desk research and interview	21 November 2019, Sarajevo BiH 11 December 2019, Sarajevo, BiH
14	**TRIAL International**	Desk research and interview	22 November 2019, Sarajevo, BiH
15	**UN International Police Task Force**	Desk research and interview	25 November 2019, via email
16	**Prosecutor's Office Banja Luka**	Desk research and interview	26 November 2019, Banja Luka, BiH
17	**BiH Ombudsmen**	Desk research and interview	26 November 2019, Banja Luka, BiH
18	**Republika Srpska Institute for Research on War, War Crimes and Missing Persons**	Desk research, interview, and field notes	27 November 2019, Banja Luka, BiH
19	**Prosecutor's Office of East Sarajevo**	Desk research and interview	29 November 2019, East Sarajevo, BiH
20	**Memorial Fund of Sarajevo Canton**	Desk research, interview, and field notes	29 November 2019, Sarajevo, BiH
21	**Municipal Court of East Sarajevo**	Desk research and interview	3 December 2019, East Sarajevo, BiH

Table A.1 (*cont.*)

	Name	Data collection	Interview date and place
22	**ICTY Outreach**	Desk research and interview	5 December 2019, Sarajevo, BiH
23	**High Judicial and Prosecutorial Council**	Desk research and interview	10 December 2019, Sarajevo BiH
24	**Youth Initiative for Human Rights BiH**	Desk research and interview	11 December 2019, Sarajevo BiH
25	**Federal Ministry of Justice**	Desk research and interview	12 December 2019, Sarajevo, BiH
26	**Anonymous**	Interview	13 December 2019, Sarajevo, BiH
27	**Ministry of Human Rights and Refugees – Human Rights Sector**	Desk research and interview	17 December 2019, Sarajevo, BiH
28	**Ministry of Human Rights and Refugees – Refugees Sector**	Desk research and interview	24 January 2020, Sarajevo, BiH
29	**Missing Persons Institute**	Desk research and interview	17 December 2019, Sarajevo, BiH
30	**NATO Defence Reform Commission**	Desk research and interview	27 December 2019, online
31	**Court BiH, War Crimes Chamber**	Desk research, interview, and field notes	10 January 2020, Sarajevo, BiH
32	**Research and Documentation Center**	Desk research, interview, and field notes	21 January 2020, Sarajevo, BiH
33	**International Independent Judicial Commission**	Desk research and interview	23 January 2020, online
34	**Center for Non-Violent Action**	Desk research, interview, and field notes	4 February 2020, Sarajevo, BiH
35	**Anonymous**	Interview	7 February 2020, Sarajevo, BiH
36	**Ministry of Justice**	Desk research and interview	10 February 2020, Sarajevo, BiH
37	**UNDP**	Desk research and interview	11 February 2020, Sarajevo, BiH

Table A.1 (*cont.*)

	Name	Data collection	Interview date and place
38	**Balkan Investigative Reporting Network**	Desk research and interview	19 February 2020, Belgrade, Serbia
39	**Humanitarian Law Fund**	Desk research and interview	26 February 2020, Belgrade, Serbia
40	**National War Crimes Strategy**	Desk research and interview	10 January 2020, Sarajevo, BiH
41	**Commission for Truth and Reconciliation in Bijeljina**	Desk research and interview	11 November 2019, Sarajevo, BiH
42	**Memorial Center Srebrenica**	Desk research and field notes	20 November 2019, Potočari, BiH
43	**Women's Court**	Desk research and field notes	January 2020, Sarajevo, BiH
44	**Municipal Court in Banja Luka**	Desk research only	–
45	**State Prosecutor's Office BiH**	Desk research, only	–
46	**Human Rights Chamber of BiH (no longer operational)**	Desk research only	–
47	**Transitional Justice, Accountability and Memory Association**	Desk research only	–
48	**Center for Democracy and Transitional Justice**	Desk research only	–
49	**The ICTY**	Desk research only	–
50	**Republika Srpska International Independent Commission on the Siege of Sarajevo**	Desk research only	–
51	**Republika Srpska International Independent Commission of Srebrenica**	Desk research only	–
52	**Youth Initiative for Human Rights Serbia**	Desk research only	–

INDEX

For EU product safety concerns, contact us at Calle de José Abascal, 56–1°, 28003 Madrid, Spain or eugpsr@cambridge.org.

www.ingramcontent.com/pod-product-compliance
Lightning Source LLC
LaVergne TN
LVHW011813200926
848484LV00005B/1173

* 9 7 8 1 0 0 9 5 8 3 9 3 0 *